TECHNIQUE IN FICTION

TECHNIQUE IN FICTION

ROBIE MACAULEY
GEORGE LANNING

EDITORS OF *The Kenyon Review*

HARPER & ROW, PUBLISHERS

NEW YORK, EVANSTON, AND LONDON

FOR JOHN CROWE RANSOM

CONTENTS

CONTENTS vii

PLOT AND STORY   *158*

9   ORGANIC FORM AND FINAL MEANING   *186*

INTRODUCTION

People who know little about writing are often pleased to re-mark, "Nobody can *teach* you how to write fiction; it isn't a subject that can be taught." Looking wise, they are likely to add, "Anyone who has a story to tell can write a novel." These are two of the most common nontheories about the craft of fiction.

Of course, the truth is that there are a great many good teachers —among them, Jane Austen, Dickens, Conrad, Joyce, Tolstoy, Chekhov, Melville, James, and Hemingway—and that every good writer learns from them before he can begin his own work. There has been hardly one fiction writer of any worth who has not (meta-phorically) apprenticed himself to a master or masters while he learned his trade. Some have been fortunate enough to have their masters alive and present before them—as fortunate as Maupassant when Flaubert used to criticize the young writer's early stories be-fore he threw them into the fire. But, whatever the circumstance, no beginning writer who has some volumes of superior fiction at hand is without teachers. The question is not whether anyone can teach you how to write fiction—good teaching is always available. It is whether you can learn.

The best and happiest way to learn would be to sit—as so many generations of young writers have done—at a café table in Paris listening to Stendhal, or Turgenev, or Joyce, or Hemingway de-bating technique with their friends. Every fiction writer who is at all good cares deeply about this matter: every great writer knows something about it that no one else knows. But, since that ideal café table is unlikely, the nearest useful thing would be to have a book that brought together a good many writers' ideas about their craft, along with examples of how they solved, didn't quite solve, or failed to solve some of the technical problems of telling a story. We have tried to do that here. This is not a how-to-do-it book; it is intended to be a how-it-was-done book. The comment and examples provided by us are simply meant to suggest to the intelligent beginning writer or the college student of fiction what are the eternal problems in putting a human story together and in making it work as a story.

There is a vast amount to be learned about technique from reading masterpieces of the novel or short story; unfortunately, there is far less to be gained from criticism. It is discouraging to observe how little of the brilliant literary criticism of our time has had to do with the essential skills of fiction. Many literary critics are prepared to discuss a novel in terms of myth, symbol, irony, ambiguity, and other elevated matters, while seeming ignorant of such fundamental ones as how the plot works, how the characters are juxtaposed, or how the novel is constructed. The two classic books on technique, Percy Lubbock's *The Craft of Fiction* and E. M. Forster's *Aspects of the Novel,* remain unrivaled. Both Lubbock and Forster are novelists—one minor and one important—and this bears on the success of these two books. The best modern critics of fiction, from the standpoint of technique, and probably the only critics that the beginning writer will find of any specific help, are those who write fiction themselves. (A selective bibliography of their work is appended to this book; one of the fine critics not listed there, however, is Allen Tate, who knows far more about the art and craft of fiction than he has ever written. Several of his articles on the subject are to be found in his *Collected Essays.*)

As far as possible, we have tried to make this a book of working information, suggestion, and example. Fiction has no absolute rules or laws. Its whole code of technique is built on precedent alone; learning about it is like reading history—a special kind of history—in order to find out which methods seem to have succeeded, and which failed, in the past. To describe this very flexible code, we have tried always to use the phrase "principles of fiction," preferring it to anything more restrictive. A *principle* is nothing more than a reasonable way of meeting one or another technical demand, and a principle's only *sanction* is that a considerable number of gifted writers seem to have followed it—to their profit. Thus, the writer who does not is taking a gamble.

Fiction, of course, lives by taking gambles, risks, or long shots, as much as it does by traditional good sense. But, before he gambles, the author must first know the difference between a meaningful risk and a pointless experiment. He must have a knowledge of principles before he can strike beyond them. He should not be like the man in Outer Mongolia who, at this very moment, is trying to invent a flying machine by means of strapping his arms into two large leather wings. This book cannot teach the beginner how to fly in a new way, but it can suggest to him why the leather-wing theory has fallen into disfavor.

The reader will find that the greater proportion of comment and example is drawn from the work of nineteenth- and early twentieth-century authors (and he may detect some slight prejudices about which ones are selected), rather than from our contemporaries. But that is where the greatest part of the history of the craft of fiction lies and it is there that the young writer ought to begin his reading and learning. Even for reasons far beyond the matter of technique, he ought to know *Remembrance of Things Past* before *The Alexandria Quartet,* and *Crime and Punishment* before *The Heart of the Matter.* There is, however, an additional reason for our selections. The past twenty-five years have shown very little in the way of new directions in fiction. The last great wave of experiment came in the preceding quarter-century, and it is simply true that most contemporary writers are contented heirs rather than self-made men.

This is a remarkable tale in itself. It is the kind of thing that one is always hearing about good or even merely successful writers; left bare, unadorned, it strikes to the heart. One feels immediately that in one's own life there is no staircase to match this writer's. All of the doors are open, but none of them reveals a significant tableau.

James, however, does not stop his anecdote on this note of mysterious perception; he goes on to tell what else went into the making of the tale. He says that the writer had got "her direct personal impression, and she turned out her type. She knew what youth was, and what Protestantism; she also had the advantage of having seen what it was to be French, so that she converted these ideas into a concrete image and produced a reality."

Direct personal impression and the subsequent bringing to bear on it of *the writer's own particular experience*: the origin of a fiction would usually seem to lie within these two areas. James put the matter this way—the novel, he said (he might equally well have been discussing the story), is "in its broadest definition a personal, a direct impression of life: that, to begin with, constitutes its value, which is greater or less according to the intensity of the impression."

In the staircase episode, the impression was that of an observer, not of a participant. The trick, then, is not simply to deck out autobiography in a thin trapping of fiction. It is true, of course, that some writers—Thomas Mann and Ernest Hemingway, among them—have been able to place themselves at the heart of an action that was based on an episode in their own lives, but even for these men there were not enough personal experiences to provide them with as many subjects as they required. In going farther afield, for example, Mann found material which commanded his imagination in the Biblical story of Joseph, in music, and in the old age of Goethe and the woman who had been his first love. Henry James, that majestic butler at the great table of Society, got a number of his ideas from country house, drawing room, or banquet gossip. Each was what he liked to call a *donnée*—something "given" to him; and he used to protest, if his informant persisted in plying him with details, that he didn't want to know too much. The "too much" would hamper his imaginative play with the anecdote; he would begin to feel confined by the facts of the real-life case. Edith Wharton said that for her every incident, every situation presented itself "in the light of story-telling material." She added that "the possibilities of a given subject are—whatever a given imagination can make of them." The New England writer Sarah Orne Jewett was the daughter of a doctor in the small town of South Berwick, Maine. She often went with her father on his rounds, and from the glimpses she had of the lives of farming families, invalids, old maids, recluses, and retired sea captains or their widows she fashioned some of her best stories. A buggy on a country road was her "staircase."

Joseph Conrad, writing of the conception of *Nostromo*, shows how anecdote, personal experience, and one's own reading may eventually combine to produce a work of powerful originality. Early in his career at sea, he heard about a man who had stolen, single-handed, a whole shipload of silver during a South American revolution. The anecdote was barren of detail and, as an account of simple crime, had no great interest for Conrad. Nearly thirty years later, however, he came upon a volume of memoirs by an American seaman; a brief portion of this book dealt with the seaman's experiences aboard a schooner whose master and owner was that same silver thief of the long-ago story. The writer represented his employer as "an unmitigated rascal, a small cheat, stupidly ferocious. . . ." This chance confirmation of a tale heard in youth evoked in Conrad "the memories of that distant time when everything was so fresh, so surprising, so venturesome, so interesting; bits of strange coasts under the stars, shadows of hills in the sunshine, men's passions in the dusk, gossip half forgotten, faces grown dim. . . ." Despite the fact that the original anecdote had now been fleshed out, despite the nostalgia it called forth, Conrad still did not feel that it offered a subject to him. "To invent a circumstantial account of the robbery did not appeal to me." Then, however, it occurred to him that the thief need not be "a confirmed rogue." In fact, he might be "a man of character, an actor and possibly a victim in the changing scenes of a revolution." It was at that moment that he had "the first vision of a twilight country which was to become the province of Sulaco, with its high shadowy Sierra and its misty Campo for mute witnesses of events flowing from the passions of men short-sighted in good and evil."

Thus—as Conrad, James, Edith Wharton, Sarah Orne Jewett show—an impression may come from anywhere: there is no particular door to look through, no astonishment which fate is saving for luckier mortals to discover and tell the tale of. The only luck lies in what Elizabeth Bowen calls "susceptibility"—and susceptibility in this particular sense is as much a matter of cultivation as of inherent disposition. The writer must learn to look hard and close at the life around him, and to relate what he sees to what his own experience has taught him. Much of the material gathered in this way may be of no immediate value to him—he may even question its eventual value. But still he will do well to store it away: whether it is an anecdote heard or overheard, the look of a countryside, or the bearing of a group of people glimpsed in a strange house.

THE USES OF NOTEBOOKS

Memory is often unresponsive; despite desperate efforts, it won't yield up that fact or emotion or sensuous apprehension which was once committed to it. For this reason, some writers keep notebooks or journals in which they jot down anything that has particularly struck them, while the impression is still fresh. Katherine Mansfield even recorded phrases and sentences, on the theory that some of them might be useful for rounding off a paragraph. It was Somerset Maugham who said that he would never live long enough to write all of the stories and novels for which his notebook provided ideas. Henry James's notebooks are full not only of ideas for possible stories but of possible ways for working out these stories. Here are two examples:

Last evening . . . Miss R. said, after the conversation had run a little upon the way Americans drag their children about Europe:

"A girl should be shown Europe—or taken to travel—by her husband—she has no business to see the world before. *He* takes her—*he* initiates her."

Struck with this as the old-fashioned French view and possible idea for a little tale. The girl whose husband is to show her everything—so that she waits at home—and who never gets a husband. . . .[1]

This is a story that James apparently never wrote and, as such, is an example of the many entries that a writer will make to no direct purpose. Here, however, in a much abridged form, is the entry James made that led to the writing of *The Spoils of Poynton:*

. . . last night at dinner at Lady Lindsay's . . . Mrs. Anstruther-Thompson [told me this history]. It is a small and ugly matter . . . a little social and psychological picture. It appears that the circumstance is about to come out in a process-at-law. Some young laird, in Scotland, inherited, by the death of his father, a large place filled with valuable things. . . . His mother was still living, and had always lived, in this rich old house, in which she took pride and delight. . . . The son married . . . and went down with his wife to take possession—possession *exclusive,* of course—according to English custom. On doing so he found that pictures and other treasures were absent—and had been removed by his mother.[2]

James goes on to tell how the son protested his mother's highhandedness, and how she responded by demanding still other possessions. There was a public quarrel which ended in the mother's announcing that the young man was illegitimate—hence not really the heir. James adds, "It presents a very fine case of the situation in which, in England, there has *always* seemed to me to be a story—the situation of the mother *deposed* . . . turned out of the big house on the son's marriage. . . ."

In mulling over how he would treat fictionally a "case" such as this one, James has left a brilliant example of the creative process at work, providing "circumstances, details, intensifications," and "deepening it and darkening it all." The evolution of *The Spoils of Poynton* from a story told at a dinner party is too long either to quote or to paraphrase here, but the reader will find it set forth in F. O. Matthiessen's and Kenneth B. Murdock's edition of *The*

[1] *The Notebooks of Henry James,* ed. F. O. Matthiessen and Kenneth B. Murdock (New York: Oxford University Press, 1947), p. 125.
[2] *Ibid.,* pp. 136–137.

Notebooks of Henry James—a book that belongs in every writer's library. Among other things, the development of James's novel illustrates the enormous difference which usually exists between conception and execution. James kept only the central fact of the feud, for he was constantly aware of the danger of being confined by the multitudinous details of an actual happening. Life, he said, is all "inclusion and confusion"—the "point" of any event is lost in the uproar. Art, however, is "discrimination and selection," and the "point" is its *raison d'être*. James found the scandal, which disgraced the Scottish laird and his mother, ugly and lacking in finish. In *The Spoils of Poynton*, he sent the great house up in flames—a far more meaningful comment on the tragedy of human covetousness and its overvaluation of material possessions.

An advantage of a notebook is that ideas entered there have a way of cooling off automatically, first, by the act of putting them down in some coherent form; and, second, by coming back to them later, when the writer has lost the original emotion and even a clear recollection of why the event seemed both strong enough and interesting enough to make a story. (Often, he will search in vain for either strength or interest—a sufficient indication that he had better turn the page and look for another idea.)

Elizabeth Bowen remarks that "A man's whole art may be rendered down, by analysis, to variations upon a single theme"; and so it is to be supposed that a particular interest—really, a ruling passion—will emerge as the notebook gets thicker. Learning to write sometimes seems like a succession of waste motions, and among the most wasteful is that one which urges us to commit to paper a fiction which—though it may look solid enough, though it may even be bought for publication—is as hollow, as much a trick, as those boxes which people make by cutting out the center of a book and gluing together the edges of the pages. These are called solanders, and few are the writers who have not perpetrated a fair number of solander-fictions in their time. When critics say that a writer is beginning to come into his own, they mean that he has finally discovered the single theme which bulks largest in his intellect, his imagination, and his emotions. All of his isolated notebook entries have, as it were, fused together: not from one episode or impression but from dozens has emerged the story which he is uniquely qualified to tell. Sarah Orne Jewett said: "The thing that teases the mind over and over for years, and at last gets itself put down rightly on paper— whether little or great, it belongs to Literature."

If the writer could read his notebooks with the eye of a stranger, that is, with the eye of detachment, it seems probable that he would come into his "own," and perhaps produce something with rightful claims to be Literature, much sooner than is usually the case. He would spot the false or fleeting impression, the phony response, the temporary interest, and strike it out. But at this point the use of notebooks passes from a practical subject to an ideal one. None of us possesses that degree of detachment—and perhaps if we did we would not be storytellers but critics.

For some writers, notebooks are of no help at all. Commenting on the method of Katherine Mansfield, Ivy Compton-Burnett said, "I cannot understand her noting phrases and sentences for future use, and find it hard to believe that they served any purpose. Rounding off a paragraph, occurring in the normal course of writing, by a tag overheard and stored up, seems to me too unnatural to be possible. She said that she never knew when such things would come in useful, and I suspect that she never found out." Miss Compton-Burnett probably expresses the common view on the jotting down of "phrases and sentences," but her objection is to notebook entries of any sort. She says, "I have not the note-book habit; that is, I do not watch or listen to strangers with a view to using the results. They do not do or say things that are of any good. They are too indefinite and too much alike and are seldom living in anything but the surface of their lives. Think how rarely we should ourselves say or do anything that would throw light on our characters or experience."

Miss Compton-Burnett is a special sort of writer who has imported elements of the Gothic novel into an Edwardian setting, which she writes about from the perspective of our own time. One can understand how the tone of contemporary talk, the quality of contemporary experience, might seem to her of no use in her craft. Yet, in the best sense, every good writer is "special"; for others, too, a notebook may offer back only a succession of snapshots of groups they can no longer identify, or of occasions which have lost their meaning. Where, for them, can ideas come from?

A BLINKING OF THE EYES

Turgenev once said that his stories originated in a vision of one or more persons who hovered before him, soliciting his attention, "appealing to him just as they were and by what they were." Henry James, who has left us this account, adds that Turgenev felt his task as a writer was to find out for these characters their "right relations, those that would most bring them out; to imagine, to invent and select and piece together the situations most useful and favourable to the sense of the creatures themselves, the complications they would be most likely to produce and feel." This process yielded the "story" that Turgenev had to tell about them. James himself worked along similar lines. He often found himself "investing some conceived or encountered individual, some brace or group of individuals, with the germinal property and authority." He could not understand the kind of author who saw his story first and then cast round for characters to launch it.

Reports such as these, especially that about Turgenev, smack of the metaphysical, of God's calling Florence Nightingale to her profession. Or they may suggest that at heart writers are occultists who see the creative process as some sort of séance which summons presences from the timeless dark. Ellen Glasgow was asked why one of her male characters blinked his eyes, and she answered, "I did not make him blink his eyes. He was blinking them when I first saw him, as a child, by the roadside."

It may be that for many writers the conception of character, and hence of story, seems to come in this mysterious way: a puff of cosmic smoke and then a scene laid bare, populated with one or more persons ready to be written about. It may especially seem to be the case when, in memoirs or prefaces, they are writing in a retrospect that covers the work of a good many years. But one may feel fairly certain that behind these real or imagined revelations lies a good

N.B. (Yes!)

deal of conscious and unconscious observation. A journal shows the emergence of the writer's dominant interest; a character usually dramatizes that interest, and the face he wears will be made up of those of a dozen different people observed at one time or another. So the process, though subterranean, is not perhaps as mysterious as writers would have their readers believe—or as they believe themselves. And other kinds of characters (often complete with stories which require only artful tinkering) require no gestation period at all, but are readily available whenever they are needed. One such is, as Ellen Glasgow puts it, the character known in legend—the grandaunt who went prospecting for gold in the Yukon; the great-great-grandfather who fought with Nelson and then, at eighty-three, established the American branch of the family by marrying an Irish servant girl in Boston. Most families have countless such characters, and any one of them may be qualified to play a major or minor role in a fiction. (In a *fiction*: the writer sinks into biography, as into autobiography, at his peril.)

There are as well those people encountered in the daily round: the widow across the street whose lights burn too late at night; the man at the carryout store whose casual remarks indicate a surprisingly cosmopolitan past; the restaurant hostess who wears a fresh gardenia every day and enjoys the reputation of possessing a mysterious suitor. All of these people might propose interesting stories—sad, remarkable, or funny, depending upon the writer's speculations and the themes that suddenly caught fire in his imagination.

Finally, there are those characters who come out of history itself to occupy a central place in one's consciousness: generals, courtesans, poets, queens and kings, and spinsters—of either sex—with sharp-edged tongues. Any of these may seem to express the writer's whole sense of things. And if they have entered sufficiently into his life, it will not always be necessary to dress them in antique clothes and put linkboys before them to light their (and the reader's) way. They will breathe the air of his own time as freely—or with the same inhibitions and distastes—as he breathes it himself. Compatriots and contemporaries, they will still have a story to tell.

A VIEW OF SALISBURY

In 1883, the year following his death, Anthony Trollope's *Autobiography* was published. The book's candor destroyed Trollope's reputation, undermined his sales, and, indeed, kept his name in disrepute until fairly recent times. For readers thought that he'd taken all of the grandeur out of the craft of fiction, reducing it to a few elementary requirements: a schedule to stick to and so many pages per day. "It was my practice to be at my table every morning at 5.30 A.M.; and it was also my practice to allow myself no mercy. . . . By beginning at that hour I could complete my literary work before I dressed for breakfast. . . . It had at this time become my custom . . . to write with my watch before me, and to require from myself 250 words every quarter of an hour." So he wrote, but to suppose he was offering, in passages such as this one, an aesthetic of fiction is to react with the same simple-mindedness that afflicted his contemporaries. For the beginning writer, Trollope is a valuable source of information on all kinds of literary considerations. His account of the genesis of the Barsetshire novels is particularly to the point here. It illustrates how the subject of a story may sometimes come ahead of the people who will act that subject out, and how conception can depend not on a notebook but on a continuing awareness of the public life.

For many years Trollope was an official of the General Post Office, and very often his job required him to travel. On one occasion it took him to the cathedral city of Salisbury where on a summer evening, while he was wandering near the cathedral, he got the idea for *The Warden* ("from whence," he wrote, "came that series of novels of which Barchester, with its bishops, deans, and archdeacon, was the central site"). Trollope adds that, at the time, this idea had "no reference to clergy in general." It was concerned instead with a practice of the Established Church that was just then receiving much public censure and bringing unhappiness to a number of people who were its innocent beneficiaries. Trollope called these "two opposite evils"—and probably they came to exercise an effect upon his imagination merely because he happened to be reminded of them by his stay in a cathedral city. The first evil was the Church's possession of monies which had been intended for charity, but "which had been allowed to become incomes for idle Church dignitaries." The "opposite" evil was the newspaper fury which had been directed against recipients of those incomes. Trollope felt that they were far from being the "chief sinners in the matter." He said, "When a man is appointed to a place it is natural that he should accept the income allotted to that place without much inquiry. It is seldom that he will be the first to find out that his services are overpaid. Though he be called upon only to look beautiful and to be dignified upon State occasions, he will think £2000 a year little enough for such beauty and dignity as he brings to the task."

Trollope, like James, required only the *donnée*—he was not interested in biography or popular sociology. As to his qualifications for beginning a series of ecclesiastical novels: "no one . . . could have had less reason . . . to presume himself to be able to write about clergymen. I have been often asked in what period of my early life I had lived so long in a cathedral city as to have become intimate with the ways of a Close. I never lived in any cathedral city,—except London, never knew anything of any Close, and at that time had enjoyed no particular intimacy with any clergyman." His characters, he said, came from his "moral consciousness" and from what he picked up, as he went along, about the clergy in general.

As a character may emerge from anywhere, so, then, may a subject or theme: from a newspaper story or any other media of communication, from gossip, from the books one reads, or from the events of one's own life or the lives of family and friends. Rose Macaulay, that brilliant, incorrigibly prankish novelist, who died a few years ago, said that one of her books "had its genesis in the reflection how manifold is human nature." She then thought "it might be fun to present one person as two, as far thro' the book as was possible." Another novel was the result of her "brooding on Cambridge life as it was about 1640; I had always read a great deal of 17th c. letters and memoirs." One of her last novels came from "a meditation on Ruin, physical and material."

The beginning writer is often told to write about what he *knows*

—but what, exactly, is this knowledge that he possesses? How much did Conrad *know* about revolution, or Henry James about the feelings of a dispossessed dowager? As much, it seems, as Trollope knew about the clergy. Understandably, the novice takes advice literally, and looking at his life he finds that what he knows is how it is to grow up, to fall in or out of love, to lose a father or mother, to go bowling or get drunk, to have a baby, to have a cold.

The great writers have dealt, certainly, with love, birth, death, illness, and folly, but it is a mistake to suppose that they have often dealt with them in terms of their own immediate experience. They have known that the ordinary facts of human life are the same for everyone, and that even biography doesn't concern itself with the commonplace. What they have sought to do is to place their emotions, their private engagements, in a larger social context; to show what is universal in the ordinary happening. In Trollope's phrase, they have set their "moral consciousness" to work.

No writer, of course, picks his subject in cold blood. Supposedly, for Conrad, the tumult and emotion of revolutions—though he had known none—somehow expressed a basic truth about the human condition; the life of the clergy—though he had known none—came to exercise a tremendous power over Trollope's imagination. Flaubert said that his imaginary characters pursued him—benevolent furies pursuing an inspired Orestes, as it were. They gave him "joy." This, surely, is the emotion that every writer feels when he falls upon a subject that is both close to him and capable of carrying him beyond himself to a dramatic statement that every reader can respond to.

2   BEGINNINGS

THE SHORT STORY

A short story occurs in the midst of life. A door opens on a scene where people are talking, acting, or reflecting. They are caught in a few moments of intensity and then the door must close; the story is finished. In comparison, the novel has infinite luxuries of time and place. It can explore without hurry, develop inevitable currents of action, watch people change and mature.

Thus, in the history of the short story, the idea has grown up that the writer must throw that door open at some arresting point. His scene, already in being, must be revealed with a dramatic intensity that compels the reader to attention and forces him to invest his interest at once:

"You make me sick," said Mrs. Egg. She spoke with force. Her three daughters murmured, "Why mamma!"

This opening, taken from a story by Thomas Beer called "Tact," is obviously contrived for its effect, for when Mrs. Egg resumes speaking we learn that the seeming violence of her outburst is merely an example of her usual rhetoric. She says:

"You make me sick, girls. . . . Dammy's been home out of the Navy precisely seven weeks an' two days, an' a hour hasn't passed but what one of you've been phonin' me from town about what he has or ain't done unbecomin' to a boy that's engaged to Edith Sims!"[1]

[1] *The Bedside Book of Famous American Stories*, ed. Angus Burrell and Bennett A. Cerf (New York: Random House, 1936), p. 943.

By selecting one of Mrs. Egg's more notable mannerisms, the author has found a way of beginning his story that will probably make any reader pause long enough to find out what Mrs. Egg is talking about. But the opening serves a more legitimate purpose: it is revelatory of Mrs. Egg's general response to criticism of her beloved "Dammy," and this protective feeling has an important part to play in the working out of the story.

Like any good principle of fiction, the dramatic opening can be exaggerated into a fallacy. Those magazine articles that dispense advice to beginning writers often speak of a "hook"—a hook that, presumably, catches the reader off-balance and drags him to his seat by main force. Mystery, violence, strangeness of character or situation, some highly tantalizing suggestion of plot—these are the reliable instruments to catch that innocent passer-by who was only on his way to look up an advertisement in the back of the magazine:

> Queer and inexplicable as the business was, on the surface it appeared fairly simple—at the time, at least; but with the passing of years, and owing to there not having been a single witness of what happened except Sara Clayburn herself, the stories about it have become so exaggerated, and often so ridiculously inaccurate, that it seems necessary that some one connected with the affair . . . should record the few facts actually known.[2]

This is how Edith Wharton begins her story called "All Souls." It is almost a classic example of one kind of hook—the genteel hook—and is not characteristic of Mrs. Wharton in her best work. What follows is a commonplace ghost story, with none of the suspense and invention that she often brought to this medium. The opening exhibits the tired slickness of a professional writer who has just been asked, by a magazine editor, to let him have something—*anything*—for a future issue.

Attention-getting devices often concentrate on the wrong objective. While they may dragoon the reader at the outset, they usually abandon the real story that remains to be told. This can happen

---

[2] Included in Mrs. Wharton's collection called *Ghosts* (New York: Appleton-Century-Crofts, 1937), p. 3.

whether the author expends ingenuity on his opening or on his title. "I Want to Know Why" is the not particularly interesting title of one of Sherwood Anderson's finest stories. It expresses with exactness, however, the theme of the story, which is that of a boy's bewildering initiation into the adult world and the relations between men and women. Given such material, Anderson might easily have selected a more sensational title, but in doing so he would have distorted his intentions in writing the story, and every reader's approach to it.

George Jean Nathan and H. L. Mencken once invented, as a game, the search for the ultimate come-on title; one of their best efforts was "The Naked Countess." It was, they concluded, a remarkable concentration of mystery, sex, and snob appeal that would arouse the curiosity of every red-blooded reader. But the difficulty was to devise a story to live up to that dramatic name—and, of course, they never found one. In this imaginary situation, there never was a naked countess, there was only a reader who had been aroused by the idea that she might exist.

All this is by way of making a plain and modest point: the story has a being first in the mind of its author, and the beginning derives from it. Probably the most sensible way to look at the matter is for the writer to establish some sort of general controls before he sets out. First, he should avoid the temptation to pack too much into the beginning of his story. All launchings are perilous—it is best to do one thing at a time. A story that commences by trying to establish, almost simultaneously, three or four characters, hinting at their relationships, making them exchange ideas, setting up their milieu, making them a part of a dramatic action, and involving them in a plot is in trouble at once.

Here, as an instance, is the beginning of a story called "England to America," by Margaret Prescott Montague (the italics are ours, and indicate how ruthlessly the author is stuffing her reader with information):

"Lord, but English people are funny!"

This was the perplexed mental ejaculation that *young Lieutenant Skipworth Cary, of Virginia,* found his thoughts constantly reiterating during his *stay* in *Devonshire*. Had he been, he wondered, a confiding fool, to accept so trustingly *Chev Sherwood's suggestion* that he spend part of his *leave*, at least, at Bishopsthorpe, where *Chev's people lived?* But why should he have anticipated any *difficulty* here, in *this very corner of England which had bred his own ancestors*, when he had always hit it off so splendidly with his *English comrades* at the *Front?* . . . The worst of it was that he had a curious feeling as if they were all—that is, *Lady Sherwood* and *Gerald; not Sir Charles* so much—protecting him from himself—keeping him from making breaks, as he phrased it. Was he a *social blunderer*, and weren't a *Virginia gentleman's* manners to be trusted in England without leading-strings?[3]

Mrs. Montague is a respected writer; this particular story of hers appeared in the *Atlantic Monthly* and subsequently received the first of the O. Henry Memorial Awards (1919). But one suspects that it was her subject (the courage of the British in wartime) which generated so much enthusiasm for the story—that, in fact, it was a kind of *White Cliffs* of World War I. A later chapter of this book deals with style in fiction, so that it is not necessary to comment here on the author's use of elaborate and artificial phrases such as "perplexed mental ejaculation." Note, instead, that all of the central characters are thrown at the reader at once; that he is given Skipworth Cary's military rank, his origin, his ancestors' origin, his social position ("Virginia gentleman"), his approximate age, and the fact that he is on leave. This is not only too much to learn all at once, before any interest in either Skipworth Cary or the Sherwood family has been established; it is more than Mrs. Montague can make later use of. The fact that Cary's ancestors came from "this very corner of England" and that he is a Virginia gentleman have no relevance to the action—unless to suggest that an AWOL private or exblacksmith from Billings, Montana, would hardly have been invited to Bishopsthorpe.

It may be true that in any story, time, place, several characters, and a hint of drama are necessary elements which must be attended to, but it is not true that all of them have equal weight and value.

[3] Included in *First-Prize Stories 1919–1963, From the O. Henry Memorial Awards* (New York: Doubleday & Company, 1963), pp. 1–2.

Thus, the second control the author might impose would be to select those elements—whether of character, action, or involvement—that represent the deepest characteristics of his story and to begin with one of them. And here he should use all his powers of definition. Whether he begins slowly or rapidly, whether his story is to be realistic or fantastic, he cannot simply point at things or simply name them. However preliminary the definition may be—and how-ever partial or misleading it may turn out to be later—he must use a clarity of line that separates his story and its entities from all the confused mass of the rest of the world.

Beginnings lead off, but they should have the seeds of finality in them. And so there is another valuable control the author might set up for himself: the habit of thinking a story through to its conclu-sion before settling on the tactics with which to start. While a half-conceived story may offer a great variety of possibilities for leading off, a story seen from the perspective of its ending will narrow those possibilities to the few most effective. Those few will be the ones most closely and richly involved with the matter and meaning of the story—and frequently they are the ones that bear the most in-evitability within them.

In the usual discussions of fictional technique, there are many false problems, and the problem of an "interesting beginning," as a separate thing, is surely artificial. If the writer has a story of worth-while interest to tell; if he takes the trouble to begin on paper only after he has finished in his mind; and if his introduction is thor-oughly a part of the life of that story; he can be sure of himself. He can be sure of his reader.

All of these controls are in the interest of economy, and, whether the writer intends to make some broad statement or only wishes to arrive at some very small and specific effect, he must waste as little as possible of his story's brief life. The beginning must be calculated and useful to the whole, but the choice of manner for the beginning is just as wide as is the range of narrative methods in fiction: scenic description, character description, dialogue, summary of past events, action in the present, generalization, a letter—or anything else. While it is seldom preferable to begin with a laundry list, an explanation of nuclear fission, or the preamble to the United States Constitution, any of these things *could* be used if it had a real function in the story that follows.

Nor is the writer limited to one method alone. In the course of its history, the short story has tended to acquire far more density and complexity of life than the simple "tale" from which it originated. Thus, there may be a necessity to introduce a number of things, by a number of methods, at the very outset. "It May Never Happen," a story by V. S. Pritchett, begins this way:

> I shall not forget the fingers that fastened me into the stiff collar. Or how I was clamped down under the bowler-hat which spread my rather large ears outwards and how, my nose full of the shop smell of the new suit, I went off for the first time to earn my living.
>
> "You are beginning life," they said.
>
> "You have your foot on the first rung of the ladder," they said.
>
> "Excelsior," my Uncle Belton said.
>
> I was going to work in the office of one of my uncles, a new uncle, the second husband of my mother's sister, who had married into the family. His name was Belton, a man of about forty-four with a tight bumptious little business in the upholstery trade, a business that sounded so full of possibilities that it would blow up and burst, out of sheer merit.[4]

Here there are several narrative methods that succeed each other quickly: the private feelings of the boy, the spoken comments of the family, a brief summary of the immediate situation, a report on everybody's generalization about the future. Along with that, there is a strong sense of the boy's bewilderment, of the platitudinous optimism in the family and pomposity in the uncle—and a suggestion that the business may indeed burst, though perhaps not out of sheer merit. Yet there is order in this variety: all of the elements have a clear relationship to each other and to the whole. The writer is at ease with what he knows and is about to tell; thus he can give the reader, too, a sense of being in the midst of fictional life.

---

[4] Included in Pritchett's collection called *It May Never Happen* (New York: Harcourt, Brace & World, 1947), p. 49.

THE NOVEL

A good novel is not merely a sizable short story. There is a qualitative difference as well as a difference in scale. Most young writers come to the novel form after a certain amount of experience in writing short fiction, and fail at first to recognize that they are in a new country. This is true of beginnings as of everything else, and one must learn to know the subtle differences in two techniques that are so greatly akin.

Whatever their methods, most good short stories begin with brevity, compression, immediate significance. A novelist's aims are longer because he is not compelled to strike for the vital moments alone and because he is traveling either a greater or a slower journey within the span of birth to death. He is not so much concerned with effect as with engrossment. He must persuade his reader to enter the labyrinth.

More than that, he should begin with something that will capture a tone or set a style of feeling that will echo throughout the book. A certain novel begins with some people in boats fishing dead men out of the Thames in the darkness. That opening is a portent; it casts its shadow over the whole long, loose course of the story. Another opens with a very succinct conversation between an English gentleman and his wife. They are discussing the themes of social status, money, and marriage: they have marriageable daughters. It is these concerns that the novel will go on to explore in their many ramifications. The beginning of a novel should have the power to persist and recur in the reader's consciousness.

And yet, so many novels begin just anywhere, just anyhow. The author is doing "finger exercises" at the keyboard; he is doing "calisthenics"; or he is standing at the window smoking his pipe and giving us the benefit of his views on life. In chapter three, he becomes desperate and buckles down to begin his story. In "Mr. Bennett and Mrs. Brown," one of the most famous of twentieth-century essays about the craft of the fiction, Virginia Woolf gives us a devastating description of an author doing calisthenics. Her subject is the novel, *Hilda Lessways,* by Arnold Bennett. Mrs. Woolf writes:

She [Hilda] shut the door in a soft, controlled way, which showed the constraint of her relations with her mother. She was fond of reading *Maud;* she was endowed with the power to feel intensely. So far, so good; in his leisurely, surefooted way Mr. Bennett is trying in these first pages, where every touch is important, to show us the kind of girl she was.

But then he begins to describe, not Hilda Lessways, but the view from her bedroom window, the excuse being that Mr. Skellorn, the man who collects rents, is coming along that way.

The passage that Mrs. Woolf then quotes is this one:

The bailiwick of Turnhill lay behind her; and all the murky district of the Five Towns, of which Turnhill is the northern outpost, lay to the south. At the foot of Chatterley Wood the canal wound in large curves on its way towards the undefiled plains of Cheshire and the sea. On the canal-side, exactly opposite to Hilda's window, was a flour-mill, that sometimes made nearly as much smoke as the kilns and the chimneys closing the prospect on either hand. From the flour-mill a bricked path, which separated a considerable row of new cottages from their appurtenant gardens, led straight into Lessways Street, in front of Mrs. Lessways' house. By this path Mr. Skellorn should have arrived, for he inhabited the farthest of the cottages.

Mrs. Woolf remarks:

One line of insight would have done more than all those lines of description, but let them pass as the necessary drudgery of the novelist. And now—where is Hilda? Alas. Hilda is still looking out of the window. Passionate and dissatisfied as she was, she was a girl with an eye for houses.[5]

Beginnings involve not only the selection of relevant detail but the problem of *time*. Where, in the long stretch of imaginary life, is the true point to begin. With the birth of the hero?—that would

[5] Included in Mrs. Woolf's collection called *The Captain's Death Bed* (New York: Harcourt, Brace & World, 1950), pp. 107–108.

seem to be the oldest and simplest answer. But there is such a thing as the backward-casting mind that cannot accept even that traditional solution. Samuel Butler, in *The Way of All Flesh,* had to unearth several generations of dead Pontifexes before he could begin to begin.

Somewhere in that flow of time must be drawn the visible line dividing past from present. All novels have a past; all novels should live in a present of their own. Only that part of *then* that is important to, that has a bearing on, *now* is worth being told. The fictional past lives only insofar as it is embodied in the fictional present.

There is a very old and trustworthy narrative principle called *in medias res*—to begin one's story "in the middle of things." This is simply to say that a novel ought to begin within the context of the events it intends to deal with. It ought to give an intimation of those events at the very start. (The word "event" is used very broadly, meaning not just happenings but any kind of motion-development in the story.)

Many of the nineteenth-century novelists—including quite a few good ones—could not bear to represent themselves, in the opening pages of their books, as writers of fiction. Rather, they pretended to be landscape painters, essayists, antiquarians, historians, or whatever. One famous example is Balzac posing as an inventory-taker. At the beginning of *Le Père Goriot,* Mme. Vauquer's boarding house is detailed foot by foot, with all its furnishings, its floor plan, its guest list, and even its smells:

The ground-floor, necessarily the part of the house where the affairs of such an establishment are carried on, consists, first, of a parlor lighted by two windows looking upon the street, which is entered through a glass door. This, the common sitting room, leads into the dining room, which is separated from the kitchen by the well of the staircase, the steps of which are of wood, square and polished. Nothing can be more dismal than this sitting room, furnished with chairs and arm-chairs covered with a species of striped horsehair. In the center stands a round table with a marble top. . . .

This dining room is pervaded by a smell for which there is no name in any language. . . . It suggests used air, rancid grease, and mildew.

It strikes a chill as of malaria to the bones; it penetrates the clothes with fetid moisture; it fills the nostrils with the mingled odors of a scullery and a hospital. . . .

The whole room is a depository of worthless furniture, rejected elsewhere and gathered here, as the battered relics of humanity are gathered in hospitals for the incurable. Here may be seen a barometer with a hooded monk who steps out when it rains. . . .[6]

There are eight pages like this of nothing but *things*. It is only on page eleven that we finally come to: "Eugène de Rastignac—such was his name—was one of that large class of young men . . ." It is a slow, cumbersome, laborious, overdetailed inventory of a beginning. Of course it is all wrong, any writer would be mad to introduce his story in this way. (Arnold Bennett, in his similar opening, was —in Mrs. Woolf's words—"trying to make us imagine for him . . . trying to hypnotize us into the belief that, because he has made a house, there must be a person living there.")

But in Balzac's case there is another factor to be considered: he was a genius. One of the odd things about genius is that it can sometimes combine all its disasters to make a brilliant success. Somehow, Balzac managed to touch all of those inanimate objects with life and to breathe an air of expectancy into that empty house. A little later the reader realizes that this is the hell of drabness and despair that Eugène must flee in order to live; all the rest of the book is an escape-attempt.

Balzac—just barely, and against heavy odds—comes off with the gamble. Nevertheless, his success is one of those infrequent exceptions to a good principle—the principle that a piece of fiction ought to begin to move forward at its very inception. There is in the range of fictional possibilities, of course, room for the set piece: extended descriptions of a scene or a character, interior monologues, lore of one kind or another. Yet these are static, the novel has to pause for them, and standing still is generally a poor way to set out.

Wuthering Heights begins: "I have just returned from a visit to my landlord—the solitary neighbour that I shall be troubled with."

[6] Trans. Katherine Prescott Wormeley (Boston: Little, Brown and Company, 1899), p. 6.

In the course of that visit, Emily Brontë manages not only to describe a good deal about the house and its surroundings but to focus on her chief concern: bringing the personality of Heathcliff to active life. He speaks, moves, and is observed—but even more revealing is the action of his dogs, a pack of "four-footed fiends," who mass for an attack on the visitor when he is left alone for a minute or two. It is all done unobtrusively but effectively, and Heathcliff, by the end of the chapter, has begun to emerge in his dark colors. The outward action is trivial and the visit of no real importance, but it does shrewdly suggest violent emotion and violence to come in its characterization of the principal actor.

Another famous beginning is that of *Anna Karenina:*

Happy families are all alike; every unhappy family is unhappy in its own way.

Everything was in confusion in the house of the Oblonskys. The wife had discovered that the husband was carrying on an intrigue with a French girl, who had been a governess in their family, and she had announced to her husband that she could not go on living in the same house with him. This position of affairs had now lasted three days, and not only the husband and wife themselves, but all the members of their household, were painfully conscious of it. . . . The wife did not leave her own room, the husband had not been home for three days. The children ran wild all over the house; the English governess quarrelled with the housekeeper. . . .[7]

It is all done in broad, general strokes. The opening of the story has nothing to do with any of the main characters—Kitty, Levin, Anna, Karenin, or Vronsky. Tolstoy's real concern here lies in just the broadness of those strokes, just the thematic essence of this situation, just the foreshadowings of the future he is able to cast by their means. This is going to be a contrasting story of happy and unhappy families. "All was in confusion in the house"—it is to be a story of domestic and emotional confusion. And it will be a story in which the fact of adultery plays a major part.

The opening is a remarkable omen. Its immediate, though quite secondary, usefulness is to begin the actual story with the Oblonskys'

[7] Trans. Constance Garnett (New York: Random House, 1939), p. 3.

"little problem." The reader discovers Stepan Arkadyevitch stirring comfortably on a sofa in his study, waking up, and remembering a delicious dream—a fine dinner served on glass tables that sang an aria, some sort of little decanters, women present. He smiles happily, gets up, reaches for his dressing gown—and only when he finds it not there does he remember that he is in his study, and why. The personal life of the novel begins.

Here, then, are three beginnings: Balzac's tour de force of elaborate scene-setting—very poor in theory but just saved from disaster by the exertion of his special powers; Emily Brontë's conservative success in leading off her story with a minor scene; Tolstoy's swift statement of his theme by one reverberating generalization and by the outlining of a microcosmic situation before passing to the narrative. But at the beginning of another classic novel—Flaubert's *Madame Bovary*—there is something especially puzzling. The novel opens by describing Charles Bovary's first day in a particular school, and it very shortly demonstrates that he is a dull, awkward, clownish boy who is to be the butt of every joke in class. It is a vivid little scene, and it makes one point very well—but for what purpose? Very soon the reader learns that the story is to have no primary business with Charles or with schooldays. It is to be the adult story of his wife and her affairs. Charles is unconscious of nearly every one of the facts or situations that are important in the novel. He *exists* in the novel but he does not *live* in it; and he does not change at all.

Until close to the end of the book it seems strange that Flaubert should have chosen to make a point of Charles's stupidity rather than to give a strong impression of Emma as quickly as possible. It seems to lay undue emphasis on a matter that Flaubert is able to establish easily a little later on in the story. Thus, the beginning seems to be a misstep, a piece of carelessness.

But Flaubert was one of the most calculating of all novelists. He knew the weight of every scene, and, when the reader arrives at the end of *Madame Bovary,* he finally understands the significance of the beginning: both beginning and ending reinforce each other. The story closes not with Emma's death by poison but with the last desolate months of Charles's life. He is unwilling and unable to recognize how completely destructive Emma had been—it was the deed of fate, he tells one of her former lovers. Thus, a story that begins with a dazed and clumsy schoolboy ends with the dazed and clumsy man, still unable to comprehend what life has done to him. The pattern of Charles's character has been the whole background of the small world against which Emma tried vainly to rebel. Technically, the relationship of the novel's beginning and ending forms an envelope. Symbolically, Charles's ineptness and stupidity are the great enveloping facts of the story, which Flaubert has emphasized by giving him the two symbolic positions. This is one of the clearest examples of the principle of viewing the beginning from the perspective of the end. Not only does Flaubert do it, but he forces the reader to do it as well.

INSERTING INFORMATION AT THE BEGINNING

One of the common difficulties for the inexperienced writer is that of communicating early the facts of what-has-gone-before. Imagine that the whole length of the circumstance the story must deal with stretches from *A* to *G*. The writer, however, has wisely chosen to begin his story, according to the principle of *in medias res,* at point *C* in the time span. That, he suggests, is the moment when events have started to move and to become really interesting. Nevertheless, he is faced with the problem of transmitting those important facts that have their basis in the era from *A* to *C*. In the drama there is an ancient device for doing this that illustrates a good many of the possible pitfalls: two minor characters, often servants, appear first on the stage and carry on a loaded conversation. Here is one very bad example:

First servant: Won't it be nice to have Miss Helen, old Mr. Butler's only daughter and the apple of his eye, back home again after her year of studying music in Paris?

Second servant: Yes, indeedy. My, she's so gay and pretty that all the young men just seem to flock around her—she's got eyes for only one, though.

First servant: Yes, poor thing! I wonder how she's going to take the shock when she hears that Mr. Locksley Hall, that young man who's studying to be a doctor at Harvard College, now in his second year and hard put to pay his way, I hear, has just about decided to marry the rich widow, Mrs. Loveless.

The (here exaggerated) absurdity comes, of course, from the fact of having people artificially exchanging information both have long known. It is an obviously bad invention. A much better method—and perhaps the most usually successful one—is by sleight of hand. The writer directs the reader's attention to something that is already proceeding and, unobtrusively and naturally, very gradually introduces the facts of the fictional case. It is frequently best to be somewhat oblique and to take advantage of inference. There is something ferocious about Heathcliff, but it is best to bring this forward by showing the behavior of his dogs, since dogs are usually supposed to reflect the personalities of their owners. A rather less (in terms of the book) significant example is that of Stepan Arkadyevitch. He wakes up from his pleasurable dream, relishes it, then reaches out for his dressing gown—and only then remembers the unhappy situation he has caused. By inference it is established that the reason for confusion in the house of the Oblonskys arises from Stepan's thoughtlessness and self-indulgence.

These are both well-placed clues that imply a certain amount of information about the situation or state of affairs at the time the novel begins. An old familiar journalistic axiom sets out the rule that all news stories should very quickly answer the questions *Who? When? What? Where?* and *How?* A novelist must, though by different methods, establish a similar frame of reference. He works most successfully—at least from the modern viewpoint—if he can first convince his reader that some interesting situation is in being, or that some interesting events are in progress, rather than by cramming him with circumstantial detail, all at once.

The question of *Who?* is answered very simply and adequately at the beginning of *Anna Karenina*: an upper-class Russian family with a self-indulgent and irresponsible father. That is all that needs to be known at the outset. With another sort of story ahead of him, a novelist might wish to remember that a crowd is not a cast and

n.b.

that nothing moves in the novel while a detailed analysis of personality is being carried on. In the beginning, the human facts are best limited to two considerations: some knowledge of the people according to their particular situation in life (are they Italian dockworkers? a farming family in the Midwest?) is the first. The second is that of individual traits, and for the moment these are kept simplified and limited to whatever is motivational. They are just the initial clues.

Again an illustration is furnished by Edith Wharton, and this time it shows her customary skill rather than a failing. Here are the first paragraphs of her novel, *The Custom of the Country*:

"Undine Spragg—how *can* you?" her mother wailed, raising a prematurely-wrinkled hand heavy with rings to defend the note which a languid "bell-boy" had just brought in.

But her defence was as feeble as her protest, and she continued to smile on her visitor while Miss Spragg, with a turn of her quick young fingers, possessed herself of the missive and withdrew to the window to read it.

"I guess it's meant for me," she merely threw over her shoulder at her mother.

"Did you *ever*, Mrs. Heeny?" Mrs. Spragg murmured with deprecating pride.[8]

The germ of Mrs. Wharton's whole narrative is contained in these seemingly casual lines. It can be assumed that Undine is young, probably very pretty, and certainly accustomed to having her own way. It is evident that she has an indulgent mother who frets about her daughter but cannot conceal her pride in the outrageous creature. The reference to Mrs. Spragg's hand, "heavy with rings," suggests that these are people of means.

Then a third character is introduced—Mrs. Heeny, a "visitor." Undine does not trim her normal conduct to meet this social situation: the impropriety of behaving to her mother in company as she might behave to her when they were alone does not occur to her—or at least is no deterrent.

Undine's selfishness and highhandedness, her parents' weakness,

[8] New York: Charles Scribner's Sons, 1913; p. 3.

and the wealth which determines them to launch their daughter
socially will direct the course of *The Custom of the Country*. Many
writers might feel that having accomplished this much in a few
beginning lines they could allow themselves a brief rest—a look
around the landscape, for instance. In fact, Mrs. Wharton soon
comes to this (the setting is an ornate, tasteless hotel suite), but not
before she has implied her setting (through the reference to the
"bell-boy") and introduced the first element of her plot: the note
which Undine snatches from her mother and withdraws to the
window to read. The message is an invitation to dinner at one of
the most august houses in New York, and it marks the beginning of
Undine's career.

The writer's next problem, answering *Where?* and *When?*, has
various degrees of difficulty. Scenes and times that are familiar to
most readers can be specified briefly and easily: "He left the shop
and began walking down the Rue Royale. At this hour in the morning it was practically deserted. A lorry full of German soldiers had
just come from the Place de la Concorde and as it passed him he
noticed that the men were staring and pointing out buildings with
the air of just-arrived tourists." But if the setting happens to be
Chandrapore, India, or Jamaica in the 1860's, place names and
topical references have little use. In such a case, the novelist often
feels that a somewhat fuller and more direct account of the setting
is required. E. M. Forster begins *A Passage to India* conventionally,
with a view:

Except for the Marabar Caves—and they are twenty miles off—the City
of Chandrapore presents nothing extraordinary. Edged rather than
washed by the River Ganges, it trails for a couple of miles along the
bank, scarcely distinguishable from the rubbish it deposits so freely.[9]

Forster then proceeds to draw a verbal map of his small fictional
territory; because the surroundings are quite alien to most of his
readers, he feels it important to give a strong sense of locality before
committing himself to events. In another kind of novel, this procedure might be simply wasteful or dull. The description of place, the

[9] New York: Harcourt, Brace & World, 1924; p. 7.

feeling for place, should be given just about as much weight in the early stages as it will have in the novel's whole course.

Any fiction writer who intends to place his story in a certain era of the past ought to establish his period fairly soon. There are standard ways of doing this by indirection: references to distinctive dress, customs, means of transportation, events of the time, contemporary personages known to history, and so on. But such things should appear as a natural part of what is being related; they should not be patent devices. A conversation about Mr. Lincoln's war policies or a description of a speakeasy should not be introduced for chronological purposes alone. If either one is there, it should be there for reasons important to the story. Many writers, on the other hand, prefer to be absolutely direct about the time. "It was one of the hottest days of the summer of 1835" is the first sentence of Turgenev's *On the Eve*. However it is done, the particular past era must be identified firmly (unless the title is something like *The Last Days of Pompeii*), because the reader tends to assume that a novel by a living author will be about contemporary times, unless advised otherwise.

But the all-important thing about the first stage of any piece of fiction is that here the author makes certain promises. If the novel or story is to be a success, those promises must be borne out. The author should be in full command of his conception, not drifting hopefully toward it. He may promise wit and precision in the analysis of human relations (as Jane Austen does at the start of *Pride and Prejudice*). He may promise a striking view of human desolation (as F. Scott Fitzgerald does in the beginning of *The Great Gatsby*). He may promise a strange, surreal vision of life (as Franz Kafka does at the beginning of *The Trial*). Or whatever else he means to carry out. In a certain sense, every beginning is a symbol; it is on the strength of its inferences or promises that a reader is willing to pursue the story.

This has a bearing on the elements of *What?* and *How?* in the introductory stage of the story. A novel or story ought to begin with some sense of movement, but that does not mean that the earliest action reported should be of dramatic significance or crucial to the

whole pattern of the fiction. The reader, beginning with no previous
knowledge and as yet having no context from which to judge, will
not recognize the relative importance of the things he is being told.
Significance—in fiction as in life—is a cumulative matter. The surprising news, for instance, that a close friend has suddenly become
rich carries with it a complex series of associated ideas and speculations; the news that the same thing has happened to a stranger is
significant only in the abstract.

The author is always in his strongest position when he is leading
toward some meaningful moment in his story; when such a moment
arrives, it always has a finer effect if it has had the advantage of a
careful narrative approach. On the other hand, if the beginning
should depict some high moment in the fictional drama, the author
is then at the psychological disadvantage of having to proceed *away*
from something rather than toward something. It is usually the best
strategy to suggest to the reader that his greatest interest lies in the
future—and this is what a good beginning should do. Henry James
once wrote a letter to Mrs. Humphry Ward, commenting critically
on one of her novels. He said,

I think your material suffers a little from the fact that the reader feels
you approach your subject too *immediately,* show him its elements, the
cards in your hand, too bang off from the first page—so that a wait to
begin to guess *what and whom the thing is going to be about* doesn't
impose itself: the antechamber or two and the crooked corridor before
he is already in the Presence.[10]

But all of these remarks are not meant to imply that the author
should avoid all facts of significance to his drama as he begins, nor
do they mean that a novel or story should not originate in an action.
They are simply cautionary suggestions against too much, too fast,
and too soon.

"HIGH" AND "LOW" BEGINNINGS

There is a related, though quite separate, question on which the
writer must decide. It is the sometimes difficult one of a certain

[10] *The Letters of Henry James,* ed. Percy Lubbock (New York: Charles Scribner's Sons, 1920), I, 322.

"tone" to be employed in the opening part of the fiction. Imagine this as the tone of voice in which the author is speaking. If it is casual, unhurried, quiet, somewhat discursive or humorous, it might be called a "low" tone. For instance, here is the opening of Vladimir Nabokov's novel, *The Real Life of Sebastian Knight*:

Sebastian Knight was born on the thirty-first of December, 1899, in the former capital of my country. An old Russian lady who has for some obscure reason begged me not to divulge her name, happened to show me in Paris the diary she had kept in the past. So uneventful had those years been (apparently) that the collecting of daily details (which is always a poor method of self-preservation) barely surpassed a short description of the day's weather; and it is curious to note in this respect that the personal diaries of sovereigns—no matter what troubles beset their realms—are mainly concerned with the same subject. Luck being what it is when left alone, here I was offered something which I might never have hunted down had it been a chosen quarry. Therefore I am able to state that the morning of Sebastian's birth was a fine windless one, with twelve degrees (Reaumur) below zero . . . this is all, however, that the good lady found worth setting down.[11]

Another example occurs in *A Room with a View*, by E. M. Forster:

"The Signora had no business to do it," said Miss Bartlett, "no business at all. She promised us south rooms with a view close together, instead of which here are north rooms, looking into a courtyard, and a long way apart. Oh, Lucy!"

"And a Cockney, besides!" said Lucy, who had been further saddened by the Signora's unexpected accent. "It might be London." She looked at the two rows of English people who were sitting at the table; at the row of white bottles of water and red bottles of wine that ran beween the English people; at the portraits of the late Queen and the late Poet Laureate that hung behind the English people.[12]

Probably a majority of all the novels that have ever been published begin in some similar quiet tone. It is a reliable way to make the reader feel easy and familiar in what is, after all, a highly artificial medium. In the first example, the main intention is not so much to

[11] New York: New Directions, 1959; p. 5.
[12] New York: Alfred A. Knopf, 1922; p. 13.

inform the reader about Sebastian Knight as it is to win his interest in a narrator who speaks with informality and charm. This would be a miscalculation, however, if it served only one purpose. As the book progresses, it becomes clear that the personality of the narrator and his ways of thought are important to the shape of the story.

The second example, while conversational and scenic, maintains the same level tone. Nothing startling, intense, or even very important is happening here; a small anomaly and a mild piece of humor set the story in motion. With all beginnings of this kind, the main effort is to engage the reader and to gain his confidence.

Yet, the beginning is most effective if it bears some relationship, in style and tone, to the whole novel—and, clearly, many novels deal with a much higher drama than either of these will. It is not good practice, however, to begin with an event of major importance within the scheme of the whole story. Robert Penn Warren's beginning to *All the King's Men* establishes the right tone by suggesting a purely hypothetical scene:

To get there you follow Highway 58, going northeast out of the city, and it is a good highway and new. Or it was new that day we went up it. You look up the highway and it is straight for miles, coming at you, with the black line down the center coming at and at you, black and slick and tarry-shining against the white of the slab, and the heat dazzles up from the white slab so that only the black line is clear, coming at you with the whine of the tires, and if you don't quit staring at that line and don't take a few deep breaths and slap yourself hard on the back of the neck you'll hypnotize yourself and you'll come to just at the moment when the right front wheel hooks over into the black dirt shoulder off the slab, and you'll try to jerk her back on but you can't because the slab is high like a curb and maybe you'll try to reach to turn off the ignition just as she starts the dive. But you won't make it, of course. Then a nigger chopping cotton a mile away, he'll look up and see the little column of black smoke standing up above the vitriolic, arsenical green of the cotton rows, and up against the violent, metallic, throbbing blue of the sky, and he'll say, "Lawd God, hit's a-nudder one done done hit!"[13]

[13] New York: Harcourt, Brace & World, 1946; p. 3.

There is, of course, no automobile crash in the opening of the story —it is simply a possibility imagined within the mind of the narrator. Thus there is no actual melodrama in the events the writer describes; yet he wishes to impart at once a sense of danger and disaster, because his story is to be about dangerous and disastrous lives. And he does it by creating an image of high speed and sudden death in a landscape where colors are "arsenical," "metallic," "throbbing." He creates an atmosphere of violence without risking the reader's incredulity by narrating unprepared-for events of violence.

The beginning that aims at dramatic intensity has great technical risks connected with it. When the story or novel seems unquestionably to demand this method, the author should respond with his best powers of invention. He must find a tactical device, as Warren has in the quoted passage, in order to do something while seeming not to do it; to transmit a charged feeling about his scene on the one hand while making it seem natural and comprehensible on the other. The beginning of *Man's Fate*, by André Malraux, finds Ch'en, a terrorist, standing in a dark hotel room about to murder a sleeping man. It is a scene as exotic to most readers as the beginning of an Eric Ambler novel of suspense. Yet Malraux brings it within the realm of comprehensibility by concentrating on Ch'en's inner feelings—and not on the act of assassination. How does it feel to be in the position of killing a living being? how does the mind react? Even at that, many readers might be alienated at the outset of this powerful novel from having too much of the merely bizarre thrust upon them. The "high" beginning, like any other, must find a way to engage the reader and to make his interest endure beyond the momentary excitements.

CHOOSING THE BEGINNING

The writer who has laid out the main lines of his story either on paper or in his mind will frequently go through some sort of questioning process in order to devise an appropriate start. That process can be indicated here in no more than a very general way. Say, for instance, that a story is to be very largely concerned with one woman's life and character. Should this be strongly impressed upon the reader at the very start? Or should she be withheld for just a short time—as Tolstoy withholds Anna Karenina and Flaubert Madame Bovary—while certain things about her milieu are displayed? Say that another story has to do with the relationships of four people over the space of a decade. Should it begin with their first meeting and proceed chronologically? Or might it be better to choose a moment, perhaps in the tenth year, in which they are about to make some decisive change in their relationships—with only that part of the past that bears on the present situation recalled to the story? Say that one's story is about a man who is both very fortunate and a fraud. He goes from one unearned success to another, but arrives, finally, at catastrophe. Should the beginning reflect alone the promising and unhampered start of his career? Or should it not give some strong intimation that here is a character who already bears within him the source of his own downfall? All of these situations are oversimplified, and yet they do suggest some of the calculation an author must apply to one of his most delicate problems.

"Once upon a time in a faraway country there lived a handsome prince." Some of the best stories in the world began that way. But, sad to say, we are all too old for them now. If the novelist or short story writer can arouse just half the anticipation the child had when he heard those words, he is in luck.

3 STYLE AND SPEECH

Style! style! complained the Goncourt brothers after an evening with Flaubert and other literary friends. They had had to listen to "a tremendous argument" about, among other things, assonance; Flaubert had said the writer must get rid of it even if it took a week to eliminate only one example. Then he and a fellow novelist, Ernest Feydeau, "started discussing a thousand different recipes for style and form, pompously and earnestly explaining little mechanical tricks of the trade, and expounding with childish gravity and ridiculous solemnity ways of writing and rules for producing good prose." The idea of a fictional work, the Goncourts decided, was nothing more to either speaker than "a peg on which to hang sound and light." They added, "We felt as if we were listening to an argument between grammarians of the Byzantine Empire."

Every writer is forced to think about style as soon as he begins to work seriously. He can hardly avoid the problem, though he may not consciously put it to himself that this is what his concern is with. But he wants to be a writer presumably because he has a particular viewpoint toward life that he feels compelled to put down on paper. To convey that viewpoint, to catch whatever emotions are attached to it, he must get it down in a certain way—in *his own* way. And so, at once, he is involved in considerations of style. What words will best convey to the reader the thing that he sees and feels? What kind of sentences give the subject its appropriate rhythm?

This is not, of course, "style" as a beginner usually understands the term. "Style," he would probably say if someone pressed him, is "fine writing." He would be rather vague about what he meant by "fine writing," but he would insist that it was something he recognized when he saw it. It involves descriptions of scenery, doesn't it? and paragraphs in which authors philosophize about their characters or theme? His own manuscripts, probably, are speckled with efforts at "style." They are the patches that fill him with pride and admiration when he goes over a particular work. They represent, in his considered opinion, the best writing he's ever done; the job is going to be to bring the rest of the narrative up to their high standard (as it is, they're a bit too conspicuous).

It goes without saying, probably, that the creative intelligence is not very sophisticated when it makes this equation between style and fine ("fancy" is a better word) writing. But this is a viewpoint that most writers have held at one time, and like other penalties of adolescence it seems to be something they must weather through and hope to get over as quickly as possible.

Luckily, something good is happening to them during this same period. Writers are usually omnivorous readers. Although pleasure may be their primary motive, the critical process is at work whether or not they are always aware of its activity. They cannot fail to ask themselves why some authors speak directly and urgently to them when others do not. Consider, for instance, two treatments of substantially the same theme; each aims to create the same reader response to what happens to its characters. Why does one seem so good and the other so flat? Why can some books be reread with pleasure, and even a sense of fresh discovery, when others that are equally serious in their treatment, equally deserving of respect, can barely be got through once? "It's the *way* X puts it," the beginner finally concludes—and there he is, pondering about style, even though another part of his mind still goes on thinking that style is concerned with grand descriptions and noble sentiments. That phase will sooner or later be left behind, and the writer will then possess, not a style of his own, certainly, but a set of examples from the work of those authors who seem most nearly to be allied to him in temperament, outlook, and interests.

It is this kind of experience that T. S. Eliot is describing when he speaks of "the influences which, so to speak, first introduce one to oneself." In his view, these influences not only appeal to one's temperament but offer "a form of expression which gives a clue to the discovery of one's own form." Eliot adds that the authors who affect us most powerfully when we are beginning to study our craft are probably not among "the great masters." He thinks that the latter "are too exalted and too remote. They are like distant ancestors who have been almost deified." The "smaller" writer, "who has directed one's first steps, is more like an admired elder brother."

In this passage, Eliot is discussing the experience of poets, but that of beginning fiction writers is analogous. Their early influences will make up a very mixed bag, and most of it will represent those authors whose techniques are essentially simple and capable of being emulated with a degree of success: Scott, perhaps; Dickens, Hawthorne, Poe. The possible choices and the combinations of choice are endless. Eventually these early influences will yield precedence to two or three writers who more closely approximate the masters of whom Eliot speaks. When the shadow of these greater eminences falls across his page, the writer is about to enter another stage of his development.

This is the terminal stage of his apprenticeship, and the most painful of all. It can also go on the longest. For the writer will first do his best to sound as nearly like his masters as he can; and then he will spend years trying to sound like anybody else under the sun—preferably himself, of course.

The greater eminences whose influence on beginners is at once baleful and beneficial are often stylists in a manner very close to the crude definition given earlier. They are not "fancy" writers (or not often), but there is no denying that they have evolved a conspicuous form of discourse. Many a small craft, manned by an amateur, has crashed on the fog-shrouded coast of Meredith. His is a siren voice not heard as often in our generation as fifty years ago, but it isn't stilled. Henry James is another old enchanter; and among more recent authors there are Faulkner, Virginia Woolf, and Hemingway. All of these writers were alert to the possibilities of language, and so it is understandable that the beginner, who is (or ought to be) alert to language, also, goes to them with so much enthusiasm. What he doesn't immediately see is that they are using language to get somewhere, to get something across. In his early intoxication with a Jamesian elaboration, or with the hard clarity of Hemingway's writing, the beginner says merely "That's it! That's the *way!*" and he immediately sets about applying the language of James or of Hemingway to his own particular subject matter and theme. It is very hard on writers that this should be the usual method by which they grope toward the style that is pecul- iarly their own, for as this phase prolongs itself they find their determination faltering. The romance of creation has faded; the act gives them no pleasure and certainly affords none to anyone else. The struggle has lasted too long and, as it seems, come to no pur- pose.

A writer's life is full of critical hours, and this is the first of them. He must either force himself to go on—he doesn't know where, or to what—or he must make the decision to give up. He will tell him- self that it's no use even as he sits down to try again. Out of this stony despair, the authentic literary personality is sometimes born —not immediately, of course, not without more dreadful failures, but finally. It is rather as if the writer found himself stripped of everyone and everything he had ever loved by a disaster as in- comprehensible as it is final. He is alone; but in this solitude he begins to emerge as himself. He begins, that is, to speak in his own way.

THE WAYS OF "SPEAKING"

Views on style are many, often contradictory, and sometimes bewildering. If there is a characteristic common to most of them, it is the effect of militancy that they give. Feeling runs high. The beginner is told that if he likes Henry James he cannot possibly approve of H. G. Wells; that a partiality for Arnold Bennett automatically deprives him of Virginia Woolf's company; that his admiration for Flaubert is quite incompatible with his affection for Trollope. The thing he hesitates to confess is that all of these writers are tumbled together in that bag containing his favorites. He has supposed that he was learning something valuable from each of them, but evidently this is not possible. For he has learned from his critical reading in the subject that one must take a side. What, then, are some of the views on style? Here are three very different ones—

Style, said Flaubert, is "in itself an absolute way of seeing things"; at another time he said: "A good prose sentence should be like a good line of poetry—*unchangeable*. . . ."

"I have never taken any very great pains about writing," H. G. Wells declared. Wells thought that literature was not "jewelry"; "it has quite other aims than perfection, and the more one thinks of 'how it is done' the less one gets it done."

"The whole secret of a living style," wrote Thomas Hardy, "and the difference between it and a dead style, lies in not having too much style—being in fact a little careless, or rather seeming to be, here and there."

Pronouncements like these could be multiplied, but they would simply illustrate more fully three common attitudes toward style: that it is everything; that it is unimportant; that it must give an effect of spontaneity or informality, however that may be contrived. Affecting each of these attitudes is the general rule that a style should be neither so elegant nor so awkward that it distracts attention from the narrative.

The reader will at once feel how unsatisfactory categorizations are—how untrue to his own experience of particular authors. Virginia Woolf was a conspicuous stylist, yet where is there language which is duller or more pedestrian than in *The Voyage Out* and the much later *The Years*? What about the splendid passages in Wells's *Tono-Bungay* and *Mr. Polly*? The point is, perhaps, that in practice the majority of writers exist in a solution of all three theories. The most that can be safely said is that, over the long haul, some are more acutely aware of language than others. That is why, no matter what anyone may suggest to the contrary, the beginner can learn something from every book he reads.

When, however, he reaches the end of his school-going days, when he confronts only his solitary self, he will need to remember whatever sensible advice writers or critics have given him. How can he achieve a style that is distinctively his own? How can he get his effects with the maximum economy of language? Most important of all, how can he tell truly?

One of the most important principles of modern fiction is associated, at least by tradition, with Flaubert, that "Byzantine grammarian." It is that the writer must pursue indefatigably the *mot juste,* or "right word"; and, beyond that, the exact rightness of phrase and sentence. Such a concern would result in the kind of style that Flaubert himself sought: "as rhythmical as verse and as precise as science, with the booming rise and fall of a cello and plumes of fire . . . a style which penetrates the idea . . . like a dagger-thrust." Flaubert had other ideas about style which seem now rather fussy and neither right nor wrong in principle. His dislike of assonance has already been noted; similarly, he was at pains to see that no word was ever repeated on the same manuscript page. Such strictures every writer will apply or ignore as he sees fit. What is important is Flaubert's concern with the right—the inevitable—cast of a sentence. In fiction, an action is done once, for all time. A line of dialogue is a permanent expression of the speaker's outlook and temperament. Everything must count.

Here is a passage from *The Mysteries of Udolpho*—one of those copious novels of the eighteenth century:

> The peasants of this gay climate were often seen on an evening, when the day's labour was done, dancing in groups on the margin of the river. Their sprightly melodies, *débonnaire* steps, the fanciful figure of their dances, with the tasteful and capricious manner in which the girls adjusted their simple dress, gave a character to the scene entirely French.[1]

[1] New York: Everyman's Library, 1931; I, 3–4.

The author, Ann Radcliffe, is taking some pains at this point to establish the setting of her story, and there is nothing unpleasing about her way of writing. But can we *see* those peasants? do we really believe that a dance is going on before us? What kind of adjustment of dress is "tasteful and capricious"? What kind of dress is "simple"? The scene is "entirely French," the author tells us, and we need her assurance.

Although English fiction from the sixteenth to the nineteenth century produced a number of examples of carefully wrought—and even overwrought—prose (Swift, Fielding, Jane Austen among the former, and Lyly's Euphues books among the latter), many writers of stories and novels were content with a conventional language. In this they were unlike English poets, who had always to think about style because of the strict requirements of meter. The idea that prose was capable of greater demands than were being made of it was slow to establish itself, and the great experiments with language belong chiefly to our century. Whatever affection, however great the admiration, one feels for Thackeray or Dickens, for Sir Walter Scott, for Samuel Richardson, even for Mrs. Radcliffe, it is no longer possible to write as they did. The *mot juste* has swept all serious writers before it.

A comment should be made here, however, about those writers for whom Wells speaks. They are the men and women who, with a minimal stylistic sensibility, appeal to the exceptional circumstances of a time. They may be not only widely read but seriously treated by their contemporaries. An example is James T. Farrell, whose naturalistic stories and novels of Chicago in the first three decades of this century were once greatly admired. Mark Schorer observes that Mr. Farrell asks his prose "to perform no service beyond communication of the most rudimentary kind of fact." Style certainly has to do with facts, but only as they serve to illuminate the theme of a fiction. Few if any novels have survived beyond their own time because of their documentation of social events, and Mr. Farrell's eventual literary fate seems to be foreshadowed in that of Wells himself. Wells's subjects were often of urgent contemporary importance, and it is impossible not to admire the earnestness and dedication with which he tackled them. But he is remembered now for *Tono-Bungay, Kipps, Mr. Polly,* and the science fiction stories. Mr. Farrell, too, has written seriously about serious subjects: poverty, sexual experience, moral disintegration. Compared with any of his books, the subject of *Mrs. Dalloway*—the party which Clarissa is getting ready for through most of the narrative—is as fragile as those flowers which she goes out to buy as her story begins. But *Mrs. Dalloway* is about love, about death, about madness, about how we apprehend each moment through which we live and what meaning we extract from the accumulation of those moments; that is the achievement of its style and theme. The Studs Lonigan and Danny O'Neill books are about how it is to be poor and young and Irish in Chicago in a period which is now closed away in history.

Both Wells and Farrell are examples of the journalistic style: Farrell of that style at its worst, Wells at something less than its best. If the present chapter were to attempt an examination of the language of popular fiction, it would be necessary to say a good deal about this kind of writing. It implies haste, careless repetition, the resorting to clichés, the use of high-flown words to give color to sentences that are flat and commonplace, and a general indifference to the rhythms of sustained prose. Here, to give an example, is a passage from Dreiser's *Sister Carrie:*

> Passion in a man of Hurstwood's nature takes a vigorous form. It is no musing, dreamy thing. There is none of the tendency to sing outside of my lady's window—to languish and repine in the face of difficulties. In the night he was long getting to sleep because of too much thinking, and in the morning he was early awake, seizing with alacrity upon the same dear subject and pursuing it with vigour.[2]

This passage has something of the terrible sentimentality of a film star's memoirs: "musing, dreamy thing"; "my lady's window"; "long getting to sleep"; "early awake"; "the same dear subject." Dreiser is one of those great, craggy objects in the American literary landscape. There is no dismissing him. How much time it will

[2] New York: The Modern Library, 1932; p. 211.

take to wear him away is something that none of us, probably, will live long enough to find out. But he is another example of the serious author of profoundly defective sensibility. Like Wells, like Farrell, he deserves respect, for he too was possessed by ideas that he felt were of social importance. Ideas will not indefinitely survive an indifferent treatment, but no one of good will can dismiss as contemptible writers who have honestly thought otherwise—or done otherwise because they could do no better. The landscapes of England and America exhibit a number of such rocky eminences: Sinclair Lewis; Sherwood Anderson, in much of his writing; Aldous Huxley, in much of his; Booth Tarkington; Jack London. It is the practitioner who is slack and fuzzy because the market asks nothing better of him who deserves his oblivion—a point which can be emphasized by a short necrology of writers whose fame once equaled the fame of many current best-selling fictionists: Myrtle Reed, Marie Conway Oemler, Eden Phillpotts, Gertrude Atherton, Rupert Hughes, Ben Ames Williams, Louis Bromfield. These are not men and women exhumed from the eighteenth and nineteenth centuries. They are our contemporaries—authors whose careers were established mainly or entirely after 1900. Few of these writers lacked for ideas, for interesting, sometimes even important, subjects. It would be wrong to base their failure on style alone, but the pedestrian quality of their language is one of the principal reasons why they are now of interest chiefly to those historians who deal with the popular tastes of former times.

The fact remains, of course, that the "subject" is the evident reason for any fictional excursion. It is the dog that has to be walked, the excuse for going out. Its owners are Style and Theme, and unfortunately there is sometimes an incongruity between the leaders and the led. A famous story by Conrad Aiken, "Silent Snow, Secret Snow," can be likened to a Chihuahua being walked by giants. Mr. Aiken's central character is a twelve-year-old boy who is sinking into madness. His delusion takes the form of snow, falling softly, falling deep, coming closer and closer to him until, at the end, the whole world is "a vast moving screen of snow": "it said peace, it said remoteness, it said cold, it said sleep."

Madness is an extremely difficult theme. To take as the subject intended to dramatize this theme a child leading an ordinary life of school, friends, and parents is to compound the difficulty. How Mr. Aiken went about planning his story one doesn't know, but it seems probable that he said to himself that, in order for the story to work, the child would have to possess uncommon intelligence and imagination. And it would be well to place him at an age when physiological changes can have a considerable effect on personality. (Mr. Aiken touches lightly on this aspect of his subject, but it is there if the reader wants to make anything of it.) And the boy had better be an only child, free to indulge his dream of snow, without the constant intrusion of brothers and sisters who would call him back to the normal world.

There would remain, at this point, the problem of language. How is madness to be described? or how brought into the story as silently and as secretly as the falling snow? Mr. Aiken tells the story from the viewpoint of the boy himself; the observations, the conclusions are his. This strategy seems inevitable, but it places marked limitations on the author's range of expression, his use of image and allusion, even though this particular boy has a greater verbal facility than the average twelve-year-old. It is here that "Silent Snow, Secret Snow" seems to go wrong. The language is eloquent; it rises fully to sustain the theme; but in doing so it soars far beyond its subject:

Queer, the effect this extraordinary surprise had had upon him—all the following morning he had kept with him a sense as of snow falling about him, a secret screen of new snow between himself and the world. . . . The delusion had been so vivid as to affect his entire behavior. . . .

This had been . . . the only distressing feature of the new experience; the fact that it so increasingly had brought him into a kind of mute misunderstanding, or even conflict, with his father and mother. It was as if he were trying to lead a double life. . . . And at school, how extraordinarily hard to conduct with success simultaneously the public life and the life that was secret! There were times when he longed—positively ached—to tell everyone about it—to burst out with it—only to be checked almost at once by a far-off feeling as of some faint absurdity which was inherent in it—but *was* it absurd?—and more importantly by a sense of mysterious power in his very secrecy.[3]

Probably no critic has ever read this story without the uneasy sense that he was being made the victim of an elaborate leg pull. It is as Jamesian as anything of James's, including his novel about a little girl, *What Maisie Knew*. In short, it can be read as precisely the kind of literary joke that inventive and irreverent authors are pleased occasionally to perpetrate. But Mr. Aiken has permitted "Silent Snow, Secret Snow" to be included in the volume of his collected stories, and this book surely would have provided him with the occasion for a public confession, if one were due. So we must suppose that he has given us the right to treat the story seriously, and to say that the style and theme are uneasily served by the subject. The failure, it must be admitted, is a noble one; "Silent Snow, Secret Snow" is a better story than many which have achieved a more perfect consonance of language, subject, and theme.

A discussion of the extremes of style—Wells and Farrell at one end of the scale, Aiken at the other—would do well to take up the case of a writer whose language settled over the subjects of his fiction as densely as the fog it was compared to earlier. Edith Wharton complained that with two exceptions she had never been able to find out what any of George Meredith's books were about. She said this in the company of Henry James, and in order to temper her criticism of such an eminent writer she added that in many passages, especially descriptive ones, Meredith's "style rose to a height of poetic imagery." At this point James broke in on her "with the cry that I had put my finger on the central weakness of Meredith's art, its unconscious insincerity. Words—words—poetic imagery, metaphors, epigrams, descriptive passages! How much did any of them weigh in the baggage of the authentic novelist? . . . Meredith [James went on] was a sentimental rhetorician."

In an essay on Meredith, James would certainly have qualified

[3] Included in *The Collected Short Stories of Conrad Aiken* (Cleveland: The World Publishing Company, 1960), pp. 219, 221–222.

this sweeping condemnation; "The Case of General Ople and Lady Camper," for instance, is a brilliant comedy. But it is generally true that Meredith's famous style rolls on regardless of its defenseless subject matter. "Style," Ellen Glasgow said, "should be [like] a transparent complexion which changes colour in response to the animation within." This is an eminently sensible observation—however difficult it may be to apply to one's own work.

Long after the beginner has got over the habit of associating style with fancy language, it is a curious fact that he goes on thinking that a great style is an esoteric one. If an example is required of him, he may cite James, although James's style, at least in his last and most discussed period, is that of oral delivery. To read him aloud is to discover that his famous "difficulty" recedes. Like any fluent conversationalist, James was aware of the rhythms of speech and of those meaningless interpolations which vary a rhythm or break it up. His language is speckled with "as it weres" and "in fines" and "at leasts" and "actuallys." Set down on the printed page and hedged with commas, they give the sentences in which they are resident a formidable look. Read aloud, they appear as the regular pauses of a good talker—for breath, or to marshal his facts, or for emphasis—and it is then possible to see how idiomatic and even colloquial James's great "manner" usually is. The reader may like or dislike such a style, but he can't call it esoteric in James's best work of this last period. It is *apparent,* certainly, on a first encounter, but in the way that a monologuist of extraordinary vigor may startle before beginning to interest.

That "elegance" of an artificial, "literary" sort is never desirable in fiction can be seen clearly in the work of second- or third-rate writers of every generation. It would be ungenerous to mention them by name, and it is unnecessary. Their failings have been acutely summarized in Willa Cather's comment on a particular group of romantic storytellers: "They always departed in that school of writing," she said; "they never went anywhere." This could be labeled the school of *Roget's Thesaurus:* "depart," don't just "go"; "eschew," don't just "avoid."

Meredith, James, those romancers whom Willa Cather disliked—

N.B.

in their various ways each sought the *mot juste;* or if not always that, at least the rightness of sentence or paragraph or scene. They may have shot absurdly far off the mark, but nevertheless their failures indicate a regard for the possibilities of language. This is generally true also of the serious writers who approximate the style that Hardy recommended: informal, seemingly spontaneous—in his word, "living." John Crowe Ransom has said that poets often write smoothly and then go back and "ruffle" their verse. His reference is to meters—the poet knows that the unfaltering iambs in which his lines are naturally written will first relax the reader's attention and then put him to sleep. Some irregularities must be introduced to snatch him back from the edge of slumber (or, worse, boredom). These should not look calculated; they ought to appear to be the happy inventions of inspiration, committed to the page quickly, before they could escape. Many prose writers enjoy a similar facility —that very fatal facility which, if it is not regularly called to a hard task, will eventually swamp its possessors in platitude or prolixity, and very probably in both. It isn't surprising that this should be so. Writers may not often come from backgrounds which are, in the strict sense, cultivated, but many emerge from bookish backgrounds. They have parents or guardians, whole families perhaps, who are more than ordinarily articulate. The example of fluency, of a range of vocabulary and allusion, is constantly before them; and to hold their own they must emulate it. Later, to hold their own, they must discover its limitations.

Anyone who has examined the facsimile manuscript edition of *The Old Wives' Tale* is bound to be struck by Bennett's sense of security in his own expression. Page after page goes by with only an occasional interlinear or marginal correction. The author even has time to draw title pages and chapter initials. It is true that Bennett began his novel partly as an exercise in calligraphy, but an edge of his attention certainly must have been caught by the story he was telling. But there it all is for the reader to marvel at— that great, flawed book, set down almost like the tables of the law, with only a scratch here and there to show where something was changed. However one may feel about the appropriate transmission of a decalogue, he may feel quite sure that novels are set down by a different method. Bennett had the fatal fluency; no inner voice warned him to beware of prolixity or of the commonplace. He said of himself, in fact, "I have never, except on one minor occasion, had the courage to write a novel, or any part of a novel, twice over. I say to myself, 'What you have written you have written, and there it is, for better or worse.'"

The good writers of our own time who belong in the category of the "living style" are not only numerous but various in their concerns. There are Eudora Welty's compulsive talkers, her old people who are poor, her men who are half erotic legend, her nubile imbecile girls; J. D. Salinger's disaffected young men with exasperated sensibilities; J. F. Powers' Roman clergy. There is Angus Wilson's great, shabby omnibus stuffed with deranged scholars and homosexuals of every conceivable taste and distaste. There are C. P. Snow's scientists and teachers and politicians.

The reader's familiarity with the work of some or all of these writers will suggest to him how various the informal style may be. But to emphasize that variety, here are a few examples:

Although Miss Quested had not made herself popular with the English, she brought out all that was fine in their character. For a few hours an exalted emotion gushed forth, which the women felt even more keenly than the men, if not for so long.

Mrs. Harris wakened at about four o'clock, as usual, before the house was stirring, and lay thinking about their position in this new town. She didn't know why the neighbours acted so; she was as much in the dark as Victoria.

There's his other wife, standing on the nightstained porch by a potted fern, screaming things to a neighbor. This wife is really worse than the other one. She is more solid, fatter, shorter, and while not so ugly, funnier looking. She looks like funny furniture. . . .

She was a great flop of a woman with a big, coarse powerful face. The other two women whose eyes were closed had their brown shawls drawn tight about their heads, but Moll's was round her shoulders and the gap above her breasts was filled with a blaze of scarlet.

Each of these passages deals with a woman, yet the reader would not be likely to think that they were the work of the same writer. (The first is by E. M. Forster, the second by Willa Cather, the third by Eudora Welty, and the fourth by Frank O'Connor.) What they do have in common is the relaxed style of narration—perhaps too relaxed in some places: "emotion *gushed forth*," "she was as much *in the dark* as Victoria." Such a style can be very effective when the writer is constantly aware of the danger of carelessness, and it is far more adaptable to a range of themes and subjects than is the high style—or even the journalistic style. It comes closest, probably, to being that "transparent complexion," changing color "in response to the animation within," of which Ellen Glasgow spoke.

Still, despite our admiration for clarity and for a style that accommodates itself to whatever is asked of it, we often reserve our highest praise for the writer who has achieved a mode of expression so peculiarly and powerfully his own that it is as if he had come into the room with us and locked the door and shut the windows against the sounds of the ordinary world. (James, Faulkner, Hemingway—Meredith, even—are examples of such writers.) Writing is a process of self-discovery, which is why even those unpublished manuscripts of ours, even those never to be published, have each done something toward making us the persons we are. The great style is the expression of the total person, and so it is not something that the writer comes to after one or two books; or, as in the case of James, after five or ten. Obviously, it is something he may never come to at all. His vision of things may not require it—as Bennett's didn't, as Willa Cather's didn't. The great style demands that the writer have that passion for the exact rightness of words and phrases that Flaubert sought; and, beyond that passion, an amplitude of vision, a sensibility continuously exposed, and perhaps a ruthlessness of dedication to the craft of fiction that is beyond the ability or the desire of the majority. One may be taught to avoid the common mistakes of the journalistic style; one may learn how to write the informal style. But the great style, with its "booming rise and fall" and "plumes of fire" and penetration of the idea "like a dagger-thrust," is the product of long experiment, of total commitment to the literary project, and of the experience and reflection of a man or woman's whole life.

ON CATEGORIES

There are a number of books on rhetoric, some of which the beginner could study to advantage, but there are not many sustained discussions of style that offer much in the way of helpful comment. Nevertheless, *style* is something that crops up, however vaguely, in almost every critical essay, and the amount of terminology attached to it is by now formidable. One of the best discussions of this elusive subject is by Cyril Connolly, in his book *Enemies of Promise*. Mr. Connolly distinguishes two kinds of writing, vernacular and mandarin, but then he is obliged to offer qualification after qualification, to invent substyles and transitional styles, and edge round those books that are exceptions to everything. The distinctions in this chapter—high style, journalistic style, informal or "living" style—are quite as arbitrary as any other labels would be. They were chosen because they seemed to describe the commonest kinds of writing, and so to offer a point of departure for comment. But the majority of writers (even some of the high stylists) exist, as noted earlier, in a solution of all three modes, and any strict critical ordering of them would have to be made from book to book. The present categories, in short, are offered not as immutable definitions but as rules of thumb by which the beginner may evaluate his own productions. On only one point does it seem possible to be inflexible. H. W. Fowler, that high-spirited authority on English usage, called the *mot juste* a "LITERARY CRITICS' WORD," which "readers would like to buy of them as one buys one's neighbour's bantam cock for the sake of hearing its voice no more." But however ubiquitous the phrase, its moral is beyond argument. The writer whose language is slack, conventional, and fuzzy can never do full justice to any subject, no matter how well chosen it may be.

SPEECH

"All good dialogue," says Elizabeth Bowen, "perhaps deals with something unprecedented." Dialogue does not consist of speeches in which two people exchange commonplaces designed to feed the reader information. It is seldom suitable as a method for describing persons or places; it is no substitute for direct narrative; and the individual speech is useless as the vehicle for the hero's metaphysical broodings or philosophical speculations.

Speech, to begin with, is necessarily rather brief:

"What about the song? Why does that make you cry?" . . .

"I am thinking about a person long ago who used to sing that song."

"And who was that person long ago?" asked Gabriel, smiling.

"It was a person I used to know in Galway when I was living with my grandmother," she said. . . .

"Someone you were in love with?" he asked ironically.

"It was a young boy I used to know," she answered, "named Michael Furey. He used to sing that song. . . . He was very delicate."[4]

This is the closing scene to Joyce's great story, "The Dead." A man and wife are alone together in their room, the snow falling outside. She is telling him for the first time about an early lover. A beginning writer, who had pushed his story to this point, would probably be tempted to have the wife go on about Michael Furey at length—what he looked like, where he came from, what the two of them did. Such a strategy would be informative but without verisimilitude. Joyce evokes Michael Furey through the quick questions prompted by the husband's jealousy and the wife's spare, reluctant answers. "Something unprecedented": not all speech deals with startling new information, but the writer's concern is always with something which *adds* to the reader's present knowledge of situation or character or event.

Speech, then, is necessarily selective: the routine exchanges of any social event— How are you? can I get you a chair? would you

[4] Included in *The Portable James Joyce* (New York: The Viking Press, 1947), pp. 236–237.

like coffee or tea? is your cold better?—should be dispensed with or summarized briefly if they are necessary to the action:

Having seen Mrs. Pence into her favorite chair and provided her with coffee laced with whiskey and honey to ease her "susceptible" throat, Mrs. Flood sat down opposite her old friend and, leaning forward expectantly, said, "You didn't telephone. I suppose that means the worst? . . ."

The speech of one person or the exchange among several is selective also in its elimination of repetitive elements. It moves forward with the kind of briskness that we *remember* a conversation possessing. (In actual fact, most of us are incapable of reporting an event without telling parts of it over two or three times, for in the rush to give the news we cannot remember how close what we *have* said has come to what we *meant* to say: "And did I tell you that he . . . ?" "Yes, you told me that." "Would you believe it? That's what he said. He said . . .")

Speech should be part of a story's or novel's organic whole, but now and again a beginner will be misled by the success of a writer who shows a brilliant command of contemporary idiom. It may not be immediately apparent that much of the talk is to no purpose, that the narrative is idling like a motor. Certainly there are those instances when a fiction is composed of conversations that seem only to dramatize a series of encounters among the characters; but then we may say that in fact this seeming pointlessness is being used by the author to illuminate his theme. Some of Eudora Welty's stories, such as "Petrified Man," make fine use of what could be called the calculated random remark. Usually, though, when authors let their conversations run on too long it is because they know they've got something good working for them and they are reluctant to cut it off. Their critical sense deserts them and the resulting fiction is ill proportioned. J. D. Salinger has an acute ear for the speech of young people of a certain portion of the middle class, but often he exercises his talent to no purpose. The interminable bathroom scene between mother and son in *Franny and Zooey* is an example. Mr. Salinger's admirers delight in this kind of talk—

evidently cannot get enough of it—and are content to view it as an end in itself. But it seems at least possible that future readers, for whom it will have no contemporary immediacy, will view it as many now view the dialect in Scott's novels, which turns so many of his pages into sludge. They skip ahead, looking for what "happens" next.

The fault, of course, is not found merely with the writer who is good at contemporary speech. There is the writer good at jokes or pointed generalizations or lively cynicisms; or simply good at keeping the whole thing going, as Henry James was. A fair number of passages in his writings would benefit from pruning—passages where the great oral stylist topples over from conversation into bull session.

One of the most important purposes of speech is to express character. As a rule, it does this obliquely. From scene to scene the evidence accumulates until at last the reader says, "Why, how vindictive (or jealous or self-sacrificing) he is!" The author no more shows his hand directly than the character does. Both of them, after all, have a life-or-death interest in keeping up appearances—You didn't know what a scoundrel Robert was? It was to be hoped that you wouldn't. Robert certainly wouldn't have told you, and it suits his creator's purposes that you should perhaps look favorably on him until just before Janet herself begins to feel uneasy. Then all those rather odd remarks he's been making come rushing together into your mind, and what has struck Janet as a frightening change in his character is for you not only understandable but truly characteristic of him at last. Most people say one thing, perhaps think the opposite, or at any rate have two or three different private opinions about what they've commented on—the view they've seemingly committed themselves to. People often express in public one set of motives and in themselves cherish another, or at least that public set very much qualified. That is why speech, insofar as its aim is characterization, moves forward by means of partial concealment. When a writer wishes to introduce a man or woman who is to be revealed almost entirely by speech, he will need all of his skill and all of his boldness to bring that character off. In James's novel,

Washington Square, Catherine Morland's aunt, Mrs. Penniman, is such a character, and she is well done: "She was romantic; she was sentimental; she had a passion for little secrets and mysteries—a very innocent passion. . . ." James manages to demonstrate all of these traits in what she says. But most characters, like most humans, are more complex.

The clues which speech can give to character include indications of intellect, of inordinate pride or humility, of education (and by inference of background), and of obsession.

Dialect and bad grammar, as usages, are to be avoided whenever possible. Dialect is wearying to read; if the writer feels that it is necessary to characterization, it should be pegged on a few typical expressions or pronunciations, and otherwise suggested by syntax—perhaps by a common inversion or elision. Grammar offers even more difficulty; in real life people sometimes affect bad grammar, or old-fashioned locutions which are now considered ungrammatical, and on occasion the writer may want to confer one usage or the other on a character in a story or novel. But he must be careful never to make a simple equation between speech and education or social background.

As well as revealing character, speech offers a revelation of relationships. In *The Wings of the Dove* there is a masterly scene between Kate Croy and Merton Densher in which she agrees to become his mistress if he will encourage Milly Theale to fall in love with him—to the eventual profit, of course, of Kate and Merton. It is all done obliquely, in the words that two cold-hearted, sensual people might use to effect such an arrangement; and yet the reader is in no doubt about what arrangement has been reached or what contempt for human dignity the participants feel as they agree upon their plan. There is no doubt, either, about how they have sized one another up, how the meeting has clarified and crystallized their relationship. "Speech," Elizabeth Bowen notes, "is what characters *do to each other.*"

A fault not confined entirely to beginners is that of making everyone in a story or book sound like the same person. Every author is prone to this, since his is the solitary intelligence, his the particular voice, at work throughout. But he must vary his rhythms, his vocabulary, the length or brevity of a speech as much as he can, and make them conform as closely as possible to what would be true of the particular character. Certain expressions that are indicative of a habitual attitude toward life may help to give color to some characters, but these expressions must be used very sparingly. Their constant repetition will spoil their effectiveness; and probably they are really only useful with minor characters. The principal figures in a fiction are confronting situations, problems, crises which are outside their former experience—or, if they are not, they had better bide their time in the writer's imagination until he finds a stronger vehicle for them.

Speech should never be used merely to give the reader information: ". . . And this is your room, John, with its single bed and worn chest of drawers and its narrow window looking out on the alley at the back." "The alley that separates this house from its neighbors facing on the opposite street?" "Yes, that alley. We only have one alley, since both streets are made up of rowhouses." It is to be hoped that the beginner will pull himself together before he perpetrates anything quite this bad, but even something better won't be readily excused by the good reader. This warning is not intended to suggest, however, that speech can never deal with knowledge which people share in common. Lovers or friends may recall the events of the past which brought them together, and in doing so may provide the reader with information which it is useful for him to know. A chronic gossip might rattle on at length to a sympathetic auditor, retelling matters known perfectly to both of them but now seen in a new light because of a fresh happening. People meeting again after a long separation usually ask one another "What ever became of _____?" or "Did you ever get that . . . ?" or "I remember the last time I saw you. You were . . ." Properly used, speech is one of the best methods for building up in a reader's mind the sense of the past of the characters, their tastes and desires, and—again—their relationships to one another. It can build not only understanding but, because of that understanding, expectation about what will happen next.

One thing very difficult to accomplish by means of speech is the reporting of physical events which are crucial to the narrative and ought to be shown directly to the reader. Too often, the author who uses this strategy is evading the responsibility of dramatizing those events. Someone appears to tell about the great happening to a group of avid listeners. This happening has, perhaps, effected a critical change in the future of the central characters, some of whom were directly involved in it. The method is usually doomed to failure. No one, for instance, would be much impressed by a novel about fighting men if the author chose to tell it through the medium of a mother whose son wrote home regularly from the front. When writers consciously choose this indirect method it is because their subject is not some large event and its participants, but the people to whom the news is brought. They are at the center of that particular fiction.

Speech may serve other purposes besides those outlined in this section, but these, in some combination, are its general aims: (1) it should be brief, because in life few of us say more than a few words at a time; (2) it should add to the reader's present knowledge; (3) it should eliminate the routine exchanges of ordinary conversation; (4) it should convey a sense of spontaneity but eliminate the repetitiveness of real talk; (5) it should keep the story steadily moving forward, and not merely exhibit the writer's skill with idiom, or his wit; (6) it should be revelatory of the speaker's character, both directly and indirectly; and (7) it should show the relationships among people.

ATTRIBUTION

"Thank you," she exploded. "Tea?" he exclaimed. "I love you, Mavis," murmured Marvin loudly. . . . The problem of attribution is chronic. Somebody offered that tea; someone is in love with Mavis. Who it is appears outside that comma and terminal quote. How is the writer to tell his reader when it is Marvin speaking and when it is Mellors the butler? Either one might press a cup of tea on a lady; either one, or both, might be crazy about Mavis. There are writers who believe that *said* is the best solution to the problem, because the most neutral:

"No," she said.
"You're making a fool of yourself," Ronnie said.
"Not trying the macaroons, Mildred?" Malcolm said, drifting up.
"I said No," she said, looking furiously at Ronnie.
"The girl says no," said Malcolm. "No macaroons this afternoon."

Like the onion in cooking, *said* is one of the basic ingredients in the attribution of dialogue, but there can be too much of it; it is better with other seasonings—and sometimes it needn't be there at all. In a brief scene between two characters, the writer need identify each speaker only once:

"I hope you'll decide to come," Margaret said.
"Oh, I don't know, I really can't decide," said Mrs. Governor. "It would be the first time since—"
"Aren't you indulging yourself in sentimental creeps? Arthur was never fond of them. It's a most unlikely place for his ghost to rise."
"But you see that's just it!—how he keeps cropping up where he's no business being. . . ."

If such a passage were to continue for several pages, it would be enough for the writer to intersperse his dialogue with an occasional "Margaret said" or "Mrs. Governor said," simply to keep the reader straight.

Often, the description of an action, if it is relevant to the general point being made in a scene, may substitute for a direct attribution:

Margaret moved impatiently in her chair. "Then you've got to learn to push him back down, or send him back here, or something."
"Here!" Mrs. Governor settled the glasses on her nose and peered at Margaret with what looked to be astonishment. "What on earth makes you think he ever comes *here?*"

However, the problem can't always be dodged in this way; characters endlessly wiggling, twitching, pushing up their glasses, raising shades, pouring tea, sneezing, gesturing, would wreak havoc with a scene. And the moment the writer embarks on a conversation involving three or more people, he cannot expect the reader always to guess correctly which one is doing the talking. He is back to *said* or its substitutes.

There are a fair number of substitutes which should never be used except in extraordinary circumstances: exploded, expostulated, ejaculated, hissed, wheezed, chortled, smirked, chuckled (people say things *with* a chuckle; it must be very hard to chuckle out a sentence), growled, groaned, trilled, breathed, croaked, snarled—and those elegant Jamesian variants: "she flung at him," "he, laughingly, tossed back."

Something that people do all of the time, in conversation, is to reply to a previous speaker; so let that be on the list of acceptable substitutes. To reply is to "tell" someone something, so told him (or her) can be added. Sometimes a speaker will offer an observation which sums up or throws fresh light on the problem under discussion, and observed is therefore of use. This comment is also one that is being pointed out. People under an exceptional stimulus may shout or cry. A surprising piece of news may cause a character to exclaim. Once in a while one person may whisper to another, or murmur a comment. There are times when everybody snaps. They also ask or inquire, and answer. Occasionally they announce or declare. Now and again they repeat or echo an earlier remark.

Here is sufficient variety for ordinary purposes.

N.B.

4 CHARACTERIZATION

"The sense of character began to fade with D. H. Lawrence," Mary McCarthy wrote recently. "After *Sons and Lovers,* we do not remember figures in Lawrence's books, except for a few short malicious sketches." Miss McCarthy doesn't especially like this decline of what might be called classic characterization, but she feels it is irreversible. The fashionable writing coming from France these days, in the form of the "objective novel," confirms her view, but she is speaking less of the convictions of a particular school of novelists than of a tendency discernible in contemporary fiction in general.

By way of contrast, here are the views of some earlier writers. The most famous is that of Henry James, expressed in his essay, "The Art of Fiction." He says, "What is character but the determination of incident? What is incident but the illustration of character?" The good novels of the eighteenth, nineteenth, and early twentieth centuries conform closely to James's dictum. In her autobiography, *A Backward Glance,* Edith Wharton tells of that "strange moment when the vaguely adumbrated characters whose adventures one is preparing to record are suddenly *there,* themselves, in the flesh, in possession of one, and in command of one's voice and hand." In *A Certain Measure,* Ellen Glasgow describes the conception of her novel, *Virginia:*

I was walking with a friend . . . in one of the older aristocratic towns of our Commonwealth, when we passed a woman of later middle age, who looked at us with eyes of a faded flowerlike blue and the smile of a wistful Madonna. As she went by, my friend glanced after her and sighed softly, "How lovely she must once have been."

That was all, but it was enough. I never heard her actual name; yet when she returned, by and by, to haunt my imagination for years, she brought with her her own unalterable name and story.[1]

Arnold Bennett describes a somewhat similar experience:

In the autumn of 1903 I used to dine frequently in a restaurant in the Rue de Clichy. . . . [One night] an old woman came into the restaurant. . . . She was fat, shapeless, ugly, and grotesque. She had a ridiculous voice and ridiculous gestures. It was easy to see that she lived alone and that in the long lapse of years she had developed the kind of peculiarity which induces guffaws among the thoughtless. She was burdened with a lot of small parcels, which she kept dropping. She chose one seat; and then, not liking it, chose another; and then another. . . .

I reflected, concerning the grotesque diner: "This woman was once young, slim, perhaps beautiful, certainly free from these ridiculous mannerisms. Very probably she is unconscious of her singularities. Her case is a tragedy. One ought to be able to make a heart-rending novel out of the history of a woman such as she." . . .

It was at this instant that I was visited by the idea of writing the book which ultimately became *The Old Wives' Tale*.[2]

The present chapter will be devoted principally to the classic view of characterization. The writer may choose eventually to abandon all of those ways by which his predecessors built up the sense of identity, but then he must find his own way—and it is not one that any textbook can help him toward. A mastery of the customary tools of characterization has the same value that an artist finds in knowing color, basic design, and drawing. If the artist does not like the effects that he gets by using his formal training, at least he knows what the things are that won't—or don't—work for him; or what he wants to get rid of. And despite the vogue of the current French "antinovel," despite the neutrality of many characters in modern English and American fiction, there are random evidences of a return to the more full-bodied characterization of earlier periods. Writers as different as Saul Bellow, Angus Wilson, Lawrence Durrell, and J. F. Powers are all deeply concerned with portraying both the particular and the general in their accounts of men and women.

There are two principal ways by which the writer may present his characters. He may choose to describe them either in a set piece or by "unrolling" them. The set piece has a long and generally honorable history. It means that from traits initially laid down, heroes, heroines, and villains seldom diverge. The reader knows the character of Crusoe or of Gulliver near the beginning of their respective stories, and this practice of Defoe and Swift was still a common one over one hundred years later. For instance, Becky Sharp and Amelia Sedley, as they appear in the early part of *Vanity Fair*, are the Becky and Amelia of the concluding chapter. As late as the present century, set-piece characterization was a familiar device of the serious writer. Wells, Bennett, Galsworthy— all relied on it to some extent: the Soames Forsyte who dies at the end of *A Modern Comedy* is essentially the man met by readers a whole trilogy earlier, in the first volume of the Forsyte story.

Set-piece characterization is not often practiced today by serious writers, although it is a commonplace of much popular fiction. It was certainly always a literary device to put people all on view at the outset of a story; earlier writers knew perfectly well that they were ignoring the common experience when they labeled their characters hero, heroine, villain, comedy relief. In life it takes some time to discover who, if anyone, is the hero, what wife or mistress he'll choose for himself, and who is going to complicate their relationship with jealousy or malice or from another motive. The way of life is the way of modern fiction, which places its emphasis more on organic form (see Chapter 9) than on plot. The decline of set-piece characterization probably stems from this decline of plot structure. Where, as in so many eighteenth- and nineteenth-

N.B.

n.b.

N.B.

century novels, the narrative consists of a series of events, each leading to the next, and all of them culminating in some kind of emphatic resolution, the writer may feel that he must state clearly which characters are going to be responsible for which kinds of happenings: those that lead to the union of the lovers, the recovery of the lost fortune, and the triumphant vindication of right; and those that throw a spanner in the works.

n.b. Most good stories and novels of today, then, depend on the unrolling of characters in the course of the narrative. This is not to say that the reader's final impression of them is always different from his initial one. He may simply have got to know them a great deal better, to have had those first impressions confirmed, and to be, now, in the position to make a many-sided judgment about them. Undine Spragg, the central figure in *The Custom of the Country,* appears at the outset of her history as a selfish, imperious girl. As her story goes on, however, it becomes plain that she is entirely without moral scruple, that she is cold hearted, self-indulgent, ambitious, and—in her effect on the lives of those around her—evil.

Since, as James says, character determines incident, and incident provides the final illumination of character, many stories and novels move forward by showing how the traits initially on view to the reader precipitate events which the character may or may not be able to cope with. In either case, these events are going to leave their mark on him, and what he has learned (or failed to learn) about himself has also deepened the reader's understanding of him. It is George Babbitt's boredom with his present life that gets him involved first with Tanis Judique and her bohemian friends and then with the cause of liberalism which affronts his conservative business colleagues. The relationship with Tanis comes to nothing, and his wife's illness restores Babbitt to his family and to "respectability," but his love affair and his excursion into liberalism have shaken him out of some of the platitudes to which he was once so firmly committed. When his son rebels, it is Babbitt who takes the boy's side and who determines that he shall find his own way, regardless of convention. That is not a decision that the man the reader meets at the beginning of *Babbitt* would make—or even dream that he would sometime face.

George Babbitt is a simple, clear-cut example of the unrolling of a character who is going to experience a change of outlook in the course of a story. As such, he offers the beginning writer a chance to grasp the elementary rules for presenting such a character. But just because the conception is so unsubtle, the beginner must be cautioned that he had better try to improve on it in his own work. Babbitt is first one thing, and then another, and finally a third. There is a certain discontinuity to the reader's image of him. Characters should seem all of a piece, and they should carry all of themselves along wherever they go or whatever they do. They may be full of surprises, but, after the reader has recovered from his shock, he should feel that this act or that one was not only perfectly intelligible but inevitable. *n.b.*

Once the writer has decided on the method by which he is going to handle his characters (and it might in some instances be a combination of those discussed above), he must determine on the best way to make them flesh and blood for the reader. He will want to use some or all of the following:

Physical appearance.
Movements, gestures, mannerisms, habits. *N.B.*
Behavior toward others.
Speech.
Attitude toward self.
Attitude of others toward the character.
Physical surroundings.
Past.
Fringe techniques such as names and figures of speech.

These are the conventional methods of characterization. Contemporary writers also employ the stream of consciousness technique. Stream of consciousness will be discussed in a separate section of this chapter, for two reasons. First, it requires a somewhat longer exposition than other methods. Second, some critics consider it a strategy of presentation (like set piece and unrolling) rather than one more device by which characterization is achieved. For instance, in *The Novel and the Modern World*, David Daiches says: "Novelists who employ the 'stream of consciousness' would deny that character *portrayal* is possible for the fiction writer at all: character is a process not a state, and the truth about men's reactions to their environment—and what is a man's character but his reactions to environment, actual and potential?—can be presented only through some attempt to show this process at work."

The present section will, then, confine itself to a closer look at the conventional methods.

PHYSICAL APPEARANCE

Nineteenth-century writers were lavish with detail: a character might be described from his widow's peak, aristocratic Roman nose, neckcloth, and faultless breeches, to his exquisitely polished boots. Here is Benjamin Disraeli writing in quick succession of two characters in *Coningsby*:

His countenance, radiant with health and the lustre of innocence, was at the same time thoughtful and resolute. The expression of his deep blue eye was serious. Without extreme regularity of features, the face was one that would never have passed unobserved. His short upper lip indicated a good breed; and his chestnut curls clustered over his open brow, while his shirt-collar thrown over his shoulders was unrestrained by handkerchief or ribbon. Add to this a limber and graceful figure, which the jacket of his boyish dress exhibited to great advantage. . . .

The gentleman for whom he had been all this time waiting entered the room. . . .

He . . . was a man of middle size and age, originally in all probability of a spare habit, but now a little inclined to corpulency. Baldness, perhaps, contributed to the spiritual expression of a brow which was, however, essentially intellectual, and gave some character of openness to a countenance which, though not ill-favoured, was unhappily stamped with a sinister cast that was not to be mistaken. His manner was easy, but rather audacious than well-bred. Indeed, while a visage which might otherwise be described as handsome was spoiled by a dishonest glance, so a demeanour that was by no means deficient in self-possession and facility, was tainted by an innate vulgarity, which in the long run, though seldom, yet surely developed itself.[3]

This is a useful passage to look at because everything is wrong with it. To begin with, the reader can't hold so much detail in his mind when it is given at one time. In striving to produce a definite visual image, the author has succeeded in producing only a succession of small images that don't result in much of a picture. Second, the author is cheating when he comes to the "man of middle size and age." There is nothing in this scene which would betray the man's "innate vulgarity"; he has done nothing to suggest that his habitual manner is "audacious" rather than "well-bred"; nor is it clear what makes his glance "dishonest." The author is telling the reader too bluntly what he wants him to know, and so abusing a principle of objective description: the reader should not feel that he has been told more about a character than an intelligent observer within the fiction would be capable of finding out.

The passage is also remarkable for its stylistic deficiencies: it is a compendium of stereotyped phrases which would do credit to Frank Sullivan's Cliché Expert: "radiant with health," "lustre of innocence," "deep blue eye," "open brow," "limber and graceful figure." The language of fiction has already been discussed, but it should be pointed out here that physical description which rests on generalities will never convey any clear picture to the reader.

Coningsby came out in 1844. As the century went on, writers became more sophisticated in their handling of physical appearance. Here is a passage from Thomas Hardy's story, "The Three Strangers" (1883):

The sad wan light revealed the lonely pedestrian to be a man of supple frame; his gait suggested that he had somewhat passed the period of perfect and instinctive agility, though not so far as to be otherwise than rapid of motion when occasion required. At a rough guess, he might have been about forty years of age. He appeared tall, but a recruiting sergeant, or other person accustomed to the judging of men's heights by the eye, would have discerned that this was chiefly owing to his gauntness, and that he was not more than five-feet-eight or nine.

[3] New York: Signet Classics, 1962; p. 28.

N.B.

Notwithstanding the regularity of his tread there was caution in it, as in that of one who mentally feels his way; and despite the fact that it was not a black coat nor a dark garment of any sort that he wore, there was something about him which suggested that he naturally belonged to the black-coated tribes of men. His clothes were of fustian, and his boots hobnailed, yet in his progress he showed not the mud-accustomed bearing of hobnailed and fustianed peasantry.[4]

This is still much too long winded, but from the various details there does emerge a single image of a strong, active man who is, or has been, up to no good.

George Meredith said, "The art of the pen . . . is to rouse the inward vision, instead of laboring with a Drop-scene brush, as if it were the eye; because our flying minds cannot contain a protracted description"—and following Meredith the tendency of modern writers has been to avoid lengthy physical descriptions, which bring the narrative to a standstill, and to seek instead the telling detail which will immediately fix a character in the reader's mind. This is difficult to do unless the writer himself has a vivid sense of that character. Too often, he resorts to the following:

She was a tall, bony woman with gray hair, dark eyes, and a forbidding expression.

He was short and thickset, and despite his obvious youth there was already a suspicion of jowls beneath his heavy beard.

There are thousands of such descriptions, thousands of such men and women. The writer is merely filling up paper, hoping that he, the reader, and the character can, among them, make shift with such vague traits. Here is something better, from Muriel Spark's *The Comforters:*

At seventy-eight, Louisa Jepp did everything very slowly but with extreme attention, as some do when they know they are slightly drunk. . . .
Louisa's hair is black, though there is not much of it. She is short, and seen from the side especially, her form resembles a neat double potato just turned up from the soil with its small round head, its body

[4] Included in Hardy's collection, *Wessex Tales* (London: Macmillan & Co., 1912), pp. 7–8.

from which hang the roots, her two thin legs below her full brown skirt and corpulence.[5]

The telling detail may take almost any form: wig, crooked teeth, lopsided smile, figure like "a neat double potato," hair or eyes of a peculiar color or brilliance, limp or shuffle. But one word of caution: no physical characteristic should be employed simply because it is capable of an immediate effect. Initially this may be its main function, but as the character is developed the reader should come to feel that this first observable trait was in its limited way a definite pointer to something basic in the character's nature.

Most serious writers use physical detail in a straightforward manner as one means for making their people real to the reader. But now and again a writer will take advantage of the stock figures that have developed in fiction—the little old lady, the dashing dark-eyed rogue, the frail timorous clerk—in order to shock the reader by showing him how different from his expectations the character really is. The device is seldom to be recommended. No character in a serious story or novel ought even superficially to resemble someone encountered many times before—or perhaps it would be more accurate to say that the resemblance should not be the first thing that strikes the reader. Furthermore, any such device runs the risk of making a fiction seem merely a trick, a sleight of hand, which either has or has not been successfully carried off. The emphasis of the fiction is falsely placed on the trick itself rather than on what, perhaps, the trick was meant to contribute to the theme and final meaning. An example is William Faulkner's "A Rose for Emily." Miss Emily is the apotheosis of the Southern lady of romantic postbellum literature: a "tradition, a duty, and a care; a sort of hereditary obligation upon the town." As a girl she was slender and after a long illness she had "a vague resemblance to those angels in colored church windows—sort of tragic and serene." In her thirties she was "still a slight woman, though thinner than usual, with cold, haughty black eyes in a face the flesh of which was strained across the temples and about the eyesockets as you imagine a lighthousekeeper's face ought

[5] Philadelphia: J. B. Lippincott Company, 1957; pp. 9, 13.

to look." In old age she became "a small, fat woman in black, with a thin gold chain descending to her waist and vanishing into her belt, leaning on an ebony cane with a tarnished gold head."

Miss Emily's life has not been an easy one, but her afflictions, too, are those proper to a Southern lady: her once-grand house has fallen into disrepair, for she has no money; and it stands now not in a fine neighborhood but among "cotton wagons and . . . gasoline pumps —an eyesore among eyesores." Worst of all, Miss Emily's one serious romance came to nothing, for her dashing suitor deserted her.

At her death, a bedroom in her house is broken into, a room "decked and furnished as for a bridal." Upon the bed lies a skeleton with a "profound and fleshless grin"—Miss Emily's faithless suitor, whom she murdered, long ago, when it became plain that he had no intention of marrying her. On the second pillow in the bed there is "the indentation of a head," and from this indentation one of the party lifts "a long strand of iron-gray hair."

Readers usually like this story and often are astonished by its grisly conclusion. The writer, however, who ought to have some knowledge of both the good and the bad tricks in fiction, may feel that Faulkner shows his hand in the first pages, and that the story is diminished by a denouement which is partly Edgar Allan Poe and partly Mary Roberts Rinehart.

The preceding comments have been directed principally toward the author's handling of the main figures in a fiction—the "round" characters, as E. M. Forster calls them. As the story or novel progresses, the writer may wish to add to his physical picture of them. But surrounding these two or three or more people there are the minor members of the cast whose appearance is occasional and whose effect on the action is often slight. Forster calls them "flat" characters: "In their purest form, they are constructed round a single idea or quality." He adds that "they are easily recognized whenever they come in."

Flat characters, of course, are not identified merely by their physical appearance: they may be known by a particular expression or by an invariable attitude or by other means. But when the writer finds it useful to evoke them in terms of how they look, obviously he must practice an economy even greater than that shown toward his major figures. They must, as it were, be captured in a glance. Balzac, who often took pages to tell about a principal character, was (perhaps surprisingly) good at catching a lesser figure in a few words. In *Eugénie Grandet,* he describes the Abbé Cruchot as "a plump, puffy little man with a red wig plastered down and a face like an old female gambler." The countess in "La Grande Bretêche" has a face "as yellow as wax, and as narrow as two folded hands."

MOVEMENTS, GESTURES, MANNERISMS, AND HABITS

Any one of these may be revelatory of character, but often the beginning writer introduces small actions which serve no purpose except to break up the dialogue: "She brushed her hair back"; "He lighted a cigarette." The number of cigarettes smoked in modern fiction is probably large enough to bury all living authors under a pile of stubs, but even such a worn-out device as this can, if properly used, make a point: "Jerry lighted the cigarette awkwardly, burning his finger." This might be revelatory of Jerry's character, showing the reader not only his awkwardness but the shyness that makes him this way. Awkwardness and shyness usually imply the presence of someone else, to whom they are a response. So let us look at Nancy, the girl with whom Jerry is talking on this rainy night in April:

A few minutes later, Nancy took a cigarette from the box for herself. She struck a match and brought it to the end of the cigarette with great concentration. It occurred to Jerry that she behaved as if she wanted to have the flame between his eyes and hers for as long as possible.

Here is a further use of the familiar device of the cigarette. Human life is made up of just such evasions as Nancy's seems to be. There are times when everyone makes a partial commitment, or a half-hearted commitment, and then has uncomfortable second thoughts. There are also those times when men and women start out on one course and then veer abruptly. It may be that Nancy, although more composed than Jerry, is equally uncertain about how this evening with him ought to go.

Movements and gestures should always be integral to the action of the fiction, as well as illustrative of character. People may point or beckon or wave through a window; they may get out of one chair and sit down in another; they may leave a room and return, stretch, scratch themselves, take a bath, or mix a drink. But when they do any one of these things, the reader must be able to say to himself: "She doesn't miss a thing that goes on next door" or "He can't sit still for any time at all; every conversation either makes him nervous or bores him" or "That's his fifth drink—something's going to happen."

Mannerisms and habits, if not used carefully, can also be irritating to the reader. They are often the prerequisite of the flat characters in a story, and are an effort of the author to provide for their easy recognition. But every reader knows how wearisome such characters can be—especially, perhaps, when they are intended to provide comic interludes. There is, for instance, the would-be fop with his affected Edwardian vocabulary; or the character who invariably forgets the most obvious piece of his equipment.

Among leading—or round—characters, Mellors, Constance Chatterley's lover in D. H. Lawrence's novel, is an example of someone with a mannerism which very quickly wears out the reader's patience: he talks part of the time like a man of some education—"The hut's not very tidy, if you don't mind"—and part of the time like the colliers he grew up among—"Ah'm gettin' th' coops ready for th' young bods." The rude form of speech is employed sometimes when he addresses his "betters," and is a defense against them or at least a wall that he erects around himself. Later, it is the language of his love for Lady Chatterley. There is also the suggestion that, since he has "come down to the ranks again," he may feel "he'd better speak as the ranks speak." But Lawrence is inconsistent in his usage; and the reader comes to feel as Lady Chatterley does: "She hated the excess of vernacular in his speech."

An especially effective use of mannerism or habit is that which constitutes a *betrayal* of a character's ostensible attitude, and a revelation of how he really feels. It is like the involuntary tic of an eyelid or twitch at the corner of the mouth which the will cannot control. Thus, someone's manner is habitually gay, but in a moment of stress the gaiety is too patently put on: it points straight at the inner anxiety. The customary manner or the usual habit suddenly strikes false; it is seen for what it is—a way of facing the world—and the character's real state of mind is dramatized in the contradiction.

BEHAVIOR TOWARD OTHERS

In one of his stories, Maupassant introduced a big man with a red beard who always went first through a door. This is an admirable example of compression: Maupassant yokes appearance to action, and gives the reader a vivid image of the man's arrogance. In a more extended passage, the narrator of Willa Cather's *My Mortal Enemy* gives us this first impression of Myra Henshawe, the novel's central character:

. . . while I was taking off my wraps in the hall I could see, at the far end of the parlour, a short, plump woman in a black velvet dress, seated upon the sofa and softly playing on Cousin Bert's guitar. She must have heard me, and, glancing up, she saw my reflection in a mirror; she put down the guitar, rose, and stood to await my approach. She stood markedly and pointedly still, with her shoulders back and her head lifted, as if to remind me that it was my business to get to her as quickly as possible and present myself as best I could. I was not accustomed to formality of any sort, but by her attitude she succeeded in conveying this idea to me.[6]

Myra Henshawe is celebrated in her hometown for having given up wealth and position in order to marry a handsome but unacceptable young man. The splendor of her love affair, of her elopement, of her sacrifice of fortune are now, a quarter-century later, as important to Myra's personal well-being as they are to the legend that has grown up around her. She must perpetuate the role of romantic heroine—which means that she must treat everyone as an audience.

Behavior toward others which is indicative of character will not necessarily be as conspicuous as Myra Henshawe's is. Someone deeply selfish might betray himself in a series of small but telling omissions of common courtesies. The overly solicitous conduct of

[6] New York: Alfred A. Knopf, 1926; p. 11.

another person might suggest calculation designed to achieve a particular end. A brutal bearing might be the defense of someone unable to reach a civil footing with society. (In romantic fiction, it sometimes conceals a gentle, diffident nature. This is not a use of behavior that can be confidently recommended to the serious writer, however.)

Flat characters behave in only one way—Lady Catherine de Bourgh in *Pride and Prejudice,* for instance, is invariably rude to her social inferiors. The conduct of round characters is always more complex, but as a fiction develops the writer should make clear the general drift of behavior, and, through it, the general moral quality of a character.

SPEECH

This, too, is the subject of an earlier chapter and therefore will be dealt with only briefly here. A fundamental rule of fiction that is worth emphasizing several times is that each character should express his personality in what he says: in its rhythms, locutions, idiosyncrasies, brevity or long-windedness, and syntactical structure. To say that Huck Finn must never speak like Joyce's Stephen Dedalus is to illustrate the rule as baldly as possible. The writer must constantly ask himself: is this how *he* or *she* would say this thing? Are these the words most typical of each of them?

N.B.

Here is a bad example of the use of speech, from *The Old Man and the Sea.* The fisherman says to a teen-aged boy:

> "You nearly were killed when I brought the fish in too green and he nearly tore the boat to pieces. Can you remember?"
>
> "I can remember [the boy replies] the tail slapping and banging and the thwart breaking and the noise of the clubbing. I can remember you throwing me into the bow where the wet coiled lines were and feeling the whole boat shiver and the noise of you clubbing him like chopping a tree down and the sweet blood smell all over me."[7]

What is wrong with this reply? Isn't it too "literary," and moreover too precise and detailed? The reader has stopped hearing the boy

[7] New York: Charles Scribner's Sons, 1952; pp. 12–13.

and is listening instead to the author, who has lost touch with his character. This is not to suggest that the boy is incapable of such impressions, but that Hemingway has confused oral expression with the boy's inward sense of experience.

Here is an unusually good example:

"Olive will come down in about ten minutes; she told me to tell you that. About ten; that is exactly like Olive. Neither five nor fifteen, and yet not ten exactly, but either nine or eleven. She didn't tell me to say she was glad to see you, because she doesn't know whether she is or not, and she wouldn't for the world expose herself to telling a fib. She is very honest, is Olive Chancellor; she is full of rectitude. Nobody tells fibs in Boston; I don't know what to make of them all. Well, I am very glad to see you, at any rate."

These words were spoken with much volubility by a fair, plump, smiling woman who entered a narrow drawing room in which a visitor, kept waiting for a few moments, was already absorbed in a book. . . . He threw it down at the approach of Mrs. Luna, laughed, shook hands with her, and said in answer to her last remark, "You imply that you do tell fibs. Perhaps that is one."

"Oh no; there is nothing wonderful in my being glad to see you," Mrs. Luna rejoined, "when I tell you that I have been three long weeks in this unprevaricating city."

"That has an unflattering sound for me," said the young man. "I pretend not to prevaricate."

"Dear me, what's the good of being a Southerner?" the lady asked. "Olive told me to tell you she hoped you will stay to dinner. And if she said it, she does really hope it. She is willing to risk that."

"Just as I am?" the visitor inquired, presenting himself with rather a work-a-day aspect.

Mrs. Luna glanced at him from head to foot, and gave a little smiling sigh, as if he had been a long sum in addition. And, indeed, he was very long, Basil Ransom, and he even looked a little hard and discouraging, like a column of figures. . . . "Are you ever different from this?" Mrs. Luna was familiar—intolerably familiar.

Basil Ransom colored a little. Then he said: "Oh yes; when I dine out I usually carry a six-shooter and a bowie knife."[8]

[8] Henry James, *The Bostonians* (New York: The Modern Library, 1956), pp. 3–5.

In these opening lines from *The Bostonians*, Henry James introduces two of his leading characters, Olive Chancellor and Basil Ransom, and Olive's sister Mrs. Luna. Mrs. Luna's first speech tells the reader a good deal about Olive, and by inference something about Mrs. Luna herself and also about the relationship between the two women. In the dialogue that follows, the reader can infer that Mrs. Luna's customary "style"—even with a stranger like Ransom—is familiarity. She is bold, a trifle flirtatious, and candid to the point of incivility. Ransom, who at first exhibits a social ease as practiced as hers, is quickly shown to be the less confident of the two. A reference to his background places him immediately on the defensive.

James's touch in this passage is so light that the reader may not immediately realize how much he has learned about Ransom, Mrs. Luna, and Olive Chancellor. Yet much of the subsequent conduct of each of them is implicit in what is laid down here. Not every novel need begin with dialogue, and not every dialogue need be as brilliantly and casually informative as this one is, but here is a model for the writer who understands that speech is not concerned merely with the exchange of information ("The Browns are coming to dinner Tuesday"; "I love you, Jean") but with the essential attitude of a character toward himself and the life around him.

ATTITUDE TOWARD SELF

Most men and women are pleased to believe that their world sees them in the terms of their own choosing, in the role they have decided to play. This is usually a role that exhibits what they regard as their essential character—a character that they themselves find either attractive or sympathetic or, ideally, both. Perhaps there are people whose attitude toward themselves—whose public evaluation of themselves, that is—is accepted by everyone around them, but these people had better not find their way into fiction. There must be drama of some sort in the encounter of characters in a story or novel, and this drama to a great extent will issue from the drama

n.b.

which is each character's preliminary encounter with himself. "How," character X says to himself, "can I get what I want without violating my role?" The question, of course, is not usually put so explicitly, since it implies a candid appraisal of deficiencies that few individuals are capable of. Rather, X may say: "How can I persuade Joan of her foolishness in wanting to marry that boy? After the sacrifices I've made for her, the example she's had of love and responsibility and proper values!—this home, her schooling, our place in the town, the care I've taken in selecting her friends. . . ."

The job of the writer is to show his readers the character's declared attitude toward himself and, if only by implication, the secret promptings that really make him behave as he does. A good example of the drama implicit in the differences between the two is the character of Mrs. Craddock in Angus Wilson's *Hemlock and After*. She is a cultivated, pretty woman with a pair of grown sons, one of whom she clings to tenaciously. When the boy, Eric, is taken up by a famous writer, who wants to establish him on his own in London, Mrs. Craddock declares herself delighted:

"I hear you're not happy about Eric's room in London," he said.
"Not *happy*?" Mrs. Craddock sounded incredulous. "But no! I think it's a wonderful idea. It's high time he had somewhere on his own. It will give him a chance to expand, and, what's really rather more important, it'll give me one too."

But she adds:

"The coal's going to be rather a strain." She made a little grimace. "Oh dear! That awful boiler! and I don't know that I can face the hens. . . . But otherwise I can manage beautifully."

Later, when they are alone, Mrs. Craddock makes a direct assault on her son:

". . . a side of me—a quite selfish side—will miss you terribly. When one gets older it's not very easy to keep one's standards up if there isn't anybody about who matters enough to do it for." Mrs. Craddock's face twitched slightly as she said this. A horrible vision of the reality of what the words might mean pierced the drama with which she had surrounded herself.[9]

Mrs. Craddock is no more a villain than her son is a hero, and this is as she should be. The beginning writer must be careful that in dramatizing the normal dichotomy in human character he doesn't tumble into melodrama. Not everyone is a smiling Uncle Silas whose immediate plans include the timely death of his ward. Mrs. Craddock, for instance, is a woman of considerable intelligence and attractiveness. There is an excellent reason why she should oppose the idea of her son's setting up in a place of his own, for the man who wishes to finance him there is a homosexual. But the point the author makes is that Eric's mother would resist *any* plan which took him away from her. Her preoccupation is not with what will be good or bad for him, but with how she can go on possessing him. Jealousy and fear have swamped the moral sense which would have provided a perfect justification for her objections.

Mention should be made here of the use of the mirror in fiction. Along with the cigarette, it is one of the most ubiquitous of props. Authors have their characters look at themselves in mirrors in order to tell the reader what they look like by a device which seems more "natural" than straight description, and in order to suggest how the character thinks about himself:

He was pleased with the way his hair shone like platinum in the light coming through the open door, and he approved again the blue of his tie, which so exactly matched that of his eyes. He looked with pleasure at his straight nose and good mouth and then he assumed the expression of intelligent responsibility which the day seemed to call for. Well-groomed, well-set-up, and—why not admit it, at least to himself?—handsome, why shouldn't he succeed with the old woman, no matter how difficult everyone said she was? Was his not the face of a man born to do well in the world?

There is nothing inherently wrong with the mirror device, but it has been used so often that it should be avoided unless it makes a very pronounced contribution to a story which no other device could do as well.

[9] New York: The Viking Press, 1952; pp. 79, 81, 127.

ATTITUDE OF OTHERS TOWARD THE CHARACTER

Here is someone seen through the eyes of one or more persons who may be friendly, unfriendly, too generous in their estimate, too unsparing, or out to make a good story. The attitudes of others can provide the reader with fresh insight into the character thus viewed or into the viewers themselves (who are sometimes the author's primary interest). A story by Aldous Huxley, "Nuns at Luncheon," does both. The "luncheon" referred to is not for nuns but for two old acquaintances who meet periodically to exchange news of themselves. One is the narrator; the other is Miss Penny, "the well-known woman journalist," whose anecdotes are "always curious." Today she reports on her "marvellous nun"—a young woman whose tragedy she unearthed while recovering from an operation in a German hospital. The nun's story occupies most of the narrative, but Huxley's real subject is the attitude of Miss Penny and her companion toward that story. In brief, then, the nun, Sister Agatha, falls in love with Kuno, a patient at the hospital who will be "taken back to jail as soon as he can stand firmly on his legs." Kuno prevails on the girl to help him escape, takes her with him, and in a shepherd's hut violates and then deserts her. Sister Agatha returns to her order, is given symbolical funeral rites, and then becomes a charwoman at the hospital.

This is all shocking and tragic—but not to Miss Penny, and perhaps not to the narrator. "Nuns at Luncheon" is an intricate piece of work, and it will reward the beginner's close study. For instance, the reader sees Sister Agatha from Miss Penny's point of view, and Miss Penny herself from the narrator's.

Miss Penny believes that she is a *femme fatale*. At the beginning of the meal she tells the narrator of her recent escape from a Russian General who assured her that her eyes drove him mad. The narrator comments bleakly that she has "eyes like a hare's, flush with her head and very bright with a superficial and expressionless brightness. What a formidable woman. I felt sorry for the Russian General." She has "long, sharp, white teeth" and always twinkles "with massive and improbable jewellery." Her long earrings swing and rattle like "corpses hanging in chains." "No, decidedly, Miss Penny was not beautiful; you could not even honestly say that she had charm or was attractive. That high Scotch colouring, those hare's eyes, the voice, the terrifying laugh, and the size of her. . . ."

Miss Penny frequently interrupts her account of Sister Agatha's romance and disgrace, and these interruptions in their careful juxta-position to various parts of the narrative are strikingly illustrative of character. Thus, telling of the nun's appearance after her return to the hospital, Miss Penny says:

"She looked as though she were dead. A walking corpse, that's what she was. It was a shocking sight. I shouldn't have thought it possible for anyone to change so much in so short a time. . . . And the general expression of unhappiness—that was something quite appalling."

This sounds compassionate, but the action that follows the state-ment illustrates how little Miss Penny's sympathies are engaged with the girl:

She leaned out into the gangway between the two rows of tables, and caught the passing waiter by the end of one of his coat-tails. . . .
"Half a pint of Guinness," ordered Miss Penny.

Then, telling of the nun's disgrace as she put it together from the gossip of hospital employees:

" 'There's been a funeral service for her in the chapel—coffin and all. She had to be present at it—her own funeral. She isn't a nun any more. She has to do charwoman's work now, the roughest in the hospital. . . . She's regarded as dead.' "

Once more the significant interruption:

Miss Penny paused to signal to the harassed little Italian. "My small 'Guinness,' " she called out.[10]

In a first-person story, the narrator's selection of dialogue and action, the story in its entirety, can be taken as illustrative of his attitude—in the case of "Nuns at Luncheon," of a man's attitude toward a heartless, garrulous woman. His account of the luncheon,

---

[10] Included in *The World of Aldous Huxley*, ed. Charles J. Rolo (New York: Harper & Row, 1947), pp. 343–344.

however, is a revelation not only of Miss Penny's character but of his own. For implicit in the story is the attitude which she has toward *him*. Few people tell their mothers dirty jokes. Nor are they likely to confide their views on the shiftlessness of the poor to a man who is out of work. In short, they pick their audience, and it is usually one which they feel to be in sympathy with what they have to say. It seems fair to assume that Miss Penny regards her companion as her male counterpart. If she didn't, she would have told her story with a long face—or, more typically, lunched with someone else.

Not every fiction makes such a sophisticated use of attitude as Huxley has here. Whether a narrative is in the first or third person, the writer's concern is with the extent to which attitude is revelatory of *someone*'s character—the speaker's or the subject's. In *Hemlock and After*, the boy Eric says to his mother: "I shall always be here at weekends . . . and in the week too, of course, if you want me particularly." Mrs. Craddock, pursuing her devious course of seeming to urge him to go to London while throwing every practical and emotional obstacle in his path, tells him that he must by all means take the opportunity.

Eric received the statement literally. "Oh! I wouldn't give the idea up," he said. "It's too important to me. There's so much that we'll both be able to get on with on our own. . . ."[11]

The reader knows that Mrs. Craddock's selfishness constitutes her real objection to the plan, but Eric, presumably, believes that she is delighted at his prospects. Therefore, when he responds to her assurances that he isn't to worry about her by declaring, in effect, that he won't, he is saying that her welfare is a good deal less important to him than his own. Eric's attitude affords the reader a glimpse into his own absorbed selfishness, which is quite as deep as his mother's. But his attitude throws fresh light, indirectly, on Mrs. Craddock herself. She has always, perhaps, been a woman on the periphery, a woman who has tragically never been at the center of anyone's life—or not since her husband's early death.

[11] Angus Wilson, p. 127.

PHYSICAL SURROUNDINGS

The general subject of the setting of a fiction is treated later in this book, but its use as a method of characterization belongs in the present chapter. In the past, some writers put almost as much emphasis on surroundings as they did on physical appearance. The reader was expected to grasp the telling detail of mansion house or tenement or countryside, and to infer from it something about the inhabitants. A good example can be found in *The Custom of the Country* (italics are ours):

Mrs. Spragg and her visitor were *enthroned* in two *heavy gilt armchairs* in one of the private drawing-rooms of the Hotel Stentorian. The Spragg rooms were known as one of the *Looey* suites, and the drawing-room walls, above their *wainscotting of highly-varnished mahogany,* were hung with *salmon-pink damask* and *adorned* with oval portraits of *Marie Antoinette* and the *Princess de Lamballe.* In the centre of the *florid carpet* a *gilt table* with a top of *Mexican onyx* sustained a *palm* in a *gilt basket* tied with a *pink bow.*[12]

Edmund Wilson calls Edith Wharton the poet of interior decoration, and this is an example of how skillfully she could use a room to characterize its occupants. Notice the emphasis on "gilt," in armchairs, table, and basket; and the dizzy combination of colors: salmon-pink damask, florid carpet, pink bow. Notice also the language: "enthroned," "adorned," "sustained"—all elaborate words which in their vulgarity are appropriate to anything as vulgar as a "Looey" suite. The other details add to the reader's sense that here are pretentious, tasteless people who have got exactly what they deserve (and admire): the table with its top of Mexican onyx; the palm; the highly varnished mahogany wainscotting; the oval portraits of classy ladies.

Unfortunately, Mrs. Wharton's impeccable sense of what is telling detail and what is excess is not the possession of every writer. In the early years of this century there was a vogue of naturalism in fiction which turned many stories and novels into sociological docu-

---

[12] Edith Wharton (New York: Charles Scribner's Sons, 1913), p. 4.

ments with tenuous claims on literature. Fiction was swamped in stockyards and slums occupied by figures who illustrated the argument but had no human dimension. In a broad sense, they were the sum of how and where they lived, silhouettes defined by detail. In reaction to this kind of writing, Willa Cather published in 1922 her famous essay called "The Novel Demeublé." Reviving a pronouncement of Dumas *père*, she wrote: "The elder Dumas enunciated a great principle when he said that to make a drama, a man needed one passion and four walls." The story or novel stripped of its "furniture" was also the concern of Virginia Woolf. "Here," she wrote in 1924, in "Mr. Bennett and Mrs. Brown," "is the British public sitting by the writer's side and saying in its vast and unanimous way, 'Old women have houses. They have fathers. They have incomes. They have servants. They have hot water bottles. That is how we know that they are old women. Mr. Wells and Mr. Bennett and Mr. Galsworthy have always taught us that this is the way to recognise them.' "

Neither Willa Cather in the United States nor Virginia Woolf in England succeeded in silencing the naturalistic writers, and characterization through physical surroundings continued for some time to enjoy an eminence. It was, for instance, a major device of writers as different as Scott Fitzgerald and Sinclair Lewis. During the Thirties it gained fresh vigor because of the Depression. Writers took to describing houses, tenements, farms, or cabins of depression victims. The epitome of this period is probably Steinbeck's *The Grapes of Wrath,* but another document of the time—and the school—is Josephine Lawrence's once-famous novel, *If I Have Four Apples* . . .

Naturalistic fiction was buried finally under its own self-imposed avalanche of trucks and public toilets, gimcrack houses on mean streets, and neighborhoods black with factory soot. Some of this fiction served a laudable social purpose, and these comments are not intended as a disparagement of that purpose. But the point for the beginner to remember is that at the center of each of the rooms of fiction must be a believable human being. It is he who gives interest alike to the furniture around him and the revolution outside the window. Neither will permanently detain the reader who enters an empty room.

One satisfactory way for incorporating physical surroundings into a story is to show them from the viewpoint of the character himself —a viewpoint inevitably affected by joy or illness, disaffection with life, or some other physical or emotional state. The reader learns about the character at the same time that he sees where he is. In Thomas Mann's "Death in Venice," the writer Gustave von Aschenbach tries to escape the guilt and secret ecstasy of his love for a beautiful boy by a long walk through the city. But his emotions do not desert him, and the Venice around him mirrors the darkness and sickness that are overtaking his life:

There was a hateful sultriness in the narrow streets. The air was so heavy that all the manifold smells wafted out of houses, shops, and cook-shops—smells of oil, perfumery, and so forth—hung low, like exhalations, not dissipating. Cigarette smoke seemed to stand in the air, it drifted so slowly away. . . . The longer he walked, the more was he in tortures under that state, which is the product of the sea air and the sirocco and which excites and enervates at once. . . . He fled from the huddled, narrow streets of the commercial city, crossed many bridges, and came into the poor quarter of Venice. Beggars waylaid him, the canals sickened him with their evil exhalations.[13]

Here, in *My Mortal Enemy,* is another, less sophisticated employment of the same method. The scene is Madison Square in New York, somewhere around the turn of the century. The viewpoint is that of an enraptured, observant (and imaginative) fifteen-year-old girl who is making her first visit to the city from her home in Illinois, and who thinks she finds there all of the cultivation, civility, and worldliness that she so much admires. The author gives a certain amount of factual detail, but the details tell as much about the narrator's state of mind as they do about the look of the square (italics are ours):

Madison Square was then at the parting of the ways; had a double personality, half commercial, half social, with shops to the south and

13 Included in Mann's collection, *Stories of Three Decades,* trans. H. T. Lowe-Porter (New York: Alfred A. Knopf, 1936), p. 404.

residences on the north. It seemed to me so *neat*, after the *raggedness* of our Western cities; so *protected* by *good manners* and *courtesy*—like an *open-air drawing-room*. I could well imagine a winter *dancing party* being given there, or a *reception* for some *distinguished European visitor*.

The snow fell lightly all the afternoon, and *friendly* old men with brooms kept sweeping the paths. . . . The trees and shrubbery seemed *well-groomed* and *sociable*, like *pleasant people*. . . . I lingered long by the intermittent fountain. Its rhythmical splash was like the voice of the place. It rose and fell *like something taking deep, happy breaths;* and the sound was musical, seemed to come from the throat of spring. . . . Here, I felt, winter brought no desolation; it was *tamed*, like a *polar bear led on a leash by a beautiful lady*.[14]

THE PAST

Edith Wharton once said to Henry James, apropos of one of his novels, "What was your idea in suspending the four principal characters . . . in the void? What sort of life did they lead when they were not watching each other, and fencing with each other? Why have you stripped them of all the *human fringes* we necessarily trail after us through life?" One of those "human fringes" is the past. Most beginning writers seem to fall into one of two opposed camps: either they give no information at all about their people, or else they swamp them in so much detail that the narrative never gets going. The writer who errs on the side of excess is probably the luckier, for excess implies that he has a vivid conception of his characters: they are not matchstick people stuck together to walk through the story. They are people in whose reality he himself believes; he knows "all" about them.

For this kind of writer, who finds it natural to provide his heroine with a father and mother and twin brothers, a childhood spent partly in the city and partly in the country, pets and schoolmates and teachers and, finally, a boy friend, the problem is going to be one of selectivity. Among these facts from the past, which are relevant to a story about, say, the heroine's efforts to put her life back together after a disastrous marriage? All of them might be; or none of

[14] Willa Cather, pp. 33–35.

them—at least, to a degree significant enough to justify their incorporation. But no harm is done if unnecessary detail gets into a first draft. The important thing is to see that all of it comes out before the final revision. It is easier to cut than to pad, and the end result is usually more persuasive.

The writer to whom such details do not come readily is in for a bad time—not merely because of the effort he's put to but because this effort may finally produce an irrelevancy and send him back to search some more. Occasionally, the trouble even extends to a name for the principal character (a name, after all, is part of the past), and the hero or heroine remains anonymous.

Characters in fiction ought to have names; they ought to come from somewhere; they ought to have standards which show them either conforming to or rebelling against the past. The appeal of much Southern writing today lies in the sense of the past which affects the decisions and actions of the present. Continuity and change: these are basic elements in life. They give to any existence its reassurance and its suspense. In fiction, they help to confer the sense of reality. The character who (in Mollie Panter-Downes's phrase) is embalmed in aspic, suspended in a transparent solid, is no more interesting or memorable than the unfortunate bug that drowns in the picnic iced tea.

FRINGE TECHNIQUES

In a *New Yorker* staff memorandum, Wolcott Gibbs once wrote: "Funny names belong to the past or to whatever is left of *Judge* magazine. Any character called Mrs. Middlebottom or Joe Zilch should be summarily changed to something else." Most creative people are enchanted by exotic or outrageous names—a peculiarity perhaps due to their general enchantment with language. Edith Wharton said:

A . . . more spectral element in my creative life is the sudden appearance of names without characters. . . . The Princess Estradina was such a name. I knew nothing of its origin, and still less of the invisible character to whom it presumably belonged. Who was she, what were her nationality, her history, her claims on my attention? She must have been there, lurking and haunting me, for years before she walked into "The Custom of the Country", in high-coloured flesh and blood, cool, dominant and thoroughly at home. Another such character haunts me today. Her name is still odder: Laura Testvalley. How I should like to change that name! . . . Several times I have tried. . . . But she is strong-willed, and even obstinate, and turns sulky and unmanageable whenever I hint at the advantages of a change; and I foresee that she will eventually force her way into my tale burdened with her impossible patronymic.[15]

It is a fact of the creative process that old characters with new names do sometimes droop and die, leaving the writer with an unfinished story or a great patch of brown in the middle of the novel. Nevertheless, he ought to examine his conscience thoroughly before he perpetrates a Princess Estradina, a Laura Testvalley, or for that matter an Undine Spragg. The trouble with such names is that they begin by being funny but may end as iron cages set around the characters, harsh barriers to their plausible development. James Purdy has sometimes succumbed to the temptations of the bizarre, and in one of his stories, "63: Dream Palace," he calls his three principal characters Fenton Riddleway, Parkhearst Cratty, and "greatwoman." "63: Dream Palace" is meant to be a tragedy, but the effect of such names is rather to turn it into a grotesque puppet drama.

Names can nevertheless play a part in characterization. Among contemporary writers, the man who probably makes the best use of the outrageous name is P. G. Wodehouse: Rollo Podmarsh, Aunt Dahlia, Maud and Reggie Byng, J. Gladstone Bott. This is to suggest that such names properly belong to light, comedic fiction. At a slight remove is the story or novel which uses caricature names: Mr. Allworthy in *Tom Jones*, the Veneerings in *Our Mutual Friend*, Dobbin in *Vanity Fair*, Lady Circumference in *Vile Bodies*; or the fiction in which names suggest the quality of a character: Roger Chillingworth in *The Scarlet Letter*, Christopher Newman in *The*

[15] *A Backward Glance* (New York: Appleton-Century-Crofts, 1934), pp. 202-203.

American; Father Urban in the J. F. Powers novel, *Morte d'Urban.*
Sometimes, writers have tried to suggest economic and social background through names. Ellen Glasgow, in *In This Our Life,* calls
two of her principal women Roy and Stanley, and in the context of
the novel thereby suggests the distinguished past of their family.
Now and again a writer—usually a British writer—will introduce
someone whose lower-class origin is to be inferred from the fact that
he or she is named for a film star: Gary, Lana, Yuh-vonne, Clark,
Marleen. Another common device is the use of a name which has
literary or mythological associations; Joyce's Stephen Dedalus is an
example.

Even the happiest choices of names, however, can never much
lessen the writer's responsibility for creating believable people. One
of the most memorable women in English literature has one of the
least remarkable of names: Jane Eyre.

Simile and metaphor have always been popular devices of characterization, and writers have ranged far afield in their pursuit of comparisons. People have been likened to fish, to bugs, to mountain
crags, to cows, sheep, horses, to food, to the gods and goddesses of
myth, to lions and gazelles, to monuments, to ideas and ideals. In
Eugénie Grandet, Balzac says of Old Grandet:

> In matters financial M. Grandet might be described as combining the
> characteristics of the Bengal tiger and the boa constrictor. He could lay
> low and wait, crouching, watching for his prey, and make his spring
> unerringly at last; then the jaws of his purse would unclose, a torrent of
> coin would be swallowed down, and, as in the case of the gorged reptile,
> there would be a period of inaction; like the serpent, moreover, he was
> cold, apathetic, methodical, keeping to his own mysterious times and
> seasons.[16]

This is an example of comparison—simile and metaphor—at both its
best and worst. The description *is* graphic; but evident, too, is that
it has to go far afield for its effects: Bengal tigers and boa con-
strictors must play a very small part in the life of citizens of provin-

---

[16] Trans. Ellen Marriage (Philadelphia: The Gebbie Publishing Company,
1899), pp. 9–10.

cial French towns. (Furthermore, the "jaws of his purse" are no part of Old Grandet himself, and for Balzac to import them into the description is illogical.) The writer must ask himself whether his comparison, however striking, is appropriate in the context of the fiction and appropriate also to the particular character. If his answer to one or both parts of the question is negative, he had better cast around for some other comparison. The description of Louisa Jepp in the Muriel Spark quotation given earlier is an example of apt linking: Louisa lives in the country among growing things and so it is appropriate to liken her to one of them.

Simile or metaphor, when it deals with minor characters, should practice the greatest economy—the Abbé Cruchot with his "face like an old female gambler." A major character can sustain a more elaborate figure—Old Grandet as part tiger and part snake—but the taste of the present time is against any passage which is too extended and too ingenious. The British writer Robert Greenwood, in his novel *Wagstaff*, captures the essential quality of his central character in this brief description: "Timing his arrival at the station to the minute, Wagstaff bustled through the barrier, looking in his brightest suit and most hilarious necktie as joyful as a tree in blossom." A subsidiary character in the book is pinpointed even more economically: she is a shy, seventeen-year-old girl who appears and disappears, says the author, "like a wren in a bramble."

One last illustration. Nigel Dennis, in a novel, *Cards of Identity* —its subject is the problem of identity—notes that one of his characters, Dr. Shubunkin, has a face marked with "dozens of seams and grooves." "When his eyes flash with analytical interest," comments Mr. Dennis, "all the lines become illuminated and run to the centre of his face, pointing. It is probable that he got this idea from the electric map system of the Paris Metro."

As a model, any one of these illustrations is superior to Muriel Spark's description of Louisa Jepp, which is a trifle laborious and complicated, and forces the reader to pause long enough to sort out and put together the details of the image. It is important to remember that a comparison should be as direct and simple as possible.

Most important of all, it must not be so striking that it sets up an independent existence in the story. Its job is to illuminate character, not to overwhelm it.

STREAM OF CONSCIOUSNESS

Around 1900, writers interested in the technical aspects of fiction began to explore the minds of their creations to an extent that hadn't been done previously. Once confronted by the unconscious, they found that new techniques of narrative—or brushed-up old techniques—were necessary if they were to make anything of what they found there. The handy old signposts, "he thought," "he vowed silently," "he was reminded," were going to have to be used sparingly, sometimes not at all, if the reader was to have a sense of direct participation in a character's mental processes—especially in those processes of which the character himself, perhaps, was unaware. More overt methods for describing mental states might have to be sacrificed altogether ("though terrified by the sound of the Holtons' carriagewheels in the drive, Fanny attempted to appear her usual composed self as she crossed the garden to greet them"). And it became evident that formal syntax would largely be absent in this new technique, since we think not in sentences but in phrases, in isolated words, in reveries that have no beginning and no end. Logic, too, was going to suffer: the unconscious throws up one subject and then, through association, another, and still another. It swoops through time, it ignores distance and geography, bringing time past, time present, time future, this place and places far away into the stream of ideas, images, sensations, memories, intuitions that flows unendingly through the mind of every man and woman. Stream of consciousness is often compared to the movie technique of montage, in which scene after scene flashes before the spectator in seemingly chaotic sequence.

Stream of consciousness is now such an accepted convention of characterization that it is difficult to realize how revolutionary it seemed fifty—even thirty—years ago. It was called the method of the "experimental" novelists—Dorothy Richardson, James Joyce, Vir-

ginia Woolf, William Faulkner. In fact, as various critics have
pointed out, in less intense form it has been a part of fiction almost
since the inception of the novel, and can be found in writers as
various as Fenimore Cooper, Dickens, Melville, and Dostoevsky.
(One critic even claims to find it in the diary entries of Fanny
Burney.) Today, stream of consciousness turns up in some form or
other in the light romance, the mystery, the Western, and the science fiction, as often as in more serious efforts. It even turns up in
the "fictionalized biographies" that ladies with three names are unable
to stop writing. Its acceptance and utilization are sometimes said to
be a result of Freud's researches; or, alternatively, of the disintegration of personal life in the twentieth century and the consequent
retreat to an interior life. Its usefulness is that it takes the reader
directly into the mind of the individual. Here is the human being
alone and unguarded—even by the censoring Self.

The primary technique of stream of consciousness is what is
called either interior or internal monologue. This is the technique
which has given stream of consciousness its notoriety and its reputation of being difficult to understand. It *can* be difficult, admittedly;
it can—what is much worse—be boring. The writer must never forget that selectivity is as important here as in any other device of
fiction. There is no censor at work on the character, but there is the
harsh censor against irrelevance at work in the author.

In his book, *Stream of Consciousness in the Modern Novel*,
Robert Humphrey makes a useful distinction between two kinds of
interior monologue—*direct* and *indirect*. The first offers a character's
thoughts without (or with a bare minimum of) author intervention
or mediation; "The monologue is represented as being completely
candid, as if there were no reader." Mr. Humphrey cites the conclusion to *Ulysses, in which* Molly Bloom thinks on and on for
nearly fifty pages, as a consummate example of direct interior monologue. Here is some of that reverie:

theyre so weak and puling when theyre sick [men in general, that is,
and Mr. Bloom in particular] they want a woman to get well if his nose
bleeds youd think it was O tragic and that dyinglooking one off the
south circular when he sprained his foot at the choir party at the sugar-

loaf Mountain the day I wore that dress Miss Stack bringing him flowers the worst old ones she could find at the bottom of the basket anything at all to get into a mans bedroom with her old maids voice trying to imagine he was dying on account of her to never see thy face again though he looked more like a man with his beard a bit grown in the bed father was the same besides I hate bandaging and dosing when he cut his toe with the razor paring his corns. . . .[17]

It is impossible to excerpt satisfactorily from this famous monologue, but in the section above the reader can at least note how a vague generalization about the male response to any kind of infirmity leads Mrs. Bloom to think of specific occasions, of the behavior of an acquaintance, of Mr. Bloom with a beard, of her father.

Indirect interior monologue uses the character's name, the third person pronoun *he* or *she,* or (but far less plausibly) the second *you.* Here, the author is more in evidence and the monologue is more controlled. Sometimes he even offers commentary or description. There is more coherence in the character's thoughts, not only in syntax but in logic. Mr. Humphrey notes that the fundamental quality of interior monologue is retained because what is presented "of consciousness is direct; that is, it is in the idiom and with the peculiarities of the character's psychic processes." As an example, he cites the opening to *Mrs. Dalloway:*

Mrs. Dalloway said she would buy the flowers herself.

For Lucy had her work cut out for her. The doors would be taken off their hinges; Rumpelmayer's men were coming. And then, thought Clarissa Dalloway, what a morning—fresh as if issued to children on a beach.

What a lark! What a plunge! For so it had always seemed to her, hen, with a little squeak of the hinges, which she could hear now, she ad burst open the French windows and plunged at Bourton into the pen air. How fresh, how calm, stiller than this of course, the air was in the early morning; like the flap of a wave; the kiss of a wave; chill and sharp and yet (for a girl of eighteen as she then was) solemn, feeling as she did, standing there at the open window, that something awful was about to happen. . . .[18]

[17] New York: Random House, 1934; p. 723.
[18] New York: Harcourt, Brace & World, 1925; pp. 3–5.

n.b.

The author is directing this passage, yet the responses, the language, are Clarissa Dalloway's. A certain amount of ellipsis remains, however: the reader gathers that "Lucy" has "her work cut out for her" because there is going to be a party (more, the reader assumes that Lucy is a maid). Then the image of morning—"fresh as if issued to children on a beach"—reminds Mrs. Dalloway of her girlhood at Bourton. Subtly, at this point, the language changes, becomes slangy—that of the girl she once was ("What a lark! What a plunge!"). And so the reader is transported directly into that past, into a "solemn" morning when "something awful was about to happen" (as it finally will, on this much later day, before the novel ends).

Indirect interior monologue is probably the most generally useful stream-of-consciousness technique. It presents the reader with a consciousness housed in a body, living somewhere, talking with other people, perhaps planning a party. The events of the fiction move forward both in reflection and in action. In the following passage, Mrs. Dalloway goes out to buy the flowers:

n.b.

For having lived in Westminster—how many years now? over twenty, —one feels even in the midst of the traffic, or waking at night, Clarissa was positive, a particular hush, or solemnity; an indescribable pause; a suspense (but that might be her heart, affected, they said, by influenza) before Big Ben strikes. There! Out it boomed. First a warning, musical; then the hour, irrevocable. The leaden circles dissolved in the air. Such fools we are, she thought, crossing Victoria Street. For Heaven only knows why one loves it so, how one sees it so, making it up, building it round one, tumbling it, creating it every moment afresh; but the veriest frumps, the most dejected of miseries sitting on doorsteps (drink their downfall) do the same; can't be dealt with, she felt positive, by Acts of Parliament for that very reason: they love life. In people's eyes, in the swing, tramp, and trudge; in the bellow and the uproar; the carriages, motor cars, omnibuses, vans, sandwich men shuffling and swinging; brass bands; barrel organs; in the triumph and the jingle and the strange high singing of some aeroplane overhead was what she loved; life; London; this moment of June.[19]

[19] *Ibid.*, pp. 3–5.

This passage serves multiple purposes. It provides information that the reader will need sooner or later to know: that the Dalloways live in Westminster, and have been there more than twenty years; that Clarissa has had a serious illness. Then there is the detail which sets off Clarissa's train of thought: Big Ben striking the hour. And Clarissa is walking down an actual street, surrounded by those carriages, motor cars, omnibuses, brass bands, and barrel organs which complete her awareness of "this moment in June." The moment is described in terms of Clarissa's sensibility, yet that sensibility is densely surrounded by the physical world. The authorial control of material, the skill of organization, evident here is probably beyond the ability of a beginner. But it is an example of what he should aim at in the use of indirect interior monologue; and to the extent that he finds himself intruding too visibly as "author," not "character," and introducing facts which are irrelevant to what the character would be thinking about at this particular moment, he knows that he is falling short of the exacting discipline required of him.

One other specifically stream-of-consciousness device is available to the writer, that of *soliloquy*. Mr. Humphrey describes this as "the technique of representing the psychic content and processes of a character directly from character to reader without the presence of an author, but with an audience tacitly assumed." This is a rather formidable definition, but a simple example may make it clear. A salesman who had failed to close an important business deal might return to his hotel room and there, in solitude, begin to rehash the events of the conference, and then proceed to a defense of himself. The "audience," of course, would be his employer, to whom he would have to give an account of himself the next day.

A more sophisticated example is Eudora Welty's story called "Why I Live at the P.O." This is the relentless monologue of the China Grove, Mississippi, postmistress, "Sister," who has lately uprooted herself from the family home after a succession of quarrels and moved to her place of business: "I like it here. It's ideal. . . . I've got everything cater-cornered, the way I like it."

"Why I Live at the P.O." is a serious story about a profound personality disturbance, but Miss Welty relates it with such gaiety that it is only in retrospect that the reader realizes how brilliantly the grim subject matter and the comedy have been played off against each other. It begins:

I was getting along fine with Mama, Papa-Daddy and Uncle Rondo until my sister Stella-Rondo just separated from her husband and came back home again. Mr. Whitaker! Of course I went with Mr. Whitaker first, when he first appeared here in China Grove, taking "Pose Yourself" photos, and Stella-Rondo broke us up. Told him I was one-sided. Bigger on one side than the other, which is a deliberate, calculated falsehood. . . .[20]

Sister's mind is totally engaged in the process of justification. Her audience is the collective world of China Grove: that world which is on Mama's and Papa-Daddy's and Stella-Rondo's side and ought to be told the "truth." Every wounding remark made by her family is remembered verbatim; her own retorts are cherished for their triumphant, unanswerable accuracy: " 'Very well,' I says. 'But I take the fern. Even you, Mama, can't stand there and deny that I'm the one watered that fern.' " "Why I Live at the P.O." offers what is almost a case history of one woman's estrangement from normal conduct and perception.

Any stream-of-consciousness technique requires not only skill but caution in its use. A fictional soliloquy or a monologue may be as fatiguing as the indescribably dull life story related by the stranger in the next seat on the train or bus. It is sad but true that the pioneers in stream of consciousness are sometimes boring—as are the new writers in France, who are its most energetic exponents at present. In its purest (that is, Joycean) form, stream of consciousness must sacrifice narrative movement to the circuitous, associative demands of the unconscious. Even in indirect interior monologue and soliloquy the reader may be asked to enter into the consciousness of someone for whom he does not immediately feel either interest or sympathy. When this happens—when, that is, it happens to the attentive reader—it may well be that the author has plunged

[20] Included in *Selected Stories of Eudora Welty* (New York: The Modern Library, 1954), p. 89.

too fast, before giving adequate attention to those other methods of characterization which bring character and reader together upon a common ground. It is true that the author has the right to expect of his reader the closest and most intelligent reading of which he is capable; it is occasionally true, however, that authors use this expectation as an escape hatch from their own ineptitude.

CHARACTER TODAY

Underlying Henry James's dictum about character and incident (see p. 59) is an assumption of human responsibility. Men live in the world they are capable of making, under those conditions they are capable of creating or of imposing upon existence. For the timid or weak or diffident, this world may be one of secondhand experience—as it is for Strether in *The Ambassadors*. It may be a world in which someone creates those conditions that make him the perfect victim for stronger, less principled people—as it is for Milly Theale in *The Wings of the Dove*. In "real" life, of course, people experience losses, deprivations, humiliations, and perhaps illnesses over which they have no control, and any one of these things may affect their vigor or judgment, or destroy them altogether; the fictionist knows these hard facts perfectly well. But the novel of character moves forward according to human impulse or decision. Man may be confined by a certain social code or by national, racial, or religious prescriptions, but within the framework of one or even all of these he is his own master.

If character has, as Mary McCarthy believes, declined in fiction, it is partly because the national and international events of the present century, being so far beyond the individual's control, have diminished the sense of personal importance and influence. In addition to worldwide wars, civil wars, cold wars, and revolutions, there have been profound changes in society and the common morality. These last two have served fiction best of all, over the years, and the present anonymous character of the one and the steady erosion of the other have evidently left some writers with the impression that they are the monarchs of a deserted kingdom. To them, Carol

Kennicott's uncultured Midwestern town seems as remote in time as one of Jane Austen's hamlets or Mrs. Gaskell's Cranford. Stately plump Buck Mulligan is as quaint as any character in Dickens. Even Mrs. Dalloway, leaving her house on that radiant June morning, is stepping into a London that vanished in the rubble of World War II. In order to restore importance to the writing of fiction, certain present-day authors have set out to destroy the classic idea that literature deals with the ordering of experience by a man or woman who is at once unique and typical of humankind, and have substituted for it an idea of literature which denies the power of the individual, the meaning of his existence, and even the fact of his identity. If this is, in the main, a negative view of man and his possibilities, they would argue that it is nonetheless a "true" view— as the perceptions of Balzac and Proust, of Dickens and Henry James, are not true for our time. And they would add that the point of any serious fiction is to mirror life as it is actually experienced. Alain Robbe-Grillet said recently:

The meaning of the world around us can no longer be considered as other than fragmentary, temporary, and even contradictory, and is always in dispute. How can a work of art set out to illustrate any sort of meaning which is known in advance? The modern novel is an enquiry, but an enquiry which creates its own meaning as it goes along. Has reality a meaning? The contemporary artist cannot reply; he does not know the answer. All he can say is that the reality may acquire a meaning through his work, and only after that work is completed.[21]

In France, this kind of writing now enjoys a great critical and popular vogue. It is known as the "objective novel," the "nouveau roman," or (in Sartre's word) the "antinovel." Bernard Pingaud has pointed out that a more apt description would be "antenovel": "what the new novelists describe or relate is what takes place before the novel in the classic sense has begun, previous to any characters or story."

In America there is no school of the antinovel which has the

[21] From "The Writer's Only Commitment Is to Literature" and included in the *Programme and Notes* for the International Writers' Conference held at Edinburgh, August 1962, pp. 43–44.

brilliance and forcefulness of the present French school (which includes Robbe-Grillet, Nathalie Sarraute, Marguerite Duras, Claude Simon, and Michel Butor). In general, the decline of character is felt here, as it is in England, in the scarcity of really memorable and convincing men and women in the fiction that is being produced. There is no rigorous philosophy of anonymity.

Nevertheless, the malaise stems from the same causes. Human consciousness has become fragmented, diffuse, incapable of generalization or definition. Life is a succession of moments—this is, then this is, then this is—and the "I" to whom this succession occurs is an accretion of "isnesses." And yet, of course, he is not, since each object, each occurrence, subtly changes him. Identity is fluid, or more drastically it is nonexistent (in the sense that this same process, which began before the story or novel opened, goes on beyond its concluding pages).

This is no longer a radical theory of identity. It is really a pushing to the limits of what David Daiches said more than twenty years ago in his discussion of stream of consciousness: that character *portrayal* is impossible. "Character is a process not a state," a process in which someone reacts to actual or potential environment. But as with any novelty, once the charm of newness has faded a dissatisfaction sets in. The reader begins to raise questions. What part, for instance, does the individual and collective past play in the life of a man? A man carries with him the sense of where he has come from, what he has done, what he wants to do again, what he must prevent himself from doing. He is a state in continuous process: but he is first a state, a unique self which is partly shaped by his own experience, by his family and theirs, by his nation and its history.

Some kind of course can be traced from the hero of early fiction to the nonhero to the abstraction enclosed in society to the present bundle of passing sensations. V. S. Pritchett, for instance, thinks that Thackeray "invented the modern non-hero." Thackeray had a strong feeling "for life as history, and particularly as class history," and the social revolution in the years between his time and the early twentieth century certainly aggravated that feeling in many subsequent writers. The notion of character as fate shifted by means of the nonhero to that of character as something shaped by the activities of a world created by the actions of men. James T. Farrell borrowed a line from Housman and called one of his books *A World I Never Made*. The title was indicative of the sense of helplessness, the attitude of "Don't blame me, I only live here," which had set in. One further result has been the novel or story in which man is reduced to the role of *voyeur,* of Peeping Tom at the spectacle of his own existence. The more general result, which Mary McCarthy is talking about, is that each character is a "dissociated outsider." He may speak to the reader's own sense of estrangement but not to that other sense which every human being possesses in spite of depressions and wars, the moral and ethical shambles of life around him, the uncertainty of the future. People continue to find the heroic in themselves, to discover it in others. They go on making some kind of order of disorder, coherence of the incoherent. "The meaning of the world around us can no longer be considered as other than fragmentary, temporary, and even contradictory, and always in dispute." But what *meaning* has Robbe-Grillet in mind? What meaning has there ever been except that imposed by the intellect?

It is true, certainly, that the parish, the provincial town, the city with its unique attributes have merged into megalopolis with its missile site and training stations, its millions of people, its sprawling suburbs, its schools and universities, television stations, factories, embassies and consulates, advertising agencies, short-order eateries. And in this vastness the writer may well stand bewildered. Where can he get hold of that which is both particular and general?

The great themes remain, however; love and hate, death, nobility, immortal longing. It is the subjects which once dramatized those themes that seem to have diminished, or to have lost their representational value for some other reason. Mary McCarthy suggests that it may be possible for the contemporary writer to create character by studying occupation: no one has done justice, she says, to the psychoanalyst; no one has described an action painter or an orthodox Freudian or a psychiatric social worker or a foundation executive. Perhaps not—at least, in a way that would win Miss McCarthy's approval. But there have been plenty of stories and books about other kinds of jobs and their incumbents, and though they have added temporary phrases to the popular vocabulary (e.g., "gray flannel suit"), they have done nothing to suggest that this is a potentially valuable method for reviving the full-bodied character. Who wore that gray flannel suit?

So there the problem rests in our time. The enclosed world is gone. There's no Gopher Prairie for Carol Kennicott to seek to enlighten; Heathcliff is in analysis and acting quite decently toward everybody; Emma Bovary is on a cruise and feeling awfully gay; and Undine Spragg is writing her memoirs for fall publication. The various worlds of fiction have been popped into a common kettle, where each of them is contributing to the general flavor of the rather bland soup.

This chapter originally bore the subtitle "Interim Report," for that is what any discussion of characterization must be at the present time. Among the techniques of fiction, it is now the most in debate; its achievements are the least satisfactory. The fact remains, however, that every fiction writer, starting out on that beautiful, formidable page one, is embarking on *somebody's* story. Unlike the historian, he is not interested simply in describing and interpreting a happening. Unlike the lyric poet, he is not concerned with a single emotion or apprehension. How he finds his way is entirely up to him; but anyone who cherishes the classic conception of character will hope that he will get considerable assistance from the extraordinary people he has to tell about.

5 POINT OF VIEW

ANGLES OF VISION

Through whose eyes should we see? The question is one that seems not to have puzzled earlier generations of novelists. Of course I shall tell my story through the words of Moll Flanders because she is obviously the best person to describe her own life. Or, of course I shall tell my story of various relationships through the different points of view of Cécile Volanges, the Vicomte de Valmont, the Présidente de Tourvel, Sophie Carnay, and so on, because they all have a part in it and no one person could possibly know all that goes on. But, with the beginning of the modern novel, specifically with Henry James, the choice of a vision or visions through which to view the story has become a more vexed and difficult question. James always sought for the right "central intelligence" or "reflector" as the personality through which to tell his story, and in the prefaces to his novels (collected as *The Art of Fiction*) he discusses his theory at frequent points. In *The Craft of Fiction*, Percy Lubbock gave an orderly but rather simplified study of James's concepts about point of view. Later critics of fiction made these concepts into a fairly rigid doctrine, in effect, *the* doctrine, which is reflected in most teaching and textbooks about writing. In 1961, Wayne Booth published a remarkable critical book, *The Rhetoric of Fiction*, a revisionist statement of theory which scrutinizes the doctrine with great care and attempts to loosen it up by pointing out several fallacies. The reader will find later reference to some of this theory.

Because point of view is a matter of angles—the angle or angles from which a story is seen—one convenient way to talk about it is by means of a diagram. The reader is warned: the diagram is fictional but is not a fiction.

THE DIAGRAM

The Gamma family is enjoying a picnic in a clearing in the woods. There are three of them, father, mother, and their son of, say, ten years of age. They think that they are alone but standing a little way off and hidden by some trees is a neighbor of theirs, Mr. Beta, who is observing them and overhearing their conversation. None of the four realizes, however, that still a fifth personality is present—it is a certain mysterious and powerful Alpha, who stands at a somewhat further distance from Mr. Beta's position and also has the advantage of being on the rise of a small hill, so that he can view the other people and all of the scene around them.

What happens in the course of the picnic does not need to be detailed; it is only important to mention one thing. Mrs. Gamma and her husband are in disagreement over something. The disagreement flares up into a quarrel and, finally, he angrily slaps her across the face. That is all.

POSSIBLE POINTS OF VIEW; THE GAMMAS

Among the three people at the picnic there are, obviously, three points of view, three different pairs of eyes, and three different minds behind them, through which the incident (or possibly the whole before-and-after story of the Gammas) can be told. The author faces a vital choice in selecting one of them, because these are not simply three different registers of the same event; each one is potentially an entirely different story. That is, the facts in the life of the Gamma family might remain much the same among the three, but the point of view is the first means by which those facts pass into fiction, into an artful treatment of the facts. It becomes, as Henry James's debates with himself show time and again, predominantly a question of *whose* story.

Assume that the author chooses Mrs. Gamma's point of view as the reflector of the incident, and assume a few more things about her. It is going to be a version of the story as told by an unappreciated, wronged, and injured person, and the story will have her special bias. She works hard and does everything to be a good wife and mother, but she is callously mistreated. She could have had another kind of life with a richer and more considerate husband; she could have had a career. But now she has chosen to sacrifice those for this man—and observe how he treats her.

Assume that the author decides against this line of development, perhaps because he dislikes portraying self-pity or perhaps because her potential personality seems less interesting than those of the others. He then chooses Mr. Gamma. Gamma is a tough-minded, self-centered man, whose main absorption is in his business dealings. He long ago shed the brief sentimentality of early marriage days and now looks at his wife and child simply as things that have happened to him and that he must bear with. On the few occasions that he is actually brought to think about his wife, he sees her as a kind of "injustice-collector," a woman who is constantly contriving small crises which will result in hurt to herself. He sees this dimly, but he cannot overcome the irritation of the moment, and so, in one way or another, he strikes out at her—not so much, he thinks, as a way of injuring her but as a way of stopping her constant jabs at him.

But the author rejects this consciousness for his story, as well. It may be that he finds the hard ego of Gamma too difficult to work with or that his intelligence is too coarse for the theme that is about to develop. A point of view must be flexible enough and subtle enough to give the author latitude and depth in telling his story. Thus he turns to the third person present, and here he finds the qualities that have attracted so many modern fiction writers. A child's point of view has the initial charm of being innocent. The author has, at hand, an immediate contrast between the reprehensible doings of adults and the fresh honesty of the child who watches them and wonders at them. As Henry James said, in his preface to *What Maisie Knew,* he wanted to show his child-observer living in its "terribly mixed little world" with "all intensity and perplexity and felicity." Further, there is a belief common to large numbers of authors that children are inordinately perceptive creatures. In the same preface James said, "I should have to invest her with perceptions easily and almost infinitely quickened." Finally, there are all those fine examples—beginning with the young Jane Eyre, David, Pip, Maisie, Jim Hawkins, and so on—of remarkable successes won by viewing the world through young eyes.

Suppose, however, that the mock author in the case decided against young Gamma. Perhaps he reminded himself that the child's point of view has grown nearly into a situational cliché in modern writing simply because so many writers have used it for exactly the purposes already noted. (Having become such a cliché, it can even be turned upside down with startling effects, as in *The Innocent Voyage*.) The charm that there once was in the combination of limited knowledge, sensitivity, and perfect candor has been replaced by a certain boredom acquired from overuse. It is no longer easy to do anything new within the convention.

Thus the author turns again, this time to the somewhat removed observer, Mr. Beta. He is, of course, that device of fiction known as the "dramatized narrator" or the "narrator-agent."

NARRATOR-AGENT

Beta lives in the same world as the Gamma family. He could, in fact, if he wanted to, step into the picnic glade and speak to them. In some fiction he plays a purely secondary role in the action, in other instances he plays even less than that; but he always has to maintain a certain distance and aloofness. He is a created personality used by the author as a substitute voice. His function is to survey the whole scope of the story and to relate it with a breadth of knowledge and a relative objectivity that one of the direct participants could not possess. He cannot give us the sudden frightening sensation of how it feels to be a child seeing his father hit his mother in the face, but on the other hand he has the advantage of being able to see all three of the actors at this moment and, through his insight, to reveal something of what they all are experiencing separately.

The skillful author draws a distinction between his own deliberately hidden personality and that of his narrator-agent. That is, he employs the strategy of giving us the story of certain events *as seen* and pulled together within the mind of an imaginary individual. The individual is first important as a selective observer, but more than that he is an interpreter, and an interpreter *in his own way. The Great Gatsby* is not just the story of Jay Gatsby; it is the story as only Nick Carraway (as distinct from Fitzgerald) could tell it.

The agent device is an ancient one in fiction, but modern novelists, beginning in the era of James and Conrad, have made it into a strategy. Conrad, in fact, was not quite aware at first of what he was doing and considered that he meant his narrator to be just the narrator-voice, the simple teller of tales, familiar from ages past. He insisted to Ford Madox Ford that the Marlow who tells many of his stories was no more than the average ship's officer, with no idiosyncrasies and a great measure of objectivity. Henry James, on the other hand, called Marlow "that preposterous master mariner." He is, in fact, an odd kind of "philosopher" figure and no one would mistake his often elaborate recitals for a plain ship's log of the events.

The idea that lay behind the use of a narrator-agent came from a revulsion against the many eighteenth- and nineteenth-century writers who made a habit of "authorial intrusions." This is a matter of banishing the story for the time being and permitting the author, in his own voice and person, to drop in for a chat with the reader. Trollope discusses what is going to happen later on in the story; Thackeray tells us that he has put aside the "puppet theatre" for the time being in order to talk to us; Fielding delights in telling us jokes and reminding us that what we have just been reading is no more than a story he has just been writing. Flaubert, Maupassant, James, Conrad, and most subsequent writers felt that this kind of "dear reader" address was a fatal invasion of the story's privacy. It destroyed whatever illusion of "real experience" the author had

cf. Conrad

been at pains to build up. What was worse, most authors, when they abandoned their stories for direct conversation, turned out to be dismal bores.[1]

Even though the author in his own person ought to be hidden, there should still remain some way in which pertinent comment and generalization can be made about the story and its people. Any author, of course, is always commenting on his material simply by selecting what to write. Even when one character is made to speak and express himself and another character consistently does not speak, the author has made a commentary on them. Still, this is rather different from a generalization, which is a matter of noting an idea that arises out of a number of particulars. The author—no matter how he may deceive himself, as he has under the influence of certain theories—is never very comfortable in the form of a camera eye. The reason he wishes to tell a story at all is closely associated with the thought that he regards the story as having certain points of general significance which he wishes to bring to the attention of the world. There will be some discussion of this particular point further on in this chapter; the important thing to recognize here is that the narrator-agent was invented to carry out a special mission. He is the author's point of view transformed (either in small ways, or in large), personified, and humanized. Because he is on the same scale and in the same setting as the actors, he does not seem like the clumsy manipulator of *Tom Jones,* who barges out of some "real" world into the middle of the play. He can move about freely and see broad areas of the story. But he does, in taking the author's place as teller, accept some limitations and make some sacrifices. He cannot be as omniscient as the author. That is, he can guess shrewdly about what is going on in the minds of the principal actors, but he cannot enter into those minds. The delicate instrument of interior exploration is denied him, and he has to rely

---

[1] Wayne Booth in *The Rhetoric of Fiction* defends (with qualifications) the intrusive author, saying that "the author has created himself as he has written the book," and that we get to know him as a friend. But bad whimsy, dull observations, and boredom can never make a friend of anybody, especially anybody who has hoped to read a story, not a second-rate essay.

on the cruder tools of attempted mind reading or insight, on what he hears, on careful observation, and on hearsay observation.

This last is true equally of any one of the principals who might be chosen to tell the story from *his* point of view. The advantage owned by the narrator-agent, however, is the fact that he is not involved emotionally in the story and that he has a greater chance to gather information from all sources. These are the things that create that small but important "distance" between him and the centers of action.

He can "gather information from all sources," but there are still certain areas, besides the interiors of other minds, that the rules of plausibility deny to him. Authors employing the narrator-agent sometimes, to the detriment of the story, forget and invade those forbidden places. Thus, Ishmael, the narrator of *Moby Dick,* is sometimes bypassed and we hear things directly that Ishmael is not privileged to hear; Nelly Dean, the narrator-agent of *Wuthering Heights,* is made to include exact transcripts of letters that she could not possibly have seen (unless she makes a habit of reading her master's mail on the sly—and we are never told that she does); Dowell, Ford Madox Ford's fascinating narrator in *The Good Soldier,* describes in detail scenes that took place in a remote country he has never visited and that are unlikely ever to have been transmitted to him by the participant. In short, the writer who uses the narrator-agent as his point of view has to accept human limitations for his representative. He cannot transfer any of his own godlike privileges.

Another, and more subtle, human limitation he has to accept is that of the individuality he gives his agent. This is both an advantage and a restriction in the way that it colors the story. At his best, the narrator-agent gives the fiction a "character," that is, a coherence of tone of voice and definite outlook on the world that is of great value. There is a kind of cohesive firmness in the method, which other methods often lack. There is a sense of command. But, to effect this, the personality given the narrator-agent has to be firm, well knit, and relatively simple.

Strange complications begin to occur when it is otherwise.

N.B

Conrad, as Murray Krieger points out in a discussion of *Youth,* had considerable trouble with the inconsistency of the early Marlow, a failing that gives *Youth* a badly fluctuating effect: there is "Marlow, the descriptive polysyllabic *raconteur,* Marlow the pompous philosopher, and Marlow the breezy drinking companion." This is one example of an excess of personality in the narrator-agent.

Another example of a somewhat different kind is the narrator who is at odds with the essential quality of the story to be told. A teller has to have some kind of congruent relationship with his tale—or else he would never choose to relate it. When he gets in the way of the story and becomes a bother to it, or when his temperament distorts and disrupts the story rather than giving a shape to it, he becomes counterproductive.

John Wain offers a good example of this in his comments on J. D. Salinger's *Raise High the Roof Beam, Carpenters and Seymour, an Introduction,* a part of the long serial about the Glass family Salinger is in the process of writing. Wain remarks:

Buddy Glass is the character who stands half-in, half-out of the fable and Tells The Story. Whether the episodes are in the first-person singular or not, we are given to understand that Buddy is holding the pen, or at the typewriter. And Buddy is a bore. He is prolix, obsessed with his subject, given to rambling confidences, and altogether the last person to be at the helm of an enterprise like this. . . .

Wain goes on to cite several examples of Buddy's "insufferable" weakness for total recall. After pointing out that the author, in several fits of archness, has more or less identified himself with Buddy, Wain adds:

And so the coy little game of pat-ball goes on, blurring the outlines, importing whimsy where whimsy has no right to be, and generally spoiling the atmosphere of seriousness, unrestrained and unpompous but complete seriousness, which a writer like Salinger needs to work in.[2]

[2] From "Go Home, Buddy Glass," *The New Republic* (February 16, 1963), p. 21.

In the person of the narrator-agent there is another rather less obvious potential for trouble—the element of ambiguity. When the hero or, alternatively, any one of the foremost participants is recounting the story, the reader is likely to be conscious of certain fallabilities already noted in that character. Not only does he have specific psychological traits that limit and define him but he has interests at stake in the drama as well. What the personally involved narrator relates as the truth is heavily qualified by what the reader knows him to be. If the author has done his work well, part of the truth is statement and part of it is good inference. Mrs. Gamma may complain that there is no apparent reason why her husband spends almost every evening away from home; yet the reader has observed how she whines and nags, and he knows that there *is* a reason.

But this clear author-reader understanding is more obscure when the agent is the narrator. There is a tendency to forget that nice equation. (For an excellent and thorough analysis of the "reliable" and the "unreliable" types of narrators, readers of this book are referred to the previously cited *The Rhetoric of Fiction.* No other critical work has gone into this difficult matter with such care and insight.)

The basic question with the narrator-agent is one of ambiguity. We do not imagine that he will lie to us deliberately but, because we lack the rich context of actions and fully developed dramatic position for him, we often find it very perplexing to judge his version of the truth. One of the most famous debates in modern criticism is over the version of the story given by the governess who narrates James's *The Turn of the Screw.* (Though she cannot be defined strictly as either narrator-agent or as a chief participant, her role has certain elements of both.) There are a number of conflicting interpretations of the "true" meaning of her story, but none that is clearly convincing. Booth remarks, ". . . few of us feel happy with a situation in which we cannot decide whether the subject is two evil children as seen by a naïve but well-meaning governess or two innocent children as seen by a hysterical, destructive governess." He adds that when James began to create the "seriously-flawed narrator" to reflect his story, he was no longer able to mediate between the peculiarities of the teller and the peculiarities of the drama. That is, the situation then became so complex with its two subjects that ambiguity, rather than one discernible version of the truth, came as a result.

I, HE, OR SHE

Both the participant and the narrator-agent discussed so far are personal points of view, and either can be presented in first person singular or third person singular form. The choice depends on whatever special quality the writer wishes to give his narration. Each choice has risks of its own.

Henry James called the first person singular "that accurst autobiographic form which puts a premium on the loose, the improvised, the cheap and the easy." He thought that it destroyed the necessary detachment between the writer and his subject. Like many other overstatements about technique, James's does the good service of indicating some wicked snares. Both the simple reader and the inexperienced writer are likely to assume a one-to-one correspondence between the real author and the "I" of the story. For the writer, the resulting temptations often prove to be great disadvantages. One of them is the effect of limiting the story to the actual events on which it is based. When the teacher of writing suggests that certain characters or certain actions might be handled in a different way to improve the story, the student may often reply that "No, she has to be just as I've described her because that's the way she was," or "I couldn't change that because it's described just the way it happened." This iron clamp of reality on the imagination is particularly heavy in the case of the first person narrative.

Another snare in this form is the kind of lavish self-indulgence found in some authors. Without any psychological separation between them and the teller, they fall into the loose, cheap, and easy habit of talking about themselves and whatever is of egotistical concern to them rather than about what is of concern to the matters in progress in the story. It is an almost fatal loss of perspective and its results are the garrulous, rambling, roguish, and irrelevant Buddy Glasses of fiction. Although every character doubtless has his origin in some facet of the author's mind, to be a *created* character he goes through the process that good craft demands. He must be objectified, tempered, and given a shape. The "I" can have the disadvantage of being nothing more than the author's undefined ego and the first person manner no more than a psychiatrist's couch on which he reclines, telling all.

On the other hand, there are certain stories and novels that have a true need for the first person teller, provided that he is a created and separate being. The autobiographic form, far from being always accurst, can give the effect of intimacy and involvement to the reader in cases where the third person cannot. There are definite, calculated reasons for stories and novels as diverse as Hemingway's *Farewell to Arms*, Tolstoy's "Family Happiness," Conrad's "The Secret Sharer," Rose Macaulay's *The Towers of Trebizond*, Robert Graves's *I, Claudius*, and hundreds of others which employ first person narration. The reader's sympathies and identification are likely to be given to the narrator who has a role in the story, and this is somewhat truer of the first person than of the third person teller. The first person voice gives an impression of being direct, candid, and honest insofar as its limitations permit, whether the voice is that of a narrator-agent or of a principal. And this kind of confidence is a little livelier and a little more quickly established than it is with the third person.

The peculiar and rather indefinable quality about first person narration is that it gives the sense of actually listening to a story being told by somebody about himself or herself. It presumes that the "I," having gone through certain experiences, now looks back at them from a more mature and knowledgeable standpoint. The reader assumes, first, that the experience was formative and expects to see a formative quality about the story; and, second, that the "I" who tells the story is somewhat different from the I who experiences it—different because he has attained the critical perspective that comes from having lived the whole of it. There is a certain interesting and lifelike quality about this twofold aspect of the narrative that only the first person voice can give—for we all look back on ourselves as we once were—while the plain "he was" or "she was" suggests a story that is told about someone else and in but one dimension of time—the time when those things happened.

The use of the third person does not automatically banish the accurst autobiographic failings—to a limited degree they appear in Hemingway's novels and to a very large degree in Thomas Wolfe's —but it helps. It is easier for the author to make "he" or "she"— even if that person is a principal and narrator—act or experience things that do not emerge from autobiography. Frequently, it is psychologically far easier for the author to put the third person principal through extremes of experience or expression than to do so for the "I." It is difficult to drop the self-identification and to make the "I" ridiculous, boastful, sordid, deceitful, stupid, or callous (though various authors have succeeded in doing one or another, either inadvertently or by design). Likewise, there are certain comments that a first person teller who is meant to be respected cannot make about himself without striking a false tone. "Being talented and clever, I was soon the best pupil in the school." "I faced the animal with coolness and courage." That is the reason why so many of the "I's" of fiction are moderate, equable, and a little colorless.

The third person point of view, then, is just slightly more removed and secondhand than is the first person. Though this sacrifices a shade of the total sympathy the reader may have with the character through whom the story is seen, it nevertheless allows the reader to have a view of some aspects of the "he" that are difficult or impossible for the "I" to recognize about itself. In André Malraux's *Man's Fate,* there is a scene in which a young man (Kyo) listens to his own voice on some records that the revolutionists are using to send secret messages. He cannot recognize the voice as his own; and so it is that there are certain things, even very common things, about ourselves of which we are not aware. It is easier for the author to show such traits about the third person without ostensibly or noticeably departing from his viewpoint.

THE OMNISCIENT MR. ALPHA

As the actual author and real teller of the fiction, Alpha is, of course, omniscient, omnipotent, and omnipresent. But even if he has discarded the idea of using any of the Gammas or Mr. Beta as the means to tell his story, he is left with the same problem that made him consider choosing one of them. He must give the impression that the story happens naturally and as the characters will it, and not that it is his arbitrary construction. There will be times when he can borrow the vision of one or another character and observe things from that person's point of view. But there will be other times when the author is entirely responsible, commenting, abridging, or taking a panoramic view. At those times he is the only possible narrator—but he must do this work plausibly, unemphatically, without proclaiming himself. Several critics of technique have spoken of the "invisible narrator," which is a somewhat misleading term. A voice is a very real presence in fiction and the sophisticated reader is usually aware of that voice's identity. The author's tone should be consonant with the fictional surroundings, tuned, as it were, to the pitch of the story and thus unobtrusive. It should not be the parade-ground voice of a sergeant major giving orders to his company of characters, nor a loud whisper giving cues from the prompter's box, nor the voice of a lecturer who has stopped the show in order to fill us in with all sorts of supplementary information and critical commentary.

Even though the risks of mismanagement are constant at every turn, Alpha's direct command of the story is, finally, the most versatile, flexible, privileged, and unrestricted of all the methods. The variety of narrative tactics open to him can be indicated more or less by these headings:

He can make selective use of a number of individual points of view, borrowing a specific character's angle of vision when it suits his purpose.

He can use the theatre of "showing not telling," for the moment presenting a quite objective look at things.

Omniscient narrator

He can analyze anything about the story by use of critical com-
    ment and generalization (as long as he does this subtly and
    harmoniously enough).
He can take a panoramic view of events, giving an account of
    simultaneous happenings or disassociated scenes that a narrator-
    agent could cover only by the use of most improbable devices.
He can discover multiple traits and facets of the characters readily
    and plausibly without having to work things around to bring
    any single point of view within discovery range.

The whole secret of this particular art of narration is the power
of metamorphosis. One of the most interesting and important meta-
morphoses is the ability to possess, for the time being, the mind
and outlook of one character; then to revert back to the all-seeing,
impersonal vision of Alpha when necessary; and then again to
accept limited sight through the eyes of a second character, etc.
The author may choose to borrow one character's point of view
either briefly and momentarily or over some longer span. In either
case, he must be sensitive about his methods because this is a
transmutation of viewpoint that must not strike the reader as an
annoying magician's trick.
    It is perhaps most difficult in the first instance—when the author
wishes to dip into the thought or feeling of a character for a moment in order to get just a touch or two of private reaction to a
scene or narration that is in general impersonal, being carried on
by the author. The method can become either a muddle or an obvious sleight of mind on the author's part if he springs too care-
lessly or recklessly from one point of view to the other:

The fire began to spread and now nearly the whole wing of the hotel
was obscured by smoke. Martin thought of the pile of banknotes in the
steel box and he could almost see them turning brown at the edges and
crisping like dead leaves. His wife, standing next to him with a stained
and troubled face, thought only of the dead child's sweater she had
carried with her all of these twelve years. She could not bear the thought
of the flames licking at it. Mrs. Parsons was thinking, "Now he'll never
be able to drag me to this hideous place again." Richard Parsons thought,

"The insurance on the clothes and things would be enough to buy a divorce, if only . . ." The fire began to sweep in gusts along the clapboards and one of the firemen yelled to them all to stand back.

This has a nervous and indecisive effect because too much is crammed into the paragraph and because the leapfrogging of different points of view is too obvious. It would be better to select only one character for an insight and to bring out whatever else necessary in the form of dialogue—or to reserve some of the reactions for further exposition. Tolstoy is sometimes guilty of this kind of indeterminate shifting. There is a scene in *War and Peace* that takes place after the battle of Borodino. The Russian army is in retreat. Kutuzov, their commander, has called his generals together for a council; they meet in a peasant's cottage. Tolstoy's main purpose was to give an account of the debate over strategy between Generals Kutuzov and Bennigsen and to show how Kutuzov decided to abandon Moscow to the French. But he also had an inspiration for getting an odd and interesting angle on the scene. Why not show it from the point of view of a little peasant girl who watches history in the making as she sits behind the stove? But the interesting idea of point of view and the necessary one do not work together. Here is some sampling of the mixture by the use of a few selections (the name indicates whose point of view is being used at the moment):

[*The adjutant Kaisarov:* he] would have drawn back a curtain from the window facing Kutuzov, but the latter shook his head angrily at him and Kaisarov saw that his highness did not care for them to see his face.

[*The author:*] Round the peasant's deal table, on which lay maps, plans, pencils and papers, there was such a crowd that the orderlies brought in another bench and set it near the table.

[*The little girl, Malasha:* she] saw the council in quite a different light. It seemed to her that the whole point at issue was a personal struggle between "Grandad" and "Longcoat," as she called Bennigsen . . . she noted with glee that "Grandad's" words had put "Longcoat" down.

[*The author:*] The words that had thus affected Bennigsen were Kutuzov's quietly and softly uttered comment.[3]

[3] Trans. Constance Garnett (New York: The Modern Library, 1931), p. 781.

It is simply evident—and it became evident to Tolstoy early—that the little girl could comprehend no more than the fact that two men, one sympathetic and one not, were quarreling. Most of the scene is presented objectively, which accomplishes its business, and the little girl's sentient presence remains no more than an unexploited idea that confuses the scene.

The moral of this is, of course, that an author should don the individual point of view of one of his characters only for well-calculated reasons and for a definite purpose. Tolstoy's half-formed thought, that it would be interesting to look through the eyes of an uncomprehending child at the high command making its fateful decision, did not come off, and no assumption of a special point of view will be successful unless the tactic is capable of presenting the scene to us *more* strikingly, and yet intelligibly, than an objective description. Along with this goes the principle of consistency. As noted before, it is better not to shift point of view within the telling of one incident or within a paragraph. Likewise, it is most effective when the author sticks close to the point of view he has adopted until he has completed some turn of his story. If he should wish, for instance, to witness a conversation among some cynical and corrupt old politicians through the eyes of an idealistic young woman, he must follow through with it, seeing, hearing, knowing, and feeling no more than she does. That is the only way that the contrast between the viewpoint and the tenor of the scene can have any effectiveness.

After the contrast has been made, the author is free to shift to another view. Percy Lubbock says:

And how? Merely by closing (when it suits him) the open consciousness of the seer, [who] can at any moment become impenetrable, a human being whose thought is sealed from us; and it may seem a small matter, but in fact it has the result that he drops into the plane of the people whom he has hitherto been seeing and judging. Hitherto, subjective, communicative in solitude, he has been in a category apart from them; but now he may mingle with the rest, engage in talk with them, and his presence and his talk are no more to the fore than theirs.[4]

[4] *The Craft of Fiction* (New York: The Viking Press, 1957), pp. 260–261.

This succeeding method of viewing the story is the objective—or what has been called the "theatre"—method. The characters are all viewed as acting and speaking equally in front of the reader and no one of them has a consciousness open to view. It is not, of course, actually objective and, if you look closely, you will see the author-director's remarks written in the speeches and attitudes of the players. Nevertheless, all of the emphasis here is on "showing, not telling." The author, ostensibly, is inviting us to view the story for ourselves, quite unattended by his commentary or direction. This way of proceeding is suited to quite different effects from that of the personal viewpoint or the author's generalizing viewpoint. It is appropriate to the spoken or acted scene whose intention is to produce a fictional dialectic: conflict, debate, the working out of a problem, the interplay of character. We are persuaded that we can see for ourselves and judge—and there is a good deal of excitement in that process of seeing and judging.

If it had not been tinged by the personal views, Tolstoy's post-Borodino council could have succeeded in being just that kind of scene. In dramatic and objective terms we could see the formidable Bennigsen sticking to his sentimental dogma ("The holy and ancient capital of Russia" must be defended), Kutuzov's eloquent argument to the contrary, and finally the emerging realization that the debate itself is meaningless and that the loss of the city is a foregone conclusion.

This "detached" point of view—particularly favored by Flaubert, Maupassant, and the French Naturalists—is so frequently employed in modern fiction that it is hardly necessary to give examples. Almost any of Hemingway's stories, for instance, will furnish a good illustration.

With the pure use of a single point of view, theorizing or judgment gets made without difficulty ("I could see that she was a clever hypocrite," or "He realized that there was, after all, such a thing as justice"), as long as it remains partial and personal. With the detached point of view, the author must direct the reader to deduce a generalization from the details he has seen and heard (we, the readers, know that X is a hypocrite, because we have concluded it out of the context of what he does and says). Consistent use of either technique is appropriate for the short story—though not for all short stories—but over the longer stretch of the novel they begin to present their serious limitations. The author is always of two minds. There is the recording, descriptive, story-telling mind and there is the purposeful, meaningful, critical mind. Therefore, when his impersonal voice is mainly responsible for the narration of the story, any judgments are assumed to be his.

Modern writers, to a great extent, have felt uneasy about this necessity and have tended to rely heavily on the apparent "telling, not showing" device of symbolism to convey their comment (see the section on symbolism in Chapter 9). But symbols are not always apposite and they can be very cumbersome. They run the risk of being either too subtle and thus ineffective with the reader or too obvious or too ambiguous. The point when an explicit comment demands to be made arises again and again, and the author cannot continue to evade without letting both intelligibility and intelligence disappear from the story.

No very exact rules can be laid down for the use of interpretative or generalizing comment except to say that the individual writer must decide carefully just where it will appear. That place, according to modern conceptions, ought to be where no other kind of expression can easily produce the meaning through a strong inference. Beyond that, the comment should bear a precise relationship to the material of the story, should be lucid, economical, and firm in its style. Here are two extended examples from Conrad's *The Nigger of the Narcissus*:

James Wait rallied again. He lifted his head and turned bravely at Donkin, who saw a strange face, an unknown face, a grimacing and fantastic mask of despair and fury. Its lips moved rapidly; and hollow, moaning, whistling sounds filled the cabin with a mutter of vague menace, complaint and desolation, like a far-off murmur of a rising wind. Wait shook his head; rolled his eyes; he denied, cursed, threatened—and not a word had the strength to pass beyond the sorrowful pout of those black lips. It was incomprehensible and disturbing, a gibberish of emo-

N.B.

tions, a frantic dumb-show of speech pleading for impossible things, promising a shadowy vengeance.[5]

Conrad has given a description here, but a description thoroughly charged with his own commentary. Only the author is capable of reading all that meaning—and it is valuable meaning for the story— into the agonized expression of James Wait. There simply is no other way to do it without obvious fakery and the small scene succeeds just because Conrad takes it into his own hands.

In another place in the same story, Conrad writes:

On men reprieved by its disdainful mercy, the immortal sea confers in its justice the full privilege of desired unrest. Through the perfect wisdom of its grace they are not permitted to meditate at ease upon the complicated and acrid savour of existence, lest they should remember and, perchance, regret the reward of a cup of inspiring bitterness, tasted so often, and so often withdrawn from before their stiffening but reluctant lips. They must without pause justify their life to the eternal pity that commands toil to be hard and unceasing from sunrise to sunset, from sunset to sunrise: the obstinate clamour of sages, demanding bliss and an empty heaven, is redeemed at last by the vast silence of pain and labour, by the dumb fear and the dumb courage of men obscure, forgetful, and enduring.[6]

Only the author is capable of making *that* observation, as well. In this case, it is mistaken. The reader is likely to feel that Conrad is shaken by a tremor of self-doubt at the beginning of Chapter Four, having evidently decided that his preceding texture of event-and-comment has failed to make his meaning clear. No reader is ever dismayed by the clarifying touch, the sure interpretation of what might otherwise remain obscure, or even the aphorism that fits into the context of the story. But the literary essay Conrad inserts here looks suspiciously like an effort to smuggle in a little Higher Thought and not to complete any facet of the story's design. Though Conrad is a splendid writer, he fairly frequently does not know when to stop. Knowing when to stop is always important to

[5] Included in *The Portable Conrad* (New York: The Viking Press, 1957), p. 432.
[6] *Ibid.*, p. 373.

a fiction writer, but it is especially important in the case of commentary and generalization.

The third advantage of the authorial-voice method is its ability to take panoramic views (the beginning of *A Passage to India*, which is quoted in Chapter 2, is a good example) or to shift scene as need be. Human viewers are limited by plausibility and available means of transportation. Alpha can, without any questions being asked, report separately on things that actually take place at the same time, move around from scene to scene, describe things in detail or in the mass, etc.

Alpha's final gift is the opportunity to deal with character in more various descriptive and developmental ways than can any limited point of view or series of particular viewpoints. The first example from *The Nigger of the Narcissus* shows Conrad observing something essential about James Wait's personality that no member of that ship's company could divine as deeply or express as well in words; nor could it be expressed at all in the detached or objective view, because Wait says nothing and presents only a tortured face which has to be interpreted for us. Wait, speaking for himself, would find it beyond his powers to articulate those chaotic feelings—at least in a precise and intelligible form, which Conrad's is. It would be well to notice the quoted examples in the chapter on characterization according to whether they are described from the impersonal author's point of view or from a certain character's viewpoint.

The final answer to the question, "Through whose eyes should we see?" is, of course, dependent on the nature of the story and the angle or angles from which the author wishes to watch it. Probably the only specific advice that can be given for practice is to suggest that, if one kind of viewpoint proves inadequate for all that the writer wishes to give about his material, he should try another or a combination of others. Point of view has an important relevance to characterization, narrative method, and final meaning. Its selection should be made with a view to aiding, rather than limiting, the development of these other essential elements.

6 BACKGROUND; PLACE; SETTING; MILIEU

"THE CROSSROADS OF CIRCUMSTANCE"

How important is setting to a work of fiction? Does it matter a great deal except in regional literature? The question might be considered by looking at a handful of famous novels and asking whether they would "work" as well, or almost as well, if the action were transferred elsewhere. How persuasive would the reader find *Wuthering Heights* if it was laid in London? What if Thackeray had moved the London scenes of *Vanity Fair* to Emily Brontë's Yorkshire? Suppose Henry James's *Washington Square* had been about a New Orleans neighborhood rather than one in New York. And William Faulkner's Mississippi novels—what if Yoknapatawpha County were in Willa Cather's Nebraska?

It is obvious that none of these authors would have written as he or she did, given a change of place. *Wuthering Heights* might have become something like Wilkie Collins' *Woman in White,* interesting chiefly because of its melodramatic plot; equally, it might have offered an "adventure" of the sort that Sir Arthur Conan Doyle, in his stories of Sherlock Holmes, later delighted his readers with. Without the magnificent desolation of those Yorkshire moors, without the violent Yorkshire weathers, without the remoteness of one household from another, not only would the action of the novel have had to be different but the terror and grandeur of its scenes would have been lost.

It would be perfectly correct to retort that the country of this novel is as much fiction as fact, the beauty and violence being equally the products of Emily Brontë's mind. But in this sense the country and the weather of a story are always those of the writer, too. He has so seized in his imagination upon a particular place that it has been transformed into something which, although it may retain a recognizable geography, depends for its "truth" upon the consistency and passion of his vision.

So, in *Wuthering Heights,* the place is Yorkshire, and could be nowhere else. Yet Yorkshire is as much a creation of Emily Brontë as are her Heathcliff and Cathy, her Mr. Lockwood and Mrs. Dean. And Yoknapatawpha County can no more move to Nebraska than Willa Cather's Red Cloud to Mississippi.

These are all clear-cut instances, and there is a mass of urban fiction, of an order generally inferior to *Washington Square,* which conceivably might be set in any large American town. Writers like Jack Kerouac persuade us, in fact, that there is really nothing to distinguish Denver from New York or San Francisco. And many Southern and Midwestern stories might seem capable—at least to a reader who has no personal experience of these areas—of being shifted a good many miles in one direction or the other—from Virginia to South Carolina, say, or from Nebraska to Iowa. Edward Eggleston called the book of his that is now remembered best, *A Hoosier Schoolmaster;* at this distance of time, however, the reader may wonder whether he might not equally have written of *A Buckeye Schoolmaster,* or of a schoolmaster in a primitive Illinois community.

Yet, given this occasional impression of elasticity of setting—an impression that authors themselves, probably, would protest—it seems evident that a fiction usually has roots that are deep in a particular area. It is hard to imagine Studs Lonigan or Danny O'Neill outside the context of his native Chicago. Even Augie March, who is so much more sophisticated, so much more of a traveler, belongs to "that somber city." The Queenborough of Ellen Glasgow's city novels could hardly be any place except Richmond.

The following generalizations can perhaps be made: stories and novels, in the main, begin with the writer's perception of one or more characters, and deal with the events that those characters precipitate; but characters belong to a particular time and place. In her booklet *Place in Fiction,* Eudora Welty observes that the setting exercises a "delicate control" over character. By confining it, setting helps toward definition.

> It was a matter of chance that I should have rented a house in one of the strangest communities in North America. It was on that slender riotous island which extends itself due east of New York. . . .

So says the narrator near the start of *The Great Gatsby,* and the reader knows that life on "that slender riotous island" is going to occupy a good deal of his attention in the following pages.

Place encompasses a story or novel; it is the mountains or hills or plains, the houses people live in, the streets of a town or city, the quality of the local life. Place is also the common speech and the subjects dealt with in that speech. It is dress and ornamentation, manners, taboos, religions. Miss Welty says: "It is by the nature of itself that fiction is all bound up in the local. The internal reason for that is surely that *feelings* are bound up in place. . . . Location is the crossroads of circumstance, the proving ground of 'What happened? Who's here? Who's coming?' . . ." She adds, "The sense of a story when the visibility [i.e., the setting] is only partial or intermittent is as endangered as Eliza crossing the ice."

In some writers' hands, unfortunately, place declines from its eminence to become merely part of that "furniture" of fiction which Willa Cather deplored. It is used for decoration, for filling out the fiction, or in the hope of achieving an effect of authority by sheer mass of ornamentation. As such, it never works. A story decorated as solidly as a Victorian parlor will first distract the reader from whatever drama is going forward, and finally stultify him.

Writers who stick to familiar ground are less prone to irrelevant detail than those who go afield for their subjects. When dealing with the unfamiliar, writers respond too often as any tourist does: they carry away masses of what might be called public information —the picture-postcard things that everyone sees. Another phrase for it is local colorism. They miss the hidden life, the quality which is unique to the particular place. And, doing so, they probably miss their characters, too.

An example of how even a good writer can err can be found in a story by Sarah Orne Jewett which is set in South Carolina. Miss Jewett, who knew her Maine life intimately, set out to tell the kind of story she had often told before, but this time laid in a South still stricken by the Civil War. It is about an old lady and a house (Miss Jewett once said that when these two subjects came together in her mind, a story was the result), and is called "The Mistress of Sydenham Plantation." Perhaps the first false note is struck here, in the title, which smacks a little of the archaic and very much of the "picturesque." (Miss Jewett usually stuck to quite simple titles: "A White Heron," "The Town Poor," "Going to Shrewsbury," "Fair Day.") The action moves from Beaufort, South Carolina, to a ruined plantation house on St. Helena's Island, and then back to Beaufort. The time is the 1880's—some twenty-odd years after the death of Mrs. Sydenham's husband and sons in the war. But for Mrs. Sydenham they are still alive, the war still in progress. On the day before Easter she determines to visit the plantation on St. Helena, to make sure that the great house there is ready for the family's annual move. Her old manservant attempts to dissuade her, fearing that the spectacle of the ruined house will kill her, but she is adamant. And presently she confronts the evidence that refutes her "dream" (as the author calls it). "The crumbled, fallen chimneys of the house were there among the weeds, and that was all" —but perhaps for Mrs. Sydenham the house stands as securely and spaciously as ever. She returns to Beaufort and there resumes the quiet, oblivious routine of her life. "Even the tragic moment of yesterday was lost already in the acquiescence of her mind, as the calm sea shines back to the morning sun when another wreck has gone down."

This is an affecting subject, but the treatment is occasionally gushy, the details are of the picture-postcard kind, and the central character has none of that clear definition, none of the texture or suggestion of depth, that readers find in Miss Jewett's best work. Here, put together in a single paragraph and italicized by us for emphasis, are a few of the false touches (notice the reporter tone which creeps in):

In the *quaint* churchyard of old St. Helena's Church . . . the grave-stones themselves were moss-grown and *ancient-looking; yet* here and there the *wounded look* of the earth *appealed to the eye,* and *betrayed* a new-made grave. The old sarcophagi and heavy tablets of the historic Beaufort families stood side by side with plain wooden crosses. The *armorial bearings* and long epitaphs of the one and the brief lettering of the other suggested the changes that had come with the war to these families, yet somehow the wooden cross *touched one's heart with closer sympathy* . . . The *five doors of the church* were standing open. On the steps of that *eastern door which opened midway up the side aisle,* where the morning sun had shone upon the *white faces of a hospital in war-time* . . . She was a very stately *gentlewoman,* for one so small and thin . . . but there was *true* elegance and dignity in the way she moved, and those who saw her—*persons who shuffled when they walked, and boasted loudly of the fallen pride of the South*—were *struck* with *sudden deference and admiration. . . .*[1]

Miss Jewett has used the church setting as an envelope for her story; the church is the reader's first introduction to Beaufort and, indirectly, to the Sydenham family, and the last scene is on Easter morning when Mrs. Sydenham attends service there. But what extraneous detail has got into this envelope!—the number of doors into the building, its use as a hospital during the war, its aisles. It is probable that Miss Jewett, with the useless conscientiousness that authors are prone to, wrote all of this down during a visit to be

[1] Included in Miss Jewett's collection, *Strangers and Wayfarers* (Boston: Houghton Mifflin Company, 1890), pp. 18–21.

sure of getting it "straight." The church has nothing to do with her real subject, which is the dream that Mrs. Sydenham sank into as an escape from the horror of her husband's and sons' deaths —and it is particularly irrelevant to that moment when reality might have destroyed the dream and killed the dreamer. As to the "sudden deference and admiration" that the Northern intruders fall into at her appearance—the reader may at least be permitted a cynical doubt. The "stately gentlewoman" is part of the picturesque cliché of the antebellum South in which Miss Jewett was caught up. An old woman who has, in the common parlance, been "loony" for more than twenty years is not likely to move the vulgar-minded to reverence.

"The Mistress of Sydenham Plantation" is a story that seems to have got going for the wrong reasons: Miss Jewett was charmed with the Sea Island country, with the aura of nobility and defeat, with the sense of antiquity, with the manners and traditions. Mrs. Sydenham occurred to her later—or perhaps was an anecdote she heard which seemed to offer just what she needed to get her impressions down on paper.

The slack and gush, the reporter's dependence on postcard pictures, are absent when Miss Jewett is writing of her own territory. Here is the opening to "The Town Poor":

Mrs. William Trimble and Miss Rebecca Wright were driving along Hampden east road, one afternoon in early spring. Their progress was slow. Mrs. Trimble's sorrel horse was old and stiff, and the wheels were clogged by clay mud. The frost was not yet out of the ground, although the snow was nearly gone, except in a few places on the north side of the woods, or where it had drifted all winter against a length of fence.

Miss Jewett is not concerned here with whether or not her ladies are "gentlewomen," with whether the Hampden east road is "quaint," with any episode of historic importance which this road was the site of, or with the emotions of passersby who have no connection with the present action. The reader is set down firmly in a wagon between these two old friends, and, without editorial comment, the author tells her story of their gentle charity to "the town poor" to whom they are about to pay a visit. The details are spare—as spare as the sunlight on this early spring day:

. . . beyond a thicket of witch-hazel and scrub-oak, they came in sight of a weather-beaten, solitary farmhouse. The barn was too far away for thrift or comfort, and they could see long lines of light between the shrunken boards as they came nearer. The fields looked both stony and sodden. . . .

[They] stared into a small, low room, brown with age, and gray, too, as if former dust and cobwebs could not be made wholly to disappear. The two elderly women who stood there looked like captives. . . . There was an uncovered small table in the middle of the floor, with some crackers on a plate; and, for some reason or other, this added a great deal to the general desolation.[2]

Beside the picture postcard hazard to which many writers are prone, there is that of telling the reader too much. The risk is one the author runs whether he is writing of home or away, and he can't save himself merely by retorting that every detail has been well and accurately observed. It is as if he were to exhibit not only the parlor of the house—the thing seen on a visit—but the dining room, the kitchen and pantry, the back hall, the shed, the bedrooms and attic, the cellar, the coal bin. "Whoever wrote up just the parlor," he says, "really didn't give you any idea of the house. I've shown you *everything*: now you really know what it's like."

But we don't; he has merely exhausted us by this prolonged tour. Excessive detail, like that which is merely picturesque, proves only that the writer has been busy about his homework. We won't dispute the information he gives us about Victorian houses, or about the workings of a great industrial firm, or the manufacture of woolen articles; but we wish he had labeled his book something other than a novel. Sinclair Lewis' *Work of Art* is an encyclopedic manual on hotel-keeping; one can get quite enthusiastic about the opportunities in the field. But *Work of Art,* as a title for this particular work of fiction, is a painful irony.

[2] Included in an edition of Miss Jewett's work called *The Country of the Pointed Firs and Other Stories* (New York: Anchor Books, 1956), pp. 278, 279, 284.

TECHNIQUE IN FICTION

If it seems necessary for the reader to have a fairly close knowledge of a setting, the writer will be wise to distribute his information through his story. Elizabeth Bowen remarks that "The weak novelist is always, compensatorily, scene-minded." It is often the case that details which initially seem crucial become less so, or become superfluous, once a fiction has begun to work itself out. After all, there is no real point to the description the writer has given of the house at the end of the village street—in fact, it begins to look as if the street itself isn't going to play much of a part in the story. And that long passage on the Indian mounds outside town, which he spent hours reading up on at the library—perhaps the mounds had better be used another time.

By way of parenthesis, it might be laid down as a general rule that the results of research must be used with the greatest caution. Most writers enjoy boning up on a subject; it is so restful, compared with the mental anguish of getting Mrs. Smythe out of her present difficulty and winding off the story at the same time. The temptation of those Indian mounds, for instance, is fierce: while one is about it, one might as well look a little way into the subject of local Indian tribes, and this leads naturally to their history, and then to the history of Indians in general, and from there . . . But the possibilities are many, and each takes the writer straight away from Mrs. Smythe, who is waiting on page twenty-four for him to come back from the library and get on with his proper business. Needless to say, by now, Indian mounds are his proper business, or seem to be, and surely there is a way to work all of this interesting material into Mrs. Smythe's story?

There isn't, of course, however hard he may try. And if this and similar ruthless deletions reduce his story to a bald and commonplace situation, he had better consign Mrs. Smythe to the wastebasket. What was charming him all along was not her dilemma but the place she lived in.

Chekhov said that descriptions "should be very brief and have an incidental nature." He thought that the best method was to "snatch at small details, grouping them in such a manner that after reading them one can obtain the picture on closing one's eyes." A moonlight night, for instance, could be evoked if one wrote "that on the dam of the mill a fragment of broken bottle flashed like a small bright star, and there rolled by, like a ball, the black shadow of a dog, or a wolf. . . ."

But supposing, the writer persists, I really *do* need to tell a good deal about my setting: should I intersperse layers of action with layers of description as if I were composing a club sandwich?

The answer is that whenever possible—whether the writer is dealing with large or small amounts of necessary scene-setting—description should be involved with the *action* of the fiction; not just the physical action but the mental and emotional events that one is telling about. "Scene can only be justified," says Miss Bowen, ". . . where it has dramatic use." *A Passage to India* contains an immense amount of information about that country, yet E. M. Forster has so skillfully involved this detail in the lives of his characters that it never strikes the reader as superimposed on their story, or as irrelevant to the working out of their destinies:

N.B.

As the elephant moved towards the hills . . . a new quality occurred, a spiritual silence which invaded more senses than the ear. Life went on as usual, but had no consequences, that is to say, sounds did not echo or thoughts develop. Everything seemed cut off at its root, and therefore infected with illusion. For instance, there were some mounds by the edge of the track, low, serrated, and touched with whitewash. What were these mounds—graves, breasts of the goddess Parvati? The villagers beneath gave both replies. Again, there was a confusion about a snake which was never cleared up. Miss Quested saw a thin, dark object reared on end at the farther side of a watercourse, and said, "A snake!" The villagers agreed, and Aziz explained: yes, a black cobra, very venomous, who had reared himself up to watch the passing of the elephant. But when she looked through Ronny's fieldglasses, she found it wasn't a snake, but the withered and twisted stump of a toddy-palm. So she said, "It isn't a snake." The villagers contradicted her. She had put the word into their minds, and they refused to abandon it. Aziz admitted that it looked like a tree through the glasses, but insisted that it was a black cobra really, and improvised some rubbish about protective mimicry. Nothing was explained, and yet there was no romance. Films of heat, radiated from the Kawa Dol precipices, increased the confusion. They came at irregular intervals and moved capriciously. A patch of field would jump as if it was being fried, and then lie quiet. As they drew closer the radiation stopped.[3]

Not all writers are as subtle as Mr. Forster, of course, and there is at least one other way to justify a density of detail. Though Virginia Woolf had a good deal of fun at the expense of Arnold Bennett, and though one still agrees with many of her strictures against his passion for rents and rates, in his better novels this kind of description provides what Mark Schorer has called the "matrix of analogy." It is there because his characters' principal frame of reference *is* a material one: they do not think, or think very much, about love, charity, friendship, loyalty, about painting or music, books, good food, fine furniture. Their deep awareness, expressed overtly sometimes and sometimes in what Mr. Schorer describes as a "buried metaphor," is of money coming in and money going out, of house properties that are keeping up, and others that are losing their value, of right and wrong investments, of economical lodgings and their drawbacks, of cheap vacations, of servants and clerks and how to get the most out of them, of the salability of buttons and ribbons and bonnets and bolts of cloth. They exude such considerations; they inhabit places where these considerations constantly distract them from minor matters like human feeling.

Another hazard faced by the writer is that of using place as a cliché. This is allied to the picture-postcard technique, but precedes it, since it is an example of the writer's use of home ground. Usually, the example is contemptible, where local colorism is merely inadequate. It is a form of exploitation of the known and familiar, and every possible drop of quaintness or squalor is wrung from salient features of the landscape, common customs, attitudes, and habits of speech. Local colorism may lead the writer into being superficial and too enthusiastic. Cliché description leads to the creation of stereotypes—the very stereotypes that the postcard users will later come along and accept as the real thing. Willa Cather summed up this kind of fiction when she said, "If a writer's atti-

[3] Pp. 140–141.

tude toward his characters and his scene is as vulgar as a showman's, as mercenary as an auctioneer's, vulgar and meretricious will his product forever remain." Generations of young people used to read—perhaps still do read—Joseph C. Lincoln's Cape Cod stories, full of cantankerous elderly bachelors, eccentric warm-hearted old maids, fogs and family furniture and family secrets, quaint Down East expressions, legends about shipwrecks, and so on. It is a shock to pick up one of these books, as an adult. What seemed so clever and vivid now seems an effect of cynical calculation. Almost all of the detail of setting is extraneous to the action. With a few modifications the story itself could be transported easily to any other coastal place—elsewhere on the Atlantic shore, for instance, or to a community on one of the Great Lakes. And the whole is as artificial as a puppet play, with the strings plainly visible (and a little slack at that), and the backdrops worn and faded from too much use.

By comparison with any of Mr. Lincoln's books, a brief novel like Edith Wharton's *Summer,* which is laid in an isolated Massachusetts village, seems barren of local detail—devoid in particular of the picturesque. And yet the action cannot be dissociated from the place: only here, the author persuades us, could have existed a society at once crude and genteel, and, in a mountain fastness nearby, another society of hideous squalor, cruelty, poverty, and moral indifference. Only here could these two cultures, superficially so different and essentially so similar, have come together to shape the life of a girl who was the product of both. There is nothing quaint in *Summer;* there is no detail which is dragged in for the sake of a quick and easy effect. The difference, in Willa Cather's word, is in "attitude." One of the writer's best possessions is the place he knows, but, without reverence for this place, it can become a vulgar device. Someone has said that traditions are those things that a society claims to revere but no longer observes. This is true not only of manners and customs but of ways of seeing the landscape. The serious writer will always view his landscape with an unsentimental, contemporary eye. He may still find fogs and old houses, bachelors and spinsters of advanced years, but he will also find limited-access highways, shopping centers, housing developments, and neon-lighted bowling palaces. His business is to make sense of the whole in terms of the people he writes about.

The commonest problem faced by anyone who is trying to compose a setting is not, however, how to avoid reducing it to the grotesquely quaint (or violent or ugly or whatever stereotype may suggest itself). It is to find a way to bring the setting vividly before the reader. Elizabeth Bowen says: "Remote memories, already distorted by the imagination, are most useful for the purposes of scene. Unfamiliar or once-seen places yield more than do familiar, often-seen places." Many writers would dispute this statement; and certainly Miss Bowen's own work does not seem to bear it out. But her comment is useful for the emphasis that it places on imagination.

As noted earlier, the country of a story is as much a creation of the writer as are his characters. Thomas Hardy took the old word "Wessex" as the county for his fiction because no single county afforded "a canvas large enough for this purpose" and he needed an imaginary territory that could sprawl across the real borders of southern England. But readers accepted Wessex as an actual place. Hardy noted that "the appellation which I had thought to reserve to the horizons and landscapes of a partly real, partly dream-country, has become more and more popular as a practical provincial definition; and the dream-country has, by degrees, solidified into a utilitarian region which people can go to, take a house in, and write to the papers from." He added, "I ask all good and idealistic readers . . . to refuse steadfastly to believe that there are any inhabitants of a Victorian Wessex outside these volumes in which their lives and conversations are detailed."

Hardy's portrait of a place had an extreme success—like Trollope's Barsetshire and Barchester—and perhaps Hardy felt a certain inconvenience as this utilitarian Wessex invaded his dream-country. But the most powerful of fictions have always had this transforming effect on geography. It is hardly possible to think of Salem, of the other towns near Boston, of Boston itself without remembering how we get them in Hawthorne; or to drive through the Hudson River country without seeing it through Washington Irving's eyes. Mrs. Gaskell, in her biography of Charlotte Brontë, has left a striking account of the extraordinary difference between the actuality of a place and its fictional reality. Here is her description of Haworth and the country surrounding it as they looked in the summer of 1855, less than a decade after the writing of *Wuthering Heights* and *Jane Eyre:*

> The town of Keighley [the nearest railroad station to Haworth] never quite melts into country on the road to Haworth, although the houses become more sparse as the traveller journeys upward to the grey round hills that seem to bound his journey in a westerly direction. . . .

> The distance is about four miles; and . . . what with villas, great worsted factories, rows of workmen's houses, with here and there an old-fashioned farm-house and outbuildings, it can hardly be called "country" any part of the way. . . . Right before the traveller on this road rises Haworth village; he can see it for two miles before he arrives, for it is situated on the side of a pretty steep hill, with a background of dun and purple moors. . . .[4]

Villas and worsted factories and workmen's houses! Surely these come as a considerable surprise. For we remember Mr. Lockwood saying, at the start of *Wuthering Heights,* "In all England, I do not believe that I could have fixed on a situation so completely removed from the stir of society." True, *Wuthering Heights* is technically a historical novel (most of the action takes place in the last quarter of the eighteenth century), but who really doubts that the landscape we see through Mr. Lockwood's eyes is the one that Emily Brontë looked out on? In *Jane Eyre,* Mr. Rochester's great house, Thornfield Hall, is in a fictitious county "seventy miles nearer London than the remote country where I now resided." The Thornfield the author gives us, although situated in lonely countryside, is two miles from the village of Hay[worth?]—"yonder on the hill"— and six miles from Millcote, "a place of considerable magnitude."

The point is that Haworth looks two ways: toward the moors and toward the town. Emily looked in one direction only; Charlotte, it

---

[4] *The Life of Charlotte Brontë* (Edinburgh: John Grant, 1924), pp. 2–3. (This is the text of the original edition.)

seems, in both. Neither spoke more "truly" than the other; neither
gives us a place we can recognize in Mrs. Gaskell's description. It
is a question of which way the writer turns his head, and of what
the outer eye sees that will satisfy the inner vision. Only the biog-
rapher or reporter looks equally in all directions. For every fictionist,
the great thing is to show the reader his chosen place through his
own solitary eyes. In this way alone can the reader understand its
peculiar influence on the people the writer wants to tell him about.

SOME USES OF DETAIL

If detail is to be effective, the writer had better have constantly
in mind those hazards listed earlier: (1) irrelevant or picture-
postcard detail; (2) excess; (3) cliché. In seeking only those details
that are deeply characteristic of a place and relevant to whatever
action is going forward, he must ask himself what precise role he
wants his setting to perform.

The Wessex novels and *Wuthering Heights,* Faulkner's Yoknapatawpha stories, the Minnesota novels of Sinclair Lewis, Willa
Cather's Nebraska fictions—all of these are dense with place; often,
in a long remembering, one's clearest recollection is of the atmosphere of a story. The characters, even, have fused with the soil and
the elements.

Not every story or novel, however, will bear such an intimate
relation to its setting. For one thing, not every fiction stays put. As
in life, characters go on journeys, take up jobs in new places, visit
friends and relations. And some characters exist in a state of total
unawareness. The writer must contrive to convince us of the vacuum in which they live, and still furnish that seeming vacuum
so that we can see what they miss. Again, an author may employ details in order to establish the period of his story: this is what
they wore, what they drove, what house they lived in. All of these
affect his characterizations, but in addition they evoke an era which
is other than that in which he is writing. The popular "costume"
novel does this all of the time; better—or at least more serious—fictions do it also, but with restraint and, again, selectivity.

Detail can also be used as a backdrop to a story. This seems to border on local colorism, but there is a difference: the author will see that nothing intrudes merely because it is unusual or picturesque. He may even choose to give a setting which is not only quick but impressionistic. Whatever happens against this backdrop would have happened somewhere else, probably, given the same set of characters; although it would have happened somewhat differently, and not at this moment in time.

Broadly speaking, it is possible to distinguish five uses of place or setting:

1. Place as character.
2. Place as destiny.
3. Place as narrative element.
4. Place as period.
5. Place as backdrop.

N. B.

Place as character is an unsatisfactory phrase, and, as the reader will understand, it does not mean that a degree of anthropomorphism is desirable in this kind of fiction. Place as character means that the setting affects the people in a story as much as they affect one another. They are subject to its weathers, hazards, beguilements, confinements. And there is the effect of a dialogue between place and person, although of course it is one-sided. At its most powerful, fiction in which place is treated as a character commands not only our imagination but our affection, and has a splendor that can scarcely be equalled in stories or novels that make a lesser use of their setting. The reason, presumably, is the one given by Miss Welty: for most human beings, *"feelings* are bound up in place"—even in the mobile present.

There is, however, one very great difficulty that the writer faces when he chooses to celebrate his setting, and that is that if he leaves it he risks his reader's disbelief. We will believe almost anything that happens within the locality that is peculiarly the author's own. But let anybody in the story take a bus or train or plane into alien territory and our credulity may be strained, the power of the illusion lost. The thing that is wrong with Willa Cather's *A Lost*

Lady, for instance, is Marian Forrester's reappearance in Buenos Aires, long years after her disgrace and disappearance from Sweet Water. Her triumph in South America is not less improbable than the fact of her being there at all. For her vanities, her gaieties, her transgressions, her assumed sophistication are effective and moving only when confined to "one of those grey towns along the Burlington railroad" and to that house "well known from Omaha to Denver for its hospitality and for a certain charm of atmosphere." The novel should have ended with Marian's going away. The forcing of Buenos Aires on our attention is an example of Willa Cather's curiously deficient aesthetic sensibility; more to our present point, it is an example of how easily even veteran writers can go wrong. In *Wuthering Heights,* people come and go (one of them even takes up residence near London), but we only see them when they are on the stage of Yorkshire.

In those writings in which place figures strongly as a character, it will often figure also as destiny. The human characters lack the possibility of choice: they must take what is at hand. Books as different as *Madame Bovary* and *Main Street* make this point. And much of their drama emerges from the difference between what the Emma Bovarys and Carol Kennicotts long for and what they can expect to get. Place may offer a benevolent, or at least tolerable, destiny—as in some of Frank O'Connor's stories of the west of Ireland—but as a rule authors will choose to write about people who are in revolt against their environment. The plain practical fact is, of course, that stories about contented people are not usually very interesting. If Nebraska was never quite as terrible as Willa Cather made it out to be in her gloomier moments, still it was in one of these moments that she found the mood for such a story as "A Wagner Matinée." The setting is Boston, but the place which dominates the narrative is the bleak, ferocious Midwest to which Georgiana Carpenter, the central character, must return, her exile there being her destiny: "For her, just outside the concert hall, lay the black pond with the cattle-tracked bluffs; the tall, unpainted house, with weather-curled boards, naked as a tower. . . ." The early novels of Robert Penn Warren, *Night Rider, At Heaven's Gate,*

All the King's Men, give a powerful sense of place as an inexorable force in human life. It might be said that they go even further and make a dramatic equation between place and death. There is nowhere else to go, and to stay is to die.

In summary, then, the uses of place as character and place as destiny are as various as the perceptions of individual writers—who will themselves feel variously about this country that is both real and of their mind and emotions.

When place is employed simply as one more narrative element, it will seldom govern those large questions that every fiction proposes. It will have little effect upon choice; it will probably not limit possibility. It will neither enhance nor much impair human dignity, courage, conviction. In the broad sense, this is place as it is ordinarily used in fiction: as milieu—the setting in which the drama goes forward. The writer will tell as much or as little as the reader needs to know in order to visualize the scene:

It was a February afternoon of smoky sunshine, as I walked home along the embankment to my wife. The river ran white in the sun, the plume from a tug's funnel came out blue as cigarette-smoke; on the far bank the reflections from windows shone through haze, and down towards Chelsea where I was walking, the smoke was so thick that the skyline, the high chimneys, had smudged themselves into it.

In this brief opening paragraph of C. P. Snow's *Homecoming,* we are given the season, the weather, and a glimpse of the city of London, through which the narrator walks on his way home. Having sketched in the setting, the author turns immediately to other demands of the story:

The day was a Tuesday, the year 1938; I had not been home since the Thursday before, which was my usual routine, as I had to spend half my week in Cambridge. I felt an anxiety, a tightness of the nerves, as I always did going home after an absence. . . .[5]

When it comes to providing background for characters who are oblivious to their surroundings, Alberto Moravia has found a good solution—although it is not one that will work in every instance.

[5] New York: Charles Scribner's Sons, 1956; p. 3.

Moravia uses what might be called the curious questioner, who says
"Where is your house? What street? What does it look like inside?
Tell me; tell me. . . ." In *The Empty Canvas*, the curious questioner is Dino, a young man who is infatuated with a beautiful girl
from a stratum of Roman society unknown to him:

"You live in a flat in the Prati district?"
"Yes."
"How many rooms have you?"
"I don't know."
"What d'you mean, you don't know?"
"I've never counted them."
"But is it a big or a small flat?"
"So-so."
"What does that mean?"
"Medium-sized."
"Well then, describe it."[6]

Henry James employed the *ficelle* or confidante in order to convey information that the central intelligence in one of his fictions
could not plausibly find out for himself. In the same way, to pre-
serve plausibility, the curious questioner can assist the author who
is dealing with a character of low-level awareness whose background
it is necessary to illuminate. The curious questioner, of course, like
the *ficelle*, is only required in a first person narrative or in one with
a restricted point of view. The omniscient author can take his
readers anywhere and show them over all kinds of houses without
anyone being present. But in these days when readers are very
conscious of point of view, and rather scornful of the writer who
turns up everywhere like a sociable bore who doesn't know enough
to stay home, a device like Moravia's may be directly usable, or at
least may suggest a solution. In *The Empty Canvas*, Dino, in an
agony of curiosity, is finally driven to go and see the girl's home for
himself. Such an action is entirely contrary to what we know of
Dino's ordinary character; Moravia makes us believe it, however,

[6] Trans. Angus Davidson (New York: Farrar, Straus & Company, 1961), pp.
154–155.

because of his earlier dramatizations of the young man's mounting obsession with everything that is connected with the girl.

Where description is used to establish the period of a story—and perhaps also its theme—the writer may find that the straightforward approach is not only simplest but most effective. For instance, *The Magnificent Ambersons* begins with a set piece about the times of the Ambersons:

In that town, in those days, all the women who wore silk or velvet knew all the other women who wore silk or velvet, and when there was a new purchase of sealskin, sick people were got to windows to see it go by. Trotters were out, in the winter afternoons, racing light sleighs on National Avenue and Tennessee Street; everybody recognized both the trotters and the drivers; and again knew them as well on summer evenings, when slim buggies whizzed by in renewals of the snow-time rivalry. For that matter, everybody knew everybody else's family horse-and-carriage, could identify such a silhouette half a mile down the street, and thereby was sure who was going to market, or to a reception, or coming home from office or store to noon dinner or evening supper.[7]

Tarkington was often very good at evoking middle-class life as it used to be in some of this country's provincial cities. Hastiness, sloppiness, and a defective sense of proportion kept him from becoming the major writer he might have been, and all of these failings are evident in the Amberson set piece, which goes on at too great length to talk about other items of clothing, about styles in beards, about architecture, servants, local customs. Nevertheless, it is in general a good example of how an author can evoke a particular era and a particular class. A subtler use of the same device can be found in Edith Wharton's *The Age of Innocence*:

On a January evening of the early seventies, Christine Nilsson was singing in Faust at the Academy of Music in New York.

Though there was already talk of the erection, in remote metropolitan distances "above the Forties," of a new Opera House which should compete in costliness and splendour with those of the great European capitals, the world of fashion was still content to reassemble every winter in the shabby red and gold boxes of the sociable old Academy.

[7] New York: Doubleday & Company, 1922; pp. 3–4.

Conservatives cherished it for being small and inconvenient, and thus keeping out the "new people" whom New York was beginning to dread and yet to be drawn to. . . .

It was Madame Nilsson's first appearance that winter, and what the daily press had already learned to describe as "an exceptionally brilliant audience" had gathered to hear her, transported through the slippery, snowy streets in private broughams, in the spacious family landau, or in the humbler but more convenient "Brown *coupé*." . . .[8]

By a roundabout route, Tarkington takes us from the general to the particular: the great Amberson mansion, which was the single most splendid sight in the city and the time he has been telling us about. Mrs. Wharton takes us back to a specific period and a specific place, and then very quickly introduces her central male character, Newland Archer; the girl he will marry, May Welland; and the woman he will love all his life, the Countess Ellen Olenska—all of whom have come to the Academy on this winter night.

Finally, there is place as the backdrop for the action of a story. Here, as a general thing, we find the author giving us a setting which is strange or exotic, or both, but giving it to us in a way that never threatens to turn into travelogue. Rose Macaulay was especially skillful in her use of backdrops—in *The Towers of Trebizond,* for instance, or *Going Abroad,* or *And No Man's Wit*—but never more so than in *Staying with Relations,* much of whose action takes place in Guatemala. Here is her description of a journey by launch into the heart of that country:

The lovely lake narrowed to its reedy end, and the launch sped up the mouth of the river Merces. And now they were indeed in a dense forest, which came down closely to the river's either side, tree interlocked with tree; trees of all kinds and shapes, their boughs vine-bound and rubber-twined, and linked together by trailing lianas above a riot of white lilies, scarlet salvias and convolvulus, giant purple and orange dahlias, little sunflowers, heliotrope, banksias, orchids, and immense tree-ferns.

It was now excessively hot and moist, after a storm in the night, and felt quite tropical and disagreeable. Wild animals crashed and made

[8] New York: Appleton-Century-Crofts, 1920; p. 1.

their appropriate noises a few yards off within the jungle, and several alligators swam after the launch with open mouths.[9]

A certain amount of specific information is given in this passage (some of it quite fake), but the few bright details are part of an otherwise indistinct background—one made up of unnamed trees of *all kinds and shapes,* of vague comment about the climate (*quite tropical and disagreeable*), and of references to wild animals who make *their appropriate noises.*

A degree of audacity is required in this kind of writing, a sense of where to point up, where to generalize; and the very clever writer who is bored with "description" may be tempted to show his indifference too boldly. Thus those "appropriate noises"—a phrase so amusing that it threatens to wreck the narrative by suggesting to the reader that fiction is entirely make-believe and mustn't ever be taken too seriously, beginning right now. Rose Macaulay perpetrated literary outrages all of her life, and no one who admires her wishes she had written differently, but the beginning writer had better not carry his backdrop painting quite as far as she did. In the main, however, this passage from *Staying with Relations* (a beautifully humdrum title for a novel laid in an exotic house in a Central American wilderness) illustrates very well the appropriate use of a setting from which nothing much is going to be asked. The human figures, despite the distractions of "appropriate noises" from the jungle, are clearly on view in the foreground.

And it is in the foreground, of course, that the business of the novel—of every kind of novel, from *Wuthering Heights* to *Homecoming*—goes forward.

[9] New York: Horace Liveright, 1930; p. 19.

7 NARRATIVE STYLE; TIME AND PACE IN FICTION

"O, pardon!" Shakespeare asked his audience; pardon for the violence that every storyteller since time began has had to do to time and space. "Can this cockpit hold/The vasty fields of France? or may we cram/Within this wooden O the very casques/That did affright the air at Agincourt?" In fact, of course not. But then, by the special laws of relativity that operate within any fiction—of course it can. One crooked figure can, in little space, stand for a million; whole kingdoms can rise; thoughts can deck out kings and "Carry them here and there; jumping o'er times,/Turning the accomplishment of many years/Into an hour-glass. . . ." Nevertheless, just because the author does have this power to compress, expand, select, to range over time and space, he must use it with the greatest skill and for the greatest advantage to his story.

The two problems, what might be called the Problem of the Wooden O and the Problem of the Hour Glass, can be discussed together because they are interdependent. Both of them are very closely connected with the important matter of pace in fiction. Each story or novel has, of course, its own pace of development, hurrying at times and slow at others. The author must judge exactly at which point he will proceed deliberately, giving us the story detail by detail, almost at the speed with which the event might have taken

n.b.

N. B.

place; and at what point he will pass quickly over a stretch of time, reporting only the general sequence of events. In between these two extremes there are various degrees of rapidity that may be employed.

All of this sounds very simple—what every storyteller has always known. There is a certain reliable tradition in telling a tale that governs what is to be dwelt on and what is to be sketched in a sentence or two: "The dwarf sat down by the fire and pulled off his long hat. His red eyes seemed to gleam. 'And now for my second question,' he said . . ." as opposed to "Ten years went by and the little princess grew into a beautiful young woman." The traditional rule is, of course, that all stages which are meant to *show* important things about the behavior of the characters or to make events dramatic are treated in a scenic or eyewitness manner. Stretches of time or occurrence which are secondary to the story's development are dealt with by means of a narrative bridge.

Although this method remains basic to fiction, the complications of modern practice have demanded variations in pace, and greater subtlety in its use. Scene and narrative must alternate, but the habit of proceeding monotonously from a block of scene to a block of narrative in regular succession is likely to give a dull and archaic feeling about the workmanship.

The various manners of proceeding ought to be looked at separately. First, there is the "scenic" mode, which brings the observer-eye very close to the setting of the fiction. It is here that visual details—the furnishings of a room, the look of a landscape, the aspect of a person—can add immediacy. Dialogue is essential. While it may be possible to summarize certain less important things that pass in conversation, a great deal should be directly quoted. The selection here is not made on the basis of mere relevance; the object is to try to persuade the reader that he is listening to the flow of talk on which the story, at this moment, is being carried. If the story happens to be told from the definite point of view of one person, his mental processes, thoughts, feelings may be part of the scenic procedure as well, usually coming as a direct response to what is passing before his eyes and ears.

This scenic method is one of the author's finest chances, and any fiction that makes no use of it has a remote and secondhand quality. It gives the author an opportunity to focus sharply, to close in on his subject; and when it is handled well it gives the story a magical illusion of life actually passing by. Just because it is so splendid a technical chance, it should never be squandered or misplaced.

cf. Naturalistic novels are full of examples of the scenic method's being drawn on and on into a dreary wasteland of words (Dreiser and Farrell are frequently guilty of this, for instance). Having begun his scene, this particular kind of writer often strains too hard after reality, trying to become a camera and tape-recorder device to gather in all, absolutely all, of the phenomena of his world. After a certain amount of this, the reader begins to realize that very little of what he sees is relevant to anything in the story, or relevant to anything, except as the proof of a power of total recall. Now, being irrelevant—or apparently irrelevant—for the moment is something that has its uses in fiction. Chekhov, for example, used that device exceptionally well for comedy, suspense, or for other effects. But irrelevancy cannot be piled on irrelevancy. Something must be proceeding in the scene, some addition to the pattern must be developing.

In order to avoid this kind of mismanagement, the beginning writer can guide himself by following a certain course. He should begin by thinking of the scene he is about to write as a small act in a drama. First of all, it is to be self-contained and to produce its own definite meanings. These meanings must, however, contribute something of value to the whole design of the fiction he has in mind. The "act" or dramatic sketch, then, must have a shape to it. It must have a beginning, a development, and a result. It may make several (but not too many) interesting points as it proceeds, but it should always work toward some culmination which justifies the scene's existence. These meanings may be large or small; they may be of incidental importance to the book as a whole or they may be of crucial importance; they may be immediately open to the reader or they may be subject to reinterpretation as more of the story is revealed. They may be quite explicit or they may be symbolical. The important thing about them is that they are meanings that are

n.b.

brought before the reader's eyes in a scenic, dramatic form—and thus they have the emphasis and impact that the simple narrative statement does not have. One of the reasons for this special impact is just that demonstration enables the reader to participate in the processes of the story by exerting his own reason. He sees certain evidence from which he forms a conclusion; thus, his intelligence has been engaged. He knows, of course, that the conclusion was foregone and that the sense of working it out is an illusion, but it is one of the most potent illusions that any writer can create.

This is a principle of high importance. The fiction writer is always more deeply concerned with ideas that emerge from some interplay of life in his story than with those that can be baldly stated for the record. If, for instance, it is essential to present a certain character as calculating and cold-hearted, the writer does best to make those qualities known in a way that seems almost inadvertent. "Mrs. Harris was a cold and calculating woman" is a statistic. Mrs. Harris talking about her recent trip, describing her daughter's marriage, remarking on the subject of money, is gradually drawn out to reveal herself—almost in spite of herself—and the scene reaches a meaning about her personality far more convincing than any list of facts could be. This is equally true of action. Generally, the unimportant, the expected, the routine actions can be left to the narrative. The interesting, revelatory, unpredictable actions that contribute most richly to story or character ought to be treated *in process*, as they gradually unfold themselves in the scene.

One of the fairly common mistakes of writers—even experienced writers—is the redundancy of telling the same thing both by way of report and by way of demonstration. The two are antagonistic, and one is likely to cancel out the other. For instance, in one scene in *The Brothers Karamazov*, Dostoevsky interrupts to say, "But the Captain was to have his hopes cruelly dashed." He then goes on to show, by scenic development, that the Captain does indeed have his hopes cruelly dashed. But Dostoevsky has damaged his scene midway by interrupting it with a narrative generalization that, properly, should have been realized by the reader himself, at the conclusion of the scene. It is equally fatal to begin by describing a character in qualitative terms and then go on with a scene that shows him living up to the description. What has happened in both of these instances is that the writer has used his story simply to adorn the initial generalization. The reader has been told rudely what to think, the dramatic continuity has been interrupted, and the narrative has been anticlimactic. In both of these cases, the writer confesses either a lack of faith in his audience—they will not be able to see for themselves—or a lack of faith in himself; he does not believe that he can show them.

N.B.

Choosing the right occasion for the pace that compresses events, time, or story-development presents a subtle problem. The bridge is used to get in all that is necessary to notice even though it may be routine and relatively unimportant. "Crawford hailed a taxi and went down to Fourteenth Street." That sentence gets him there although nothing significant happens on the way. "Years passed and MacGregor became an embittered old man." The sentence moves the story from one point in time to another. "Later on that spring Mrs. Meadows died and Catherine was free to marry Brian, which she did on the first of June, even though his sister prolonged the old bitterness by refusing to appear at the wedding." This sentence spans a series of events that we might have predicted, and nothing would be accomplished by relating them in detail.

N.B.

Formerly, a naïve or primitive kind of storytelling tended to put a great deal of the work in terms of narrative summary. The modern tendency has been to use this kind of summary much more sparingly. A great many of the successful modern short stories are almost entirely scenic; there is often an old-fashioned air about one that drops into the vein of narrative summary for very long. There has even been a vogue for the twenty-four hour novel, or at least the novel that takes place in a very short space of time. The greatest example of this is, of course, Joyce's *Ulysses*. Nevertheless, even today, most short stories or novels will reach certain points that cannot be got over without falling back on the old necessity of summarizing secondary events that have a bearing on the story as a whole.

There is one principle here that is a sound one, even though some very good writers have neglected it now and then. It is the idea that extended narrative summary ought, whenever possible, to be subsequent to and to derive from a scenic part of the story. The dramatic scenes are meant to provide the primary life of the story—they hold the real development of event, interest in character, and almost all of the tension. It is this that the narrative summary must depend on; if the scenes have built up enough momentum for the story, the narrative will roll along on the force of it, relying on the fact that the reader has now enough interest in Mr. A to hear about how he boarded his ship, entered his cabin, and unpacked his bag.

—Or almost enough interest. There was once a time when the majority of readers could be counted on to be quite curious about just the simple details of crossing a gangplank, entering a ship, about what the interior of a liner's cabin looked like. Nowadays our visual experience is far wider and more sophisticated—we have looked at the very scene, if not personally, at least in the movies or on television; or a dozen other novelists have detailed it for us before this. Thus, the mere impression of the eye and ear are no longer sufficient. If this business of getting on the ship is to be narrated at all, it must have some weight of significance for the person who is passing through the action. It may be that certain small things he does in the course of this ordinary happening—or certain things he may think—will refer back to the traits we have already observed in him. These incidentals, although they propound nothing new, continue our observation of his personality. We have, say, seen him be angry with his wife. Now we are told that he is rude to the steward —and we begin to get some consistent sense of him.

Even though the narrative summary will derive most of its strength from the interest already established by previous scenes, it can equally point toward some new direction in the story. For the sake of economy and unity, it works as an extremely useful device. In its simplest and least effective employment, the narrative bridge does no more than transport the reader rapidly over a stretch of time or space in order to arrive at the next significant happening. A more skillful use of it is to make it serve as preparation or to set the atmosphere or to provide the initial material for the next scene or sequence of scenes. This may take any number of different forms: it could be described as a clue, an inference, an event that points to fuller consequences. It may be incidental, and for the moment unexplained; or it may be emphasized in such a way that the reader knows that something will come of it. Nevertheless, it cannot be fully explored during the fast pace of narration; it is meant to lead on to some kind of scenic exploration. For an example or two of its use, it might be worthwhile to return to the hypothetical traveler, Mr. A.

"When A was finally alone in his cabin and began to open his suitcases, he was astonished to discover that none of the clothes in them belonged to him. There were pink shirts three sizes too large for him, a bright purple bathrobe he had never seen, some highly decorated ties—the clothes of a large, loud stranger whose identity he could not begin to imagine." This is a fairly obvious example of an incident in the narrative that directs the story toward some scenic explanation. It is a preparation for a development of the plot.

"During the five days of crossing, A, who had been so cheerful when he boarded the ship, began to change. He found that the infinity of ocean, the heavy meals, the fatuous tourists playing endless games of shuffleboard, all reminded him somehow of the tedious relatives he was going to visit." This would be a preparation for some new moods or attitudes to be developed in what is to come after A's arrival.

There is another thing that is appropriate to the passages of narrative and that is the author's generalization about the life of his story. When the reader has accepted the fact that the author is in the process of bridging between scenes, he will also accept the "anonymous" generalization without feeling that it interrupts. Carson McCullers, an author skillful at narration, is likely to draw back in the course of her story and observe it in such terms as—"Once you have lived with another, it is a great torture to have to live alone. The silence of a firelit room when suddenly the clock stops ticking, the nervous shadows in an empty house—it is better to take in your mortal enemy than face the terror of living alone" (from "The Ballad of the Sad Café"). In this case—as is true in the case

N.B.

of many other stories—only the author could have made that statement, which is both sensitive to the realities of the story and at the same time abstract. None of her characters is capable of formulating ideas in just this way; to have one of them voice this sentiment in a dialogue would be wildly improbable. Thus Mrs. McCullers chooses to draw this conclusion herself, in the midst of narration; and the effect is to give this portion of her story a focus that it might not otherwise have had.

This is just one example of the variety of elements that the author may use in the course of his narrative exposition. That exposition should never settle down to a mere listing of events in chronology. It should have a definite style, should shift its ground, should use a diversity of tactics. Even though its basic use is for transition and information, in the hands of the best writers it goes far beyond the merely utilitarian.

Description of the physical setting can often be used as an interesting element of the extended narrative, but such description, when given in the context of a dramatic scene, ought to have an immediacy about it; it should contribute something significant to the look of the moment. Description in the narrative, however, can be more leisurely or can range more widely. One example of an author who uses elaborate description to enrich his narrative is the great nineteenth-century author of comedy, Nicolai Gogol (see particularly the beginning of *Dead Souls*).

Or, on the other hand, description can be used impressionistically. Carson McCullers, in the story of hers just referred to, uses it briefly and intermingled with other things in the course of her narrative:

That autumn was a happy time. The crops around the countryside were good, and over at the Forks Falls market the price of tobacco held firm that year. After the long hot summer the first cool days had a clean bright sweetness. Goldenrod grew along the dusty roads and the sugar cane was ripe and purple. . . . Boys hunted foxes in the pinewoods, winter quilts were aired out on the wash lines and sweet potatoes bedded in the straw against the colder months to come.

And a little later, describing "the night it had snowed":

In the dark hours after midnight the dim flakes started falling softly on the town. By dawn the ground was covered, and the strange snow banked the ruby windows of the church, and whitened the roofs of the houses. The snow gave the town a drawn, bleak look. The two-room houses near the mill were dirty, crooked, and seemed about to collapse, and somehow everything was dark and shrunken. But the snow itself— there was a beauty about it few people around here had ever known before.[1]

While "dramatic" illusion is fragile, so that a little interruption will break the spell, narrative passages can be varied with a good deal of freedom—for instance, by the occasional notice of episodes or the inclusion of a line or two of dialogue. "One day Julia sat down at the desk in her room to write the long-delayed letter to her mother. But as she sat there staring past the pen and the sheet of paper in front of her, she found that she had nothing at all to say." This is a fleeting event, not important enough in itself to warrant development into a full scene, yet interesting enough to mention as an episode. The long stride of the narrative is slowed for just a moment and we get a scenic glimpse. Brief dialogue can be put to exactly the same use. The general survey of a passage of time halts for a moment to focus on a remark or on a question and answer. All of these things—generalization, description, episodes, dialogue, etc. —can be used to break the monotonous tone of narrative survey and to give it a flexible, lively impression.

But none of this answers the most difficult question: exactly what parts of the story should be developed by scenes and what parts left to be related in narrative. The exact assignment differs, of course, with every novel or short story. The author always begins with a general idea of what may lend itself to dramatic treatment, and what does not; but the inexperienced writer frequently misjudges. Charles Dickens was a novelist who had a keen sense of the two different functions—the dramatic and the narrative—and his advice on this score to a beginning novelist (Jane Brookfield) is worth quoting at some length:

[1] Included in Mrs. McCullers' collection, *The Ballad of the Sad Café* (Boston: Houghton Mifflin Company, 1951), pp. 41, 53.

It strikes me that you constantly hurry your narrative (and yet without getting on) *by telling it, in a sort of impetuous breathless way, in your own person, when the people should tell it and act it for themselves.* My notion always is, that when I have made the people to play out the play, it is, as it were, their business to do it, and not mine. Then, unless you have really led up to a great situation like Basil's death, you are bound in art to make more of it. Such a scene should form a chapter of itself. Impressed upon the reader's memory, it would go far to make the fortune of the book. Suppose yourself telling that affecting incident in a letter to a friend. Wouldn't you describe how you went through the life and stir of the streets to the sickroom? Wouldn't you say what kind of a room it was, whether it was sunlight, starlight, or moonlight? Wouldn't you have a strong impression on your mind of how you were received, when you first met the look of the dying man, what strange contrasts were about you and struck you? I don't want you, in a novel, to present *yourself* to tell such things, but I want the things to be there. You make no more of the situation than the index might, or a descriptive playbill might in giving a summary of the tragedy under representation.[2]

This is an almost classic description of a fault that dogs most student short stories and novels. The grand scene that is led up to—and then disappointingly skated over; the opportunity for some kind of development that is quite overlooked by the "impetuous, breathless" author. There is, of course, no formula that will solve this problem neatly. Every author will have to survey his story's concept and decide which portions of it suggest themselves as primary, dramatic occurrences and which portions can be left to the schematic treatment of narrative. If his story is worth telling, there will be places where his characters demand to talk and act as if on a stage. Those are the crucial moments in their lives. Most short stories are, by necessity, almost limited to crucial moments. The novelist's problem, on the other hand, is somewhat different. Usually he will want to have many of his scenes in a quieter key—scenes that may bear as much meaning as the more striking ones, but that develop it gradu-

2 *The Letters of Charles Dickens 1833–1870* (London: Macmillan & Co., 1893), p. 599.

ally, indirectly, and in depth. It is here that the decision becomes difficult between what can be told best in a scenic fashion and what cannot.

In trying to deal with this problem, the novelist should be concerned first of all with the balance or design of his book. Too extensive narrative will become tedious; overlong scenes will lose any dramatic form or unity. It is unlikely that a novel whose first half was pure narrative and whose second half was pure scene would be a success; and just as unlikely that one whose beginning and end were scenic, and whose entire middle section was narrative, would turn out well. Thus, in most novels scene and narration succeed each other. Probably the most reliable method is to work out a pattern of scenes for the entire book, one scene being followed by another of a different and contrasting kind, and a number of developmental scenes leading the way toward a conclusive one, so as to form a clear scheme of relationship for the "enacted" story.

Of course, in its first primitive form, every piece of fiction occurs to the mind as a little narrative. But, once that is confirmed as a usable idea, the writer will usually find it greatly to his advantage to begin immediately to translate it into this pattern of scenes—figuratively speaking, his scenario. Doing this, he is able to decide—in a preliminary way, at least—what portions or aspects of the story he wishes to present as dramatic and which will be left to narration. He is further able to order the scenes into a design which will serve as a general chart to the whole novel. It is clear that the unfortunate Mrs. Brookfield had failed to do this. The concept of her story remained no more than a narrative outline, undoubtedly fleshed out with certain dialogue and scenic episodes, but missing any chance of convincing the reader that the characters "tell it and act it for themselves." On the other hand, Mrs. Brookfield's correspondent himself would have profited from a clear idea of how his scenes were to unite to form a dramatic pattern. The lack of such an idea accounts, in part, for what George Orwell called Dickens' "rotten architecture."

What has just been said is not to be taken as a neat formula.

Most short stories and novels will go through many agonizing transformations in the course of being written. Concepts will change and, with them, any preconceived pattern. Nevertheless, this scenario procedure is suggested as the first act of strategy on the writer's part. It is a strategy that should forewarn him against writing scenes that are irrelevant or redundant, and against placing a scene in what is obviously the wrong spot. It should give him some sense of how to pace his novel so that it does not seem to advance with jerky speed in one place and to slow down to a crawl at others. Most useful of all, it engages his imagination at once with what will be his primary presentation; with all that is to appear in the foreground of his novel.

A plan of this kind is not a substitute for a plot outline (which the writer may wish to construct in addition), but it forces the writer to make several important decisions about how the story or the novel will be done. Plot, it is noted in Chapter 8, is based on the action of cause and effect. The scene pattern is a matter of relativity; it decides on the value given to each element of the story, how they are to be balanced in the design, and the pace at which they will succeed each other. It is a way of relating the parts to each other and to the whole.

When the strategy is used well, the novel not only gains a coherent form but is likely to be successful in developing the writer's themes to their fullest. Henry James was particularly aware of this objective, and he discussed it at some length in relation to *What Maisie Knew*. Explaining his method, James said that there the "treatment by 'scene,' regularly, quite rhythmically occurs." He noted that the "intervals between"—the narrative links—are all preparatory to the scenic occasions, and that the latter are *"wholly* and logically scenic," and function as illustrations of the themes. He felt, finally, that the great advantage to the total effect of his story came from the fact that he had carefully recognized the different responsibilities of scene and narrative. The reader is thus able to sense exactly how the theme is being developed.

Here, by way of review, are the various possible ways of narrating a story—short or long—that have been referred to thus far:

1. One scene alone which comprises the whole story.
2. Several separate scenes, with the transition from one to another noted briefly, but without any real narrative links.
3. Scene and narrative both used, succeeding each other as required throughout.
4. Narrative alone.

Nearly all successful novels employ the third method. The first three are equally available to the short story writer; but the fourth method is almost never used today, belonging as it does to the tale rather than to modern fiction.

TIME AND HOW TO SHIFT IT

The element of time in fiction has so far been dealt with almost wholly in terms of the pace at which the story proceeds, and a simple chronological progression from one event to the next has been assumed. But such a straight and narrow time line would be difficult for the modern writer to endure: it, too, belongs to the age of the straightforward tale. One of fiction's best inventions was the idea that imagination is not ruled by clock and calendar. It comes from what Marcel Proust called "the inseparableness of us from the past"—the concept that something of the past is always present to influence each new moment. In order to make use of this idea, the novelist had to put aside the classical dramatic rule of "unity of time" and to discover techniques by which he might show the presentness of the past in his story. But, before discussing any of these techniques, it will be worthwhile to mention something the critics call "enveloping action."

Enveloping action is a term to indicate the entire history of events relevant to the story, its past, present, and conceivable future. It is obvious, of course, that no fiction writer could ever deal with this whole scope, because his purpose as an artist is to choose certain salient points in that long stretch of time and, by bringing these to life, create his story. The enveloping action is, in a way, the story's prehistoric past and the story itself a historic era. As archaeologists have demonstrated, a good many significant facts of prehistory can

N. B.

be discovered. In the same way, the fiction writer may go backward in time to disclose moments of the past that are intimately involved with the present event. As E. M. Forster observes, Proust could so mesh two different times in his imagination "that his hero was at the same period entertaining a mistress to supper and playing ball with his nurse in the park."

The most primitive form of movement through fictional time is that device called the "flashback." Having arrived at a point where reference to some previous period will be helpful, the writer halts and sends up signals to the reader: "When his eye fell on that photograph of himself and Ellen as they sat together on the sand at Nag's Head, Arthur's mind went back to that memorable day in the June of 1949 . . ." The trouble with this trusty and aged device is that it immediately announces itself as a device—as in an old movie when the camera interrupts the scene to show the pages of a calendar flipping backward. The reader is reminded, rather too pointedly, of the fact that what he is reading is a matter of artifice, and his willing suspension of disbelief may get a sharp jolt. Still, an attempt at transition is usually better than no transition at all: "Arthur sat down to clean out his desk. Many years ago in 1949, he and Ellen had gone to Nag's Head to spend a vacation at the beach."

n.6

While its occasional use may not work too much harm, the simple flashback becomes more and more awkward and obvious with repetition. For the writer who—like Henry James, Proust, or Ford Madox Ford—wishes to bring a number and variety of past experiences to bear on his present story, it is impossible. A subtler, far more inconspicuous method has to be discovered to accomplish the same effect: the solution those writers found was something which has been given the label of "time-shift."

If the writer simply announces that he wishes to return to some bygone period, he appears to be arbitrary. It is in his best interests to persuade the reader that the excursion is natural, even inevitable, in the terms of the present story. The most reliable way of making the move is to go from the external scene and enter into the consciousness of the character who is providing the point of view. Thus far, there is no real difference from the example of the flashback given above. But, in the more sophisticated use of the method, phrases like "an episode from the past loomed up before him . . ."; "her memory suddenly went back to that day when . . ."; "he was reminded of the time . . ."; and similar noises of counterclockwork are dropped. Instead, the author concentrates on writing a passage of real transition. He draws the reader's attention discreetly from the present scene to something subjective, and this subjectivity usually takes the form of pertinent generalization. The generalization arises from what has just been happening but, almost before we know it, we find that the abstract statement has led into another period of time and another scene where it applies equally.

n.b.

One of the most elaborate uses of the time-shift in fiction occurs throughout Ford Madox Ford's novel, *The Good Soldier*. An important strand of the story concerns a British officer, Edward Ashburnham, and his complicated relationship with his wife, Leonora. In the course of events, they return from a German spa to their home in England—this is the novelistic present tense. But, before anything occurs in England, Ford wishes to return to the scene of their first meeting; he has his narrator begin by relating that Leonora suffers an emotional breakdown (this is in the "present"). The narrator then proceeds to generalize about the reasons why this has happened—he believes that she now realizes that she can trust her husband, after years of tension and treachery. "And then," the narrator observes, "with the slackening of her vigilance, came the slackening of her entire mind. This is perhaps the most miserable part of the entire story. For it is miserable to see a clear intelligence waver; and Leonora wavered."

That generalization suggests another one. "You are to understand that Leonora loved Edward with a passion that was yet like an agony of hatred. And she had lived with him for years and years without addressing to him one word of tenderness." At this point, the story is no longer inhabiting any actual moment in time—it is in some abstract area of the emotions—and, before we are quite aware that we have descended to earth again, we are with the nineteen-year-old Leonora in the garden of her father's run-down Irish

N.B.

manor house where she is being lined up with her six sisters for a family photograph, just before she is to meet young Edward.

This is no more than a very small and limited notice of the time-shift employed in *The Good Soldier*. It is far more than a sophisticated version of the flashback; it is the over-all technique of the novel. Ford uses time as a kind of montage, moving back and forth in it at will, never quite finishing one event or analysis of character before bringing in another, but always returning to what he has begun earlier in order to deepen it, give it another cast, or to stress some new aspect of it.

Even in books that work such complicated stratagems with time, however, there must be some calendar of the present that goes from Monday to Tuesday and from 1962 to 1963. This is what we have called "the novelistic present" (even though the actual tense in most cases will be the past). It is the line of continuity from which the time-shift departs and to which the time-shift must inevitably return, and the writer must never forget that this is the main line of his story. Excursions into the past are always the summoning of memory to help explain or illuminate the present in some significant way—they have no other point or purpose. They should never, either through garrulity or their own fascinations, swamp the intentions of the present story. If the beginning writer suddenly discovers that the part of his story he has gone backward to recover is fuller and more interesting than what is proceeding in the novelistic present, he must stop to realize that he has cast his story badly. He has begun too late. The only sure thing to do in such a case is to begin again with another plan and at an earlier point in time.

A similar difficulty sometimes encountered is the urge to get a great deal of the past described in one long stretch, or in several long stretches. This is equally harmful. Time present cannot stand motionless for too long or it will have lost all its momentum of interest for the reader; again the sense of forward pace has had violence done to it. The best solution is to separate the block of past event into several different elements and to work these into the present story separately and at appropriate places. The past, of course, can be alluded to, suggested, or brought into the present without a formal journey in the time machine. The characters of the story can easily recall certain points of it through incidental reference. In most cases, it is best to keep the description of time past to the minimum that is clearly meaningful and illuminating; additional insights or details of it can come out through thoughts, dialogue, or events.

Finally, all of these things relate back to the varying tempo or pace of every novel—and each novel has its own. There is no accepted over-all pattern available, and ultimately—as is true of all the important things about writing fiction—the author has to rely on his own sense of rhythm and change. Among such writers as James, Conrad, and Ford, there was considerable confidence in the principle of *progression d'effet*. As Ford explained it, the phrase meant that "every word set on paper must carry the story forward and that . . . the story must be carried forward faster and faster and with more and more intensity." But take this pattern of pace and try to impose it on *The Magic Mountain, Mrs. Dalloway,* or *A Portrait of the Artist as a Young Man* and it will be clear how special this theory is and how impossible it is for books whose themes do not fit it.

The wisest remark on the whole matter of pace in fiction remains E. M. Forster's. He says that human beings lead two lives, "the life in time and the life by values." In other words, two clocks run on, the regular chronometer and the eccentric clock of the emotions. "He waited for her only half an hour, but it seemed like forever" is a familiar example. Thirty minutes is real time, forever is value-time. As noticed earlier, the technique of direct narrative severely condenses real time, while the extended scene gives value-time. And nothing differs more drastically among individual authors than value-time. The romantic novelist, for instance, would find that it takes one long chapter for his heroine to collapse and die. He prolongs the scene, wringing every drop of emotion from it. The naturalistic novelist, having prepared us for the sad event, might do it starkly, briefly, and with understatement. "The agony of parting seemed to stretch on endlessly," the first, in effect, is saying. "It happened so quickly that we had no time to say goodbye" implies the other. (Only the doctor noted that death occurred exactly thirty-seven minutes after the first hemorrhage; but he did not write a novel.)

Thus, at the very beginning of a work of fiction, the writer should be prepared to record actual time so that the work makes sense; but, more than that, he should be prepared to make his stresses, his meanings, his pattern of life occur in accordance with value-time. And, to do that, he must know his values.

8   PLOT AND STORY

"As regards plots I find real life no help at all. Real life seems to have no plots," says Ivy Compton-Burnett. "The author always loads his dice, but he must never let the reader see that he has done so, and by the manipulation of his plot he can engage the reader's attention so that he does not perceive what violence has been done him," says Somerset Maugham. "Plot must further the novel towards its object. Plot is the knowing of destination," says Elizabeth Bowen. "The plot, being an imitation of an action, must imitate one action and that a whole, the structural union of the parts being such that, if any one of them is displaced or removed, the whole will be disjointed and disturbed," says Aristotle.

Each of these commentators is noting, from a different angle, the principal thing that distinguishes fiction from the artless chronicle of events. Thus: plot is an artifice. It arouses and directs the reader's *N.B.* expectations. It has the sense of predestination. It imposes a unity on the narration so that all of the happenings interrelate, in the end, to make a whole. In fact, the application of this kind of strategy is what has made the art of modern fiction possible.

E. M. Forster, in *Aspects of the Novel*, has given a useful description of the differences between *story*, which is the most ancient and fundamental element of any narration of events, and *plot*, which is a sophisticated invention of later date. Story, he says, is a simple arrangement of events in their time sequence, and he gives as an example, "The king died and then the queen died." But plot, on the other hand, is that same time sequence with the addition of causality: "The king died and then the queen died of grief"; or, to strengthen the plot element with a little suspense, "The queen died, no one knew why, until it was discovered that it was through grief at the death of the king." Forster comments that the question asked of the story is always "and then?" but that the question asked of the plot is always "why?".

To add a little further to this distinction: the story is the road of time, proceeding from the known to the unknown and meeting each event in succession. A plot, on the other hand, is a pattern of cause and effect. One event forces another to occur or one happening causes something hitherto withheld to be revealed. The plot is always a matter of a situation as it undergoes change and development. It is only at the end, when the events have reached culmination, that the pattern is complete.

This is the place for a word of caution. The terms *plot* and *story* have been employed as E. M. Forster uses them in *Aspects of the Novel*. Other authors have frequently regarded them as interchangeable or have blurred the difference between the two. Forster's distinction, however, is extremely useful and thus it will be followed in this chapter. Elsewhere in the book, the word "story" has the more general sense of any coherent recital of events, in the form of fiction.

Forster not only distinguishes between the two, but he sees a qualitative difference. The interest in pure story, he says, is a primitive one that depends on curiosity alone as to what happens next. In contrast, the ability to grasp a plot requires both memory and intelligence. The constant suggestion of "why?" in a plot poses mystery and, he says, "To appreciate a mystery, part of the mind must be left behind, brooding, while the other part goes marching on." Finally, Forster notes, the result of a successful plot is "something aesthetically compact . . . beauty at which a novelist should never aim, though he fails if he does not achieve it."

The idea of plot entered into fiction slowly and hesitantly. Despite Aristotle's adequate critical definition and the long tradition of plot in drama, fiction remained more or less a matter of story throughout its early history, up to the nineteenth century. *Don Quixote* is an example of the story-novel in a pure state (and even though the form, by Forster's definition, is primitive, there are many other things in it to engage the intelligence). Defoe and Smollett followed the same methods. It was in the work of their contemporaries, Fielding and Richardson, that novels began to take on a plot formation, and this is one reason why they are often called the first modern novelists in English. In the nineteenth century, fiction writers at last achieved a thorough command of plot and, being delighted with the knowledge, discovered various virtuoso ways of using it—to the point of sterile artificiality at times. The mystery story, with its puzzle-plot, and the surprise-ending story are examples of the ingenious toys they invented. The reaction set in with the writers of the early twentieth century, many of whom felt that the theory tended to make fiction too narrow and mechanical. It had become an end in itself.

The Russian writers of the nineteenth century, however, had avoided an overdependence on plot, and their influence now rose considerably. Chekhov's style of short story was preferred to Maupassant's, and Tolstoy loomed larger than Dickens or Balzac in the novel. The tendency to minimize plot in favor of other values can be seen clearly in the stories of Sherwood Anderson, Katherine Mansfield, and Ernest Hemingway, and in such novelists as Joyce and Virginia Woolf. Today, plot has regained a certain respectability, but most serious fiction writers employ it with a sense of moderation; they realize that it is only one of the means toward their end.

THE CLASSIC PLOT

To begin talking in specific terms, it is necessary to go back to the foundations of the concept of plot. Aristotle's was, of course, the classic definition and his *Poetics* gave an orderly description of principles that have affected the practice of writers ever since. But Aristotle's chief point of reference was Greek drama and his discussion of plot was applied to tragedy. Quite a few of his formulations have been much debated and much modified, though their relevance, even to the craft of fiction, is still important.

The primary thing is shape. Aristotle saw plot as an action that is complete and whole; that has a beginning, a middle, and an end. It originates in one of life's natural situations; the situation is changed as the logic of probability or necessity brings new events; all of these events are aimed to result in a single and (in terms of the plot) inevitable outcome. Along with this goes the idea of the three unities—of action, time, and place (Aristotle himself demanded the first one only; neoclassical critics of the sixteenth century developed the idea of the other two). The time covered by the drama, the area of its physical setting, and the scope of its action all ought to be strictly limited to a small compass. The unities, however, proved too binding for the romantic writer and they are, of course, too narrow for most fiction. Classical tragedy required a burning concentration to create its pity, terror, and final purging of the emotions. It is too fierce a discipline for fiction, which always wants to take in far more of the great mixed bag of life's experience.

Aristotle distinguished two kinds of plot—the "simple" plot, which closely resembles Forster's "story," and the "complex" plot. The secret of the complex plot is change, which is its dynamic element. That change is embodied in several indicated turning points which serve to revolutionize our whole outlook on the situation of the drama. To see how these work, observe a standard working model of the Aristotelian mechanism.

At the beginning there is the establishment of the situation. Characters are defined; they are placed in some kind of relationship (allied, opposed, or simply observational). The situation is in progress; that is, one or more of the characters is supplied with intentions (and these intentions are usually of the most straightforward kind—a young girl looks forward to her marriage, or a young man leaves his poor surroundings and plans to find some room at the top, etc.).

The next stage of the plot has been called the "rising action." Developments follow the course that has been indicated for them

at the beginning and the intentions are pursued, not without conflict and opposition, but with seeming success. This "rising action"
leads to the first great turning point of the plot, one which Aristotle
specified as the "reversal of the situation." An event which at first
seems to be a normal part of what we have known and seen hitherto
suddenly puts a new (and frequently disastrous) face on the situation. Aristotle gives, as an example, the arrival of the messenger
who comes to relieve Oedipus' fears about his mother, but who ends
by revealing the king's true identity and thus forces a complete reappraisal of the circumstances.

This reappraisal, which is the second turning point, follows
swiftly and inevitably. Aristotle calls it the "recognition." It is the
moment when characters become aware of the drastic change that
has been made in their relationships. The "reversal" alters the world
they live in by introducing new or unknown facts; the revolution of
facts then produces a revolution of ideas and emotions, which is
"recognition."

The trouble with these definitions, however, is that they are
rather too peculiar to the tragic drama Aristotle was discussing.
One substitute for "reversal" is the term "crisis," which is somewhat
broader and more useful in the understanding of fiction. Aristotle's
"reversal" depends on a thunderbolt of fate. It is true that the men
of tragedy have unwittingly demanded it and have made themselves
targets for it, but it still arrives from the skies. A fictional crisis, on
the other hand, may be a decisive turning point in a conflict of
forces that have already been put into opposition during the "rising
action" of the story. It may be, and frequently is, a climax of character that forces a showdown in the drama. It may be that a number of the developments sketched out in the "rising action"—things
inconsequential in their separate selves—are brought together to
form an explosive mixture. Such methods are far less artificial.

(Aristotle felt that he was describing a kind of drama that was
consistent and logical. He speaks of it as following the "law of probability or necessity," and wants only development that is "inevitable." Yet it is heavily and obviously dependent on a chain of
coincidence—the sudden revelation of secret information in the

"reversal" scene being a prime example. In another place, he mentions "the statue of Mitys at Argos which fell upon his murderer and killed him." Aristotle goes on to observe that "Such events seem not to be due to mere chance.")

To Aristotle, the "reversal" is the past, like a time bomb, taking revenge on the present. However limiting this theory may be in the specific formulation, it gives rise to the more inclusive idea of crisis. Coupled with it is that invaluable insight about "recognition." ("Recognition" is the psychological transformation that must occur as the result of crisis—one or more of the characters has had to take on an entirely new vision of the world around him. The old pattern of human relationships is broken up and a new one has to be formed. This is where the writer of serious fiction places the main stress and where he finds the most interest.

Succeeding that, in the classical formula, comes the "falling action," the postclimax events that lead toward the final resolution. In classical tragedy, of course, this final scene is called the "catastrophe," and that implies an ending in deep sorrow, destruction, or death. In comedy, and in that peculiarly mixed form called fiction, the resolution scene is given the name of "denouement." This is a general term signifying the point at which everything comes clear. It used to be the grand moment when disguises were cast off, mistaken identities revealed, long-lost relatives reunited, parted lovers joined, mysteries solved, and villains jailed. When the playwright or storyteller was particularly at a loss for something to tie the package neatly, he would send out for what the Romans called a *deus ex machina*—a god from the machine (lowered, quite literally, onto the stage by mechanism in some early dramas), who would quickly solve any pending problems. In somewhat more modern drama, he takes on the form of the rich uncle, or whatever; he is from India, or wherever; and he forgives Clarence, reunites him with Arabella, and provides a liberal cash settlement.

This, then, is a simplified drawing of the structure called plot. It does not take into consideration the dozens of elaborations or variations that can be made on it; such things as double plots, the use of mystery, surprise endings, etc. Nor does it suggest how the invention can be used for better or for worse, how it can give form and strength to fiction, or how it can give a false and concocted impression. Following are some writers' opinions and some actual practice.

ONE EXAMPLE OF THE CLASSIC PLOT

The first example is a very unpretentious story, one of those in Alberto Moravia's *Roman Tales*. It is told by a man who goes from one restaurant to another playing his guitar. The story is about this man and Milone, a clownish singer who is the other half of the act. It is an interesting story, in regard to plot, because it follows the classical structure—but so simply and unobtrusively that the reader is hardly aware of the method. Here, then, is a description of that structure.

1 (Establishment:) The narrator describes their occupation and his partner at the same time. Milone is a heavy, awkward man who has no talent for singing but some small gift for parody. Whatever he does, he overdoes, especially in his broad burlesque of women singers. The narrator finds this kind of clowning indecent and despises Milone; but he sticks with him because the act is popular and brings in a good income.

2 (Rising action:) He goes on to describe a typical scene in a middle-class restaurant where Milone is doing something highly vulgar with a simple and beautiful popular ballad. The audience enjoys it; far from being offended, the ladies are the most enthusiastic. Later, Milone has the idea of dressing up in women's clothes and he wants his accompanist to do likewise. The narrator is disgusted. " 'Isn't it about time you invented something attractive, something moving?' " he asks. " 'People want to laugh,' " says Milone, " 'and I make them laugh.' "

3 (Crisis:) One day the two entertainers happen into a poor wine shop and Milone, for no particular reason except vanity, decides to sing. As usual, he distorts and destroys a beautiful song. But after he finishes, a handsome young man in workman's overalls steps up and says furiously, " 'Now *I'll* sing it for you.' " And he does, making the song beautiful again. The onlookers are indifferent, but, when the young man goes back to his table, the girl who has been waiting for him throws her arms around him. Milone and the narrator know why he has sung the song.

(Recognition:) All that the narrator ever sees is "a bitter expression" on Milone's face. He has to suppose, to supply for us, what must have gone on in the clown's mind after this blow:

4

I have said that Milone's head had been turned, and that he believed himself to be a great artist of some kind whereas in reality he was just a poor wretch who played the buffoon to amuse people while they were eating; so much the greater, therefore, was the fall brought about by that gesture on the part of the fair-haired young man in overalls. I think that, while the young man was singing, he must have seen himself, all of a sudden, not as he had hitherto believed himself to be, but as he really was—a clumsy, big man of fifty who put on a bib and recited nursery poems. But I also think he must have realized that he would never be able to sing, even if he made a pact with the devil. All he could do, in fact, was to make people laugh; and the only way he was able to make them laugh was by holding certain things up to ridicule. And those things, it so happened, were just the things he had never succeeded in having in his own life.[1]

(Catastrophe:) The next morning it is discovered that Milone has hanged himself in his room. The narrator is the only one who goes along to see him buried. With an appropriately grotesque touch, he notes that the landlady sells the rope, piece by piece.

5

This is no more than a thumbnail tragedy, but it is almost a success—and its success comes from the fact that the author is sure of nearly every move. He does not describe the narrator's love affair; he doesn't inquire into how Milone invests his money or what letters he receives from home. He quietly bases his story on the traditional scheme of the plot, adapting here and there as necessary. The result is a compact and economical story, with no false trails or wasteful disgressions.

Beyond that, the story gets its strength from exactly the same source as tragedy. Only a man who is capable of feeling is capable of disastrous self-recognition. The narrator and thus the reader are

---

[1] New York: Farrar, Straus & Company, 1957; p. 44.

led to misjudge Milone in the first part of the story; he seems incapable of any shame. Paradoxically, it is his very ability to think and to apply a moral judgment to himself that is his hidden flaw—and that is fatal.

Now there is one very awkward aspect to the plotting of this story. Moravia reached the recognition scene and found that he could do it by supposition only. The reason for this seems to lie in the fact that he has left all of the telling to the narrator and has shown Milone silently, as a rather inarticulate creature. It would be a mistake in characterization to have him begin to talk after the scene in the wine shop and to express the shock and revulsion he must feel. Therefore, in the quoted passage, the narrator must guess the whole of the recognition. He guesses shrewdly and, without much doubt, accurately. Still, there is no hiding the fact that the one important character has departed, leaving us without a single real clue except that "bitter expression." The author (disguised as the narrator) is sitting there summarizing for us what must or what might have happened in Milone's heart. As nearly every good dramatic writer has realized, the recognition has to take place within our view. Watching and listening to a man as his world goes to pieces before his eyes is a shocking thing. But it is essential to the presentation of tragedy—even to this minor one.

The moral is useful. Any writer who sets out to employ a very definite plot has certain obligations. He may shift plot elements around as he pleases, turn them inside out, invent any sort of striking variation that helps him to accomplish a purpose. He cannot, however, ignore certain large principles—perhaps they might be called the "rational principles" of the plot. If he uses mystery for plot purposes, he is obligated to give a solution somewhere. If his plot scheme follows the general pattern of tragedy, there must, in some form, be a crisis and a recognition.

CHANCE AND COINCIDENCE

When fiction first began to borrow the idea of interlocking action from the drama, it sacrificed a certain fidelity to life. As Ivy Compton-Burnett says, "Real life seems to have no plot." The prac-

N.B.

tice of fitting believable events to a dramatic pattern carried far greater risks of artificiality in fiction than it did in Greek drama— where the accepted idea of fate could account for a great deal.

Any writer of more or less realistic fiction depends very heavily on his credit with the reader. He is seeking to persuade the reader that his fiction is directed toward some observation of values in life; he puts that motive into great jeopardy when he seems to abandon the plausible interaction of events for something that is obviously an intrigue. It is a thin line that separates the two, but it is crucial. We believe in cause and effect in human relationships. When that cause and effect begins to seem rigged, the author is in trouble with the ordinary scepticism of his reader. A jury will accept evidence that is selected and arranged in some sort of pattern that leads to a point; it should not accept evidence that is cleverly cooked.

Chance or coincidence has always been the bad magic of the plot. An example of one of its more outrageous forms was the "god from the machine," that meddling fairy godparent who so frequently used to deliver happy endings and destroy credulity at the same time. In the present day, the obvious use of coincidence is identified with commercial or second-rate fiction. It is easy to forget the many good writers who, struggling with the stubborn material of plot, have resorted to it, or how tempting it may be to an inexperienced writer.

First, it ought to be said that there is a perfectly natural kind of chance. It is by chance, of course, that Anna Karenina meets, of all the cavalry officers in the Russian army, just the man named Vronsky. But, because she has an affinity to that kind of man, we accept the notion without any question. If we can say, of this or that character in fiction, "She would have had a disastrous love affair anyway, whether it was with X or with somebody else," or "He would have succeeded in getting rich no matter where or when he lived," chance is nicely balanced with causality to make a convincing fiction. It is only when the writer deserts the kind of fate that arises from character and finds events depending on the cast of the dice that he must be extremely wary. There *is*, of course, the chance that is seemingly quite unpredictable and entirely fortuitous.

But when a writer employs it unscrupulously to make some plot dovetail or to have things "turn out," it becomes in fact no longer acceptable as mere chance but a trick that the author has played in the name of chance. The old saw that "Life is stranger than fiction" stems from this matter. The wildest kind of coincidence can happen in real life, but the realistic writer has to avoid the suspicion that "his fiction is stranger than life."

Mark Twain, in his famous essay on Fenimore Cooper's literary offenses, said, "the personages of a tale shall confine themselves to possibilities and let miracles alone; or, if they venture a miracle, the author must so plausibly set it forth as to make it look possible and reasonable." This is, as it should be, not so much a plea for strictly naturalistic fiction as it is a plea for fair play on the part of the author. Literature offers a considerable number of examples of unscrupulous plot miracles, even among good authors or great authors.

Shakespeare is a particular offender in *Othello,* constructing his plot out of the most incredible patchwork of chance—a lost handkerchief, an overheard conversation which is misunderstood, characters failing to say the obvious thing and instead saying the obviously wrong thing. Dickens, of course, is the greatest inventor of fantastic coincidence in the whole of English literature. His plots thrive on the purely fortuitous—but so openly and so systematically that they seem a special case. He uses coincidence not simply with a stroke here or there to rationalize a difficulty, but almost as a universal connective by which one character or group of characters has its interests involved with another. Thomas Hardy even more deliberately raised the idea of chance (or, as he called it, "hap") to the status of a philosophical principle in his work. Hardy's plots often turn on what seems to be random luck, yet the use is something different from the conventional one of creating surprise, rescuing a character from a dilemma, or making possible a happy ending. Hardy thought that hap was the perverse, blind, and wanton force that brought human wishes to nothing, appearing at the crucial moment to upset lives and bring down disaster.

A few examples of the calculated accident will serve to illustrate its bad effects. In *Jane Eyre,* the situation finally develops into a stubborn plot problem: Jane, though she loves Rochester, refuses to live with him while his wife is still alive. This impasse comes directly and naturally from her strong moral sense and, as Edwin Muir remarks, "The story should have been worked out to end on this assumption." But, instead of finding a way to loose this knot, the author simply slashes it. Muir goes on to say, "Charlotte Brontë has the insane Mrs. Rochester conveniently burned to death; she defeats fate, she defeats Jane, making her qualities irrelevant and meaningless, by introducing an accident containing a curious mixture of amiability, cruelty, and nonsense."

Frequently, however, the occurrence of chance is not so damaging to the whole structure; it is simply used to make the necessary plot connections. The notorious devices of the Victorian novelist included the discovery of a significant letter, the overhearing of a private conversation, the leaving behind of some such material clue as a glove or handkerchief. No one today, except Miss Compton-Burnett, would use such antiques, yet inexplicable things still happen in fiction. Most of Sherwood Anderson's short stories are told in a natural way and without reliance on devices. Yet, in "I Want to Know Why," he meets a small problem of connecting his plot and solves it with coincidence. The boy narrator has to see his hero, the racehorse trainer with whom he associates everything "brave or wonderful," in a totally different situation—in a country bawdy house, drunken, bragging, and lecherous. Anderson has no plausible way of getting the boy to the scene, so he simply has him walk down a road outside Saratoga. "Pretty soon I went up the side road—I don't know why—and came to the rummy farm house." Anderson can't take the boy inside and so he provides him with a convenient window through which to view the scene. Along with the view, he can overhear the conversation. Thus the revelation rests on a precarious pile of three devices of chance.

There is a curious example of another kind of coincidence in Stendhal's great novel, *The Red and the Black*. It is a matter of forecasting a future event in very exact terms rather than a means of hooking the plot together at one point. The hero, Julien Sorel, as a young boy, sets out to be interviewed for a job as tutor to the

Mayor's children. On his way, he stops at the village church and sits down in the pew belonging to the Mayor's family. He finds a slip of newspaper which says, " 'Details of the execution and of the last moments of Louis Jenrel, executed at Besançon, on the . . .' " On the other side of the paper are the words, " 'The first step.' " On his way out, he thinks he sees blood near the holy water stoup, but it is only a red reflection. He has an obscure fright, but then says to himself, " 'Should I prove coward? *To arms!*' "

The odd thing about this incident is that it cannot be taken as a vague omen of some sort; it is a highly detailed set of clues to events still far in the future. Louis Jenrel is a rhyme for Julien Sorel (as he sees). Julien is to be executed at Besançon. He is, with the tutor's job, about to take his first step on the road to his crime. It is in this very pew that he will shoot Madame de Rênal and her blood will fall on the same floor. " *To arms!*' " suggests the literal pistol. Looking back from the end of the book, the reader remembers this little prophecy as a startling wrong note. Stendhal's superb development of his hero's psychology has persuaded us that Julien's rise and sudden self-destruction come inevitably from the kind of personality he has. But can we be so sure? Doesn't that little slip of paper suggest some mechanical and vulgar idea of predestination?

"It so happened that . . . ," "Now by chance it occurred . . . ," "Quite unexpectedly he found himself. . . ." These and their equivalents are signs of danger for the fiction writer. Some plot requirement is about to take a costly victory at the expense of naturalness.

PREVIEWS OF EVENTS TO COME

Stendhal's forecast of Julien's fate suggests mention of a somewhat different device, once favored by writers but nowadays seen much less frequently. It is the trick of borrowing some piece of information from the still unknown future of the story or novel in order to point up the circumstance being presently related. It is sometimes called the "had-I-but-known" method. This phrase refers to the practice of creating suspense through an arbitrary preview. It is embodied in such introductory sentences as, "Had I but known what danger awaited me, I never should have entered that house"; or "Little did Catherine realize that she was about to make her greatest triumph"; or "Looking back on it later, I knew that I should have taken warning from her words."

Sometimes the information is given not to arouse suspense but to dispel it, as in this very specific example from Trollope's *Barchester Towers*: "But let the gentle-hearted reader be under no apprehension whatsoever. It is not destined that Eleanor shall marry Mr. Slope or Bertie Stanhope."

There are two questions of technique here—the question of the intrusive authorial point of view, which is of no concern just now, and the question of orderly plot development. It is an unfortunate blunder to remind the reader so plainly of "the violence that is being done to him." If there is one illusion that the writer should take most pains to foster, it is the reader's feeling that he is observing the process of people working out certain problems of life in their own terms. When he casts ahead in this way, he is, in effect, admitting that his plot is predetermined, arbitrary, already entombed. After one such excursion in *David Copperfield*, Dickens rather sheepishly apologizes: "This may be premature. I have set it down too soon, perhaps. But let it stand."

Graham Greene nearly succeeds in spoiling a fine short story, "The Basement Room," with an obnoxious version of this device. He wants to tell us that his small boy protagonist is going through a traumatic experience that will blight all his life thereafter and so Greene keeps stepping in to inform us that "he would never escape that scene. In a week he had forgotten it, but it would condition his career, the long austerity of his life." This observation has no connection with the plot because the story does not deal with the rest of the boy's life, but those sententious bits of popular psychology do succeed in damping some of the reader's interest in the present drama.

Quite distinct from this kind of ruse, there is a perfectly legitimate way of anticipating the future. One of the indispensable ingredients in fiction is that of always promising something. It is a sort of low common denominator of all readable books. In the best kind of fiction the promises are put with subtlety—it may be simply that we have seen a certain trait of character in Mrs. A and we are tantalized by the thought of her coming into collision with Mrs. B, who is just her opposite. It may be that we have seen a character embarked on a certain course which, we anticipate, will run him into trouble; our prediction being based on the fact that we know more of the circumstances than he does. Anything, in short, that is proposed to the reader as interestingly incomplete suggests a prediction of the future to him.

THE DEVICE OF MYSTERY

Withholding certain information until it can be revealed most effectively has always been an important part of plot construction. Every plot has an element of mystery in it that raises the question "why?" about people and their actions, but (excluding the pure mystery or detective story, which has its own conventions and is something of a special case) the matter of tactics in raising that question and later in answering it is all-important. The tactics to avoid might be listed as follows:

It is a mistake to confide in the reader through one character's point of view while withholding something known to that character.

It is a mistake to conceal something merely for the sake of mystification.

It is a mistake to sensationalize any mystery with huggermugger devices.

It is a mistake to introduce extraneous mystery that contributes nothing to the unfolding of the plot.

To the intelligent reader, these tactics seem deceitful and cheapening. One of the useful guidelines for avoiding them is a clear sense of the reader's knowledge of the plot at any given point as compared with that of the protagonist or protagonists. It is perfectly legitimate (and a frequent practice) to permit the reader to be ahead of the character who is acting as point of view. This is true of

N.B.

almost every story whose narrator or whose point of view is a child, an adult of limited intelligence, or any person who is excluded from a full understanding of events. In these cases, the reader comprehends, in a "superior" way, what is going on and what is likely to happen. (An example of this is in the last-cited Graham Greene story. The boy Philip sees his friend Baines, the butler, who is married to the terrible-tempered Mrs. Baines, having a rendezvous with a pretty young woman. At first it does not enter his head to be suspicious of this, but it does ours.)

On the other hand, the narrator or point of view must never be ahead of the reader. That is, he cannot seem to be confiding in the reader (as Esther Summerson, who narrates part of *Bleak House,* does), while withholding certain secret information. If John is the point of view and if John finds the lost letter with the significant message and reads it, the author cannot suppress what that message is. If he does, he is guilty of mystification.

Most modern writers who use some element of mystery prefer to lay the emphasis on *how?*, not *who?* That is, they direct the interest of the reader to the motivations of their characters in order to make him wonder why, for example, character A has so behaved in the past as to bring about the situation we now find him in. Or, we may see a long-standing enmity between characters B and C and be intrigued to find out how and why they first clashed. The mystery of *who?*, in contrast, is that of the classic detective story, the effort to identify the "guilty"—in effect, the responsible—person. *Who* committed the murders in the Rue Morgue? *Who* killed Roger Ackroyd? Two more variants, which again stress the uncovering of hidden facts: *where* is the missing will concealed? *what* is it that lies behind the bricked-up wall in the cellar? When a writer centers interest on the discovery of facts in this way, he is concentrating on a trick of plot, to the detriment of the serious elements in his story. When he centers the mystery on motivation, on the desires and actions of his people, he is generally succeeding in making the "mystery" contribute to the mainstream of his story. The solution of a factual mystery is usually a letdown, being not nearly so interesting as the elaborate buildup that has prepared for it. The solution of a motivational mystery—if well handled—is a valuable way of disclosing something about a personality and it adds to the fiction.

A good example of delicate balance in the treatment of a mystery is Machado de Assis' remarkable novel *Quintas Borba,* in which the reader's surmises may be quite different from the narrator's, although they are always based on the same evidence.

THE TWIST AT THE END

The surprise ending, or a reversal of the situation at the close of a short story, was a favorite device of Maupassant and was popularized in American fiction by O. Henry. It is sometimes used to prove the ingenuity of the author or otherwise to provide a stroke of irony—those diamonds the woman worked all her life to pay for are discovered to be paste. It belongs to the anecdote more than to serious writing and its use is now confined to the mystery novel (where it is quite legitimate, as a trick among tricks), the commercial short story, and television dramas.

THE DOUBLE PLOT, THE SUBPLOT, AND THE MULTIPLE PLOT

A great many novels, though few short stories, carry forward two or more plots at the same time. The tradition, in English literature, comes largely from the Elizabethan drama, in which the play with two plots is a favorite convention. The general rule here was to develop a main plot whose highborn characters were to be the objects of sympathy and identification. The subplot which accompanied it usually involved people of lower social status and was frequently comic. The two plots were often different sides of the same theme, and the subplot could act as a joking comment on the main action or as an ironic mirror. The tribulations of love between the aristocratic lovers, for instance, could be seen as the humorous mishaps of love between two of their servants. Customarily, the denouement brought about the simultaneous resolution of both plots.

This kind of parallel construction had great attractions, one of the chief being the playwright's chance to exploit a theme from two different angles. There could be a serious comparison as well as comic contrast; *King Lear* is a good example of the theme's gaining power from two different views of parent-children relationships. Whatever its purpose, a skillful use of the double plot could give the onlooker a sense of moving about freely in the world of the play, of knowing what the Duke was like and also knowing what his servants and soldiers thought of him. It was the same tendency to expand and explore that gave so much energy to the nineteenth-century novel.

Although the general purposes of the double plot have remained much the same in fiction as in the drama, novelists have discovered a considerable range of imaginative variation. One of the most daring experiments in the form is *Wuthering Heights*. The traditional method of working the two plots is to keep them roughly parallel in chronology and to alternate the narrative between them. Emily Brontë's striking conception is to tell, in effect, the same story twice, once with a tragic ending and once with a happy solution. Rather than alternating, one follows the other. The main plot is that of Heathcliff, Catherine, and Edgar, and this leads to the subplot enacted by the children, young Cathy, Linton, and Hareton. In the second generation, roles correspond to those of the first but the characters within them have altered—and the romantic violence of Heathcliff and Catherine has burnt itself out. This becomes more than a double-plot device; in effect, the author answers the same question twice with opposite visions of what might have happened.

Jane Austen's *Pride and Prejudice* has a totally different use of the double plot. Here the plots are so closely alike in substance that it is only the small reversal of events from one to the other (Bingley is prevailed upon to reject Jane; Elizabeth then rejects Darcy) and shadings of character that separate the two. It is like watching two slightly different aspects of the same experience and thus concentrating our attention on the theme. (There is, of course, the second subplot of Lydia and Wickham, which is a contrasting one that shows the dangers of making love a game rather than a serious business of the moral nature and the intellect.) Jane Austen's kind of fiction was intensive. She was more interested in varieties of the same experience than in varieties of experience that bear wide contrast and make broad comparisons.

With Dickens the division of plot has almost approached the stage of anarchy. That tendency of the Elizabethan drama to reach out for wider experience is exaggerated into an effort to organize a multitude of people and many widely differing areas of society into related schemes of plot. There is a main plot, which is accompanied by a subplot, but then new and remarkable characters keep crowding in, many of whom have a tendency to generate plots of their own. As Frank O'Connor remarks about *Dombey and Son:*

. . . we get a straightforward picture of a hard-hearted, arrogant business man who pays no attention to his little daughter, Florence, and whose life is bound up with his son, Paul, who he hopes will succeed him in the business. But Paul's mother has died, so he acquires a wet-nurse, Mrs. Toodle, who in turn fans out into a number of entertaining characters; while in the sub-plot, the hero, Walter, who loves Florence, is the nephew of a wonderful old character called Solomon Gills, and Solomon has as friend an equally wonderful character, Captain Cuttle, who, in turn, has a friend—[2]

It often happens that Dickens' energy and imagination seem to turn away from his pale, conventional hero and heroine and their plot, toward the comic or melodramatic possibilities in other lives. Thus, the center does not hold. The reliable rule of the drama was to assume that we are all a part of the same life and that the same human motives only work themselves out somewhat differently on different levels. The relationship between two plots was natural. Dickens' fantastic imagination did not permit him to believe this. His multiple worlds do not reflect but exclude each other; such places as the aristocratic house of Chesney Wold are connected with a slum like Tom-all-Alone's by lines of pure coincidence and intrigue. This is one of the great weaknesses of the manifold method. Plots insist on becoming idiosyncratic and do not work together to produce a theme. Aristotle was sound in demanding "a single effect" for any drama. It is not fair, however, to leave

[2] *Mirror in the Roadway* (New York: Alfred A. Knopf, 1956), p. 80.

Dickens without mentioning his most unified novel, *Great Expectations,* where his splendid inventions do cohere.

Perhaps the most famous example of a novel with a split in its structure is Tolstoy's *War and Peace.* Percy Lubbock has made a careful examination of this in *The Craft of Fiction.* Lubbock argues that there are two "stories" (and he uses the word, roughly, in the sense of "plot"), which have no real, but merely a coincidental, relationship. One is the story of private people; Pierre, Natasha, Andrei, plus their friends and families; and the other is the drama of the conflict of nations, with the Czar, Napoleon, Kutuzov, and other figures as the actors. The first treats the theme of the cycle of life from youth to age, while the theme of the second is a historic clash. Lubbock says:

I can discover no angle at which the two stories will appear to unite and merge into a single impression. Neither is subordinate to the other, and there is nothing above them (what more *could* there be?) to which they are both related. Nor are they placed together to illustrate a contrast; nothing *results* from their juxtaposition. Only from time to time, upon no apparent principle and without a word of warning, one of them is dropped and the other resumed.[3]

He adds that Tolstoy was trying, at the same time and without knowing it, to write an *Iliad,* the story of particular men; and an *Aeneid,* the story of a nation. This does not deny the greatness of *War and Peace,* but Lubbock suggests that it could have been even greater had Tolstoy recognized the incongruity in its form.

Vanity Fair is another case of two plots that have generally the same weight and that balance each other off without having a great deal of connection. Thackeray had their paths cross now and then, notably in the Brussels scene before Waterloo, when the Amelia Sedley plot and the Becky Sharp plot are thrown together under the same roof, but generally they remain independent. Independent—but balancing each other, and this is more or less the open secret of why the book does not fall apart. It cannot be said to be unified, either, but still there is a system of correspondences that pre-

---

[3] New York: The Viking Press, 1957; p. 33.

vents a fatal crack. Contrasts and comparisons are always being made back and forth between the two plots, not only in the general roles played by the characters but also in some of the finer detail of personality. A very good example of this is Amelia's attitude toward children versus Becky's attitude, which has been commented on pointedly, first by Lord David Cecil in *Early Victorian Novelists* and then by Frank O'Connor in *Mirror in the Roadway*. Thackeray was most skillful in introducing a scene or detail about Amelia, for instance, at which the reader cannot help thinking of Becky and how different it would be with her. And so the two plots, not twins but siblings, share a good deal simply by having one refer us to the other.

All of this suggests that the writer who wishes to use some scheme of double or multiple plot should carefully consider what his different lines have in common. Where they come together, where they refer to each other, where each reinforces a definite theme—these are the points that are important to the unity of his novel or, occasionally, his short story. If the coincidence of the two is haphazard or artificial, the book itself is likely to seem fragmentary. On the other hand, it is advantageous to make the separation between them distinct enough so that they seem to be two different explorations. *Pride and Prejudice* gets no great advantages from its too similar plot lines. It is probably best to think first of the theme that is to run through the fiction and then to decide how either or all of the elements of plot will relate themselves to it.

ECONOMY VERSUS DIGRESSION

Chekhov made one of the remarks that is most frequently quoted about plot. He said that if a shotgun hangs on the wall in the first act, it must go off in the last act. There is a certain ambiguity about this statement, but it is usually taken to mean that a plotmaker should never put anything useless or extraneous to the plot into his play. (Chekhov violated this rule frequently and with great pleasure.) Some other expert witnesses ought to be called in on either side:

[*Lawrence Sterne:*] Digressions, incontestably, are the sunshine;—they are the life and soul of reading!—take them out of this book [*Tristram Shandy*] for instance,—you might as well take the book along with them;—one cold eternal winter would reign in every page of it; restore them to the writer;—he steps forth like a bridegroom,—bids All-hail; brings in variety and forbids the appetite to fail.[4]

[*V. S. Pritchett:*] What is it that attracts us to the Russian novelists of the nineteenth century? . . . The real attraction of that censored literature is its freedom—the freedom from our kind of didacticism and our plots. The characters of our novels, from Fielding to Forster, get up in the morning, wash, dress and are then drilled for their roles. They are propelled to some practical issue in morality, psychology or Fortune before the book is done. In nineteenth-century Russia . . . there is more room to breathe, to let the will drift, and the disparate impulses have their ancient solitary reign. . . . Turgenev, who knew English literature well, used to say that he envied the English novelists their power to make plots; but, of course, he really disdained it. The surprises of life, the sudden shudders of its skin, are fresher and more astonishing than the imposed surprises of literary convention or the teacher's lesson.[5]

[*Fyodor Dostoevsky:*] I can never control my material. Whenever I write a novel, I crowd it up with a lot of separate stories and episodes; therefore the whole lacks proportion and harmony. . . . how frightfully I have always suffered from it, for I have always been aware it was so.[6]

[*André Gide:*] He [Paul Claudel] speaks . . . with the greatest scorn of English writers in general "who have never learned that the rule of 'nothing unessential' is the first condition of art."[7]

[*Anthony Trollope:*] There should be no episodes in a novel. Every sentence, every word, through all those pages, should tend to the telling of the story. Such episodes distract the attention of the reader, and always do so disagreeably.[8]

[4] *The Life and Opinions of Tristram Shandy, Gentleman* (New York: The Clonmel Society, 1899), I, 118.

[5] *The Living Novel* (New York: Harcourt, Brace & World, 1947), p. 216.

[6] *Letters of Fyodor Michailovitch Dostoevsky*, trans. Ethel Colbourn Mayne (New York: The Macmillan Company, 1914), p. 217.

[7] *The Journals of André Gide* (New York: Alfred A. Knopf, 1947), I, 163.

[8] *An Autobiography* (New York: Oxford University Press, 1950), p. 237.

An odd budget of conflicting testimony! A famous English novelist passionately defends his own tangents and digressions. Another English novelist says that the trouble with English fiction is that it is so regimented by plot—whereas, look at the Russians, how freely they wandered. A great Russian novelist castigates his own work for its freedom of digression and lack of form. A Frenchman says that the English novel is stuffed full of irrelevance. Still another English novelist says that the first rule of fiction is to make everything absolutely relevant. The only thing lacking is a Bulgarian to remark that *all* other European fiction is bad because it has not learned the Bulgarian rule of being absolutely relevant while being irrelevant at the same time.

In fact, this is the answer—though not a Bulgarian one. It is the particularly lucid comment by Ford Madox Ford, which strikes the heart of the problem as none of these other writers could:

The first thing that you have to consider when writing a novel is your story, and then your story—and then your story! . . . Any digression will make a *longueur,* a patch over which the mind will progress heavily. You may have the most wonderful scene from real life that you might introduce into your book. But if it does not make your subject progress, it will divert the attention of the reader. A good novel needs all the attention the reader can give it. And then some more.

Of course, you must appear to digress. That is the art which conceals your Art. The reader, you should premise, will always dislike you and your book. He thinks it an insult that you dare to claim his attention, and if lunch is announced or there is a ring at the bell he will welcome the digression. So you will provide him with what he thinks are digressions—with occasions on which he thinks he may let his attention relax. . . . But really not one single thread must ever escape your purpose.[9]

THE EFFECT OF PLOT ON FICTION

It is time to try some generalizations as to what plot *is* in a larger sense and what it *does* for fiction. Its long history of trial and error is the history of an attempt to organize the raw material of human

[9] *It Was the Nightingale* (Philadelphia: J. B. Lippincott Company, 1933), p. 211.

experience into one kind of pattern, a causal pattern of beginning, middle, and end that does not waste anything in the telling. What are the advantages, finally, of this kind of craftsmanship? Does its expert use result in art, or does it result in artifice?

As such questions have a habit of doing, these revert to Aristotle. Aristotle put "action" first, as the main business of drama, and "character" second. This is a philosophical distinction of great significance. Once we accept action as the primary thing, we have set ourselves on the road to plot. The next great principle is the organization of human action in a pattern of cause and effect. Once this is done, the course has been set and the development is inevitable. Character, the secondary consideration, has to fall into line; it has to be cut and tailored to fit into the pattern of action.

Actually, what we have here are two basic ways of looking at life. The Aristotelian way is to say that we cannot expect to look directly into human minds. The primary evidence, the only reliable evidence we have about human life is the way people act and the things they do. What one man does impels another to do something else and all of the side considerations, the incidental thoughts, or the irrelevant things that may possibly occur to him are of no great importance because they are not finally expressed in what he does. Character is inferred by action; the only true way to read character is through action.

This is a very reassuring idea; it seems both a realistic way and a most convenient way of grasping human life. But, even beyond that, it opens the way to moral judgment. One of the things that plot leads most powerfully toward is a moral judgment on the people it has dealt with. Even if the judgment is implicit, it is nevertheless there. The very idea of denouement demands a sorting-out of life; a plot cannot end without the assigning of values, without the identification of right and wrong. This, in an abstract way, is what the denouement really is.

The opposite view is that knowledge of human beings begins with a knowledge of character, and thus literary art should begin there as well. What a man is dictates what he does and, although his reactions are partly a response to the actions of others, there is always the element of individuality. Thus fiction, if it is to have truth as art, cannot follow the imposed scheme of a plot. It must take as its main subject character, with all its ramifications and contradictions. The novelist's main task is to know character and only then to decide what actions proceed from it. The author who begins from these premises may have some evident moral ideas, but he does not let them restrict his final conclusions—his main search is for psychological truth. This is a very sketchy statement of one modern objection to plot and it must be filled in later, but for the moment it is well to return to the examination of how plot affects all the other elements of story.

A scheme based on action, as the dramatists were quick to see, is a very useful way of selecting what should be said and what should not be—hence the very deep belief most plot-makers have in economy. The idea of the three unities is a good, though rather too doctrinaire, formulation of that belief. "Nothing unessential," everything contributory to the royal scheme of action—these are the watchwords. When carefully observed, this principle had the admirable effect of galvanizing other elements or refining them, all in the high interests of the plot. The notion of setting as a landscape or cityscape which the writer may sit down to paint in luxuriant detail is ruled out. Characters do not just happen to be any place; they are either put in a scene that contributes something to the mode of the action or they appear in a neutral setting that does not impede the action. The idea of a precise style and the exact use of words comes from the general concept of economy that stems from plot. Choosing just the right and most telling moments of time out of all the possibilities in life is also part of that economy.

As suggested, it is the matter of character where the main dissent comes. Yet, laying aside for a moment the philosophical objection posed by the individual-centered view, it is possible to say that the plot scheme of action has often been able to mobilize character in a brilliant way—even if purely for its own uses. As Frank O'Connor says, "Intrigue [i.e., plot] has the great advantage of enabling a novelist to make his characters show their paces, to submit them to a variety of tests and to develop them in unexpected ways. Without the missing check in *The Last Chronicle of Barset* we should never have been able to plumb the full depth of Crawley's misanthropy. But, above all, intrigue imposes a standard of mere relevance, and saves the English novel from the atmosphere of utter irrelevance we so often find in Russian novels. . . ."

Plot has the remarkable capacity of compelling a fiction writer to *show* character positively. "Francis Macomber was a coward." "Jay Gatsby dreamed of recovering the past." These are passive statements. We have the author's word for it, but his word may or may not be true. In a plot situation, the character must act in order to prove himself, in order to attain being.

Even so, plot probably never would have exercised so much fascination for authors had it been only a way of organizing the material of life into a scheme of action. Its ultimate aim, which is the outcome of the technical performance, is a moral solution of all the issues. It offers the writer a ready-made and efficient way of articulating his ideas. Right and wrong, blame and amnesty, punishment and reward, guilt and innocence, celebration and condemnation—these are all possibilities of the denouement. It is a kind of miniature Last Judgment in the small world of the fiction.

A good many writers and critics, particularly the modern ones, have pointed out that something may go drastically wrong at this point. They observe how often the traditional plot seems to go dead at the end. Young love is rewarded too regularly, ambition is punished too automatically; in fact, the most interesting speculations aroused by the early parts of the drama end in a terrible banality. In reply to this it might be said that the fault frequently lies with the individual author, the author who is thoughtlessly using a moral instrument with no regard to the fact that he is quite without any interesting or complicated moral view of his own—thus he simply borrows an accepted one. His imagination, which was lively enough in setting things in motion, fails when it comes to consequences. It might be argued that the gifted author does *not* fail this test. *The Vicar of Wakefield*, for instance, is moribund at its close, but *Le Père Goriot* is not.

Still, the formal charge against plot remains. And it rests very largely on the point that an author's conception of individuals must be the source of fiction—not his observation of their motions. The point gains its great significance from the fact that the conception of the individual grew so immensely more complex, extensive, and subtle in the late nineteenth and early twentieth centuries. Plot exerts a tyranny in making its characters display themselves just in the certain actions that are functional. That could be accepted perfectly well in an age that took a relatively simple view of human personality. In the work of Fyodor Dostoevsky and Henry James, to single out two great transitional novelists, that tyranny was already becoming impossible. Both of these writers knew too much and felt too much about the inner life, or human psychology, to be able to machine their characters down into efficient functions of the plot. This is not to deny that complex psychological portraits had ever existed in literature before the middle of the nineteenth century, but they were the exceptional strokes of a Shakespeare or a Stendhal.

As noted earlier, this was a vast though gradual shift in one of the basic assumptions of fiction. It was not simply a boredom with plot technique or a distaste for worn-out devices; it was a totally different idea of how man can be known and understood. The "consistent" character of plotted drama is one who exists only in public. As Aristotle said, "Within the action, there should be nothing irrational. If the irrational cannot be excluded, it should be outside the scope of the tragedy." The new theory demanded that the writer know the full range of the private or inner life of his central characters, not just the springs of action. He should know as many sides of them as possible whether or not that knowledge contributes anything specific to the events of the story or novel. This led to a new conception of the whole pattern of fiction that has N.B. been called "organic form"; it will be discussed in the last chapter.

PRACTICAL SUGGESTIONS—A PLOT OUTLINE

The beginning writer is usually wise to follow the traditional principles of construction in writing his first stories or novel. This practice gives him some guidelines that he can follow until he is quite confident of the departures he wants to make and in which ways his originality will best operate. On the other hand, it is hardly necessary or profitable to try to fit his story rigidly into such traditional plot regulations as are outlined below. Some freer version of the plot design, which nevertheless does not abandon the idea of consistent development, is probably the most useful kind of reference.

Introduction of oppositions. In establishing the primary situation of his story, the writer should delineate some opposing forces or ideas in order to produce the essential element of tension. More specific words for this are: conflict, doubt, problem, struggle, division. It may be a matter of conflict within the mind of one person or it may be a more external conflict; the important thing is to make the reader aware that there is a pressure to decide between or among alternatives.

Deepening of the oppositions. If oppositions remain in constant balance, repressed, or latent, there will never be a story. But once set up, they must grow more grave, heading toward a point of intolerance. This part is the development of the fiction and it is here that the tensions are made clearer and more forceful.

The point of intolerance, or crisis. The oppositions reach a stage at which they can no longer exist with each other. They are now fully realized and fully focused and they must reach a showdown in some occurrence.

The resolution. After the crisis, things can never be quite the same. The world of the fiction has changed for better or for worse. It may be that the characters whose part the author has taken have been blessed with success, or half-success. Perhaps they have been deceived by an apparent success and we know better. Perhaps they have failed completely. Or perhaps they have failed in gaining a small objective but have won in a larger sense. These are just a few of the many possibilities the resolution may bring about.

The main thing to observe in constructing a story is that everything should originate in character. It is what impresses the reader —the characters are what he remembers long after the intricacies of the plot have been forgotten.

9 ORGANIC FORM AND
FINAL MEANING

A MILLION WINDOWS

A novel is a mirror carried along the roadway of life. Not at all; a novel is a pulpit, both agreeable and salutary, from which the writer directs his sermons. On the contrary; it is an art that takes us out of our perishable activity into the light of imperishable consciousness. . . . But there are any number of definitions.[1] The interesting thing is that when any critic or writer sets out to say what fiction *is*, he usually ends up by saying what he thinks fiction ought to *do*. It ought to be a realistic mirror of life; it ought to have a moral purpose; it ought to take us into an ideal realm of the imagination. Thus, the final meaning of any work of fiction is shaped to a greater or lesser extent by what each individual author thinks of as his artistic responsibility. And is there any superior or correct theory? Henry James answered by saying that "The house of fiction has . . . not one window, but a million," each one an outlook for some individual vision or individual will. He thought of it as a vast house front full of watchers, "one seeing more where the other sees less, one seeing coarse where the other sees fine, one seeing black where the other sees white, one seeing big where the other sees small." They are all looking out on the human scene,

[1] The present three are slight paraphrases of statements by Stendhal, Trollope, and Conrad, in that order.

but each perceives it in his unique way. No one of them is *the* way to measure what is going on before their eyes.

One of the special qualities of each personal vision comes from the particular *ought to* in it, the intention of the writer in his abstract conviction, his general sense of mission. It was suggested in the last chapter that the idea of formal plot had a powerful attraction for the kind of fiction writer who wishes to make moral evaluation the outcome of his work. That has proved to be one of the best inventions through which a judgment of man's actions could be expressed.

The revolt against the formal plot which originated in the late nineteenth century, and continues in our own times, was twofold. The first great dissent was against the accepted idea of the primacy of an outward view of man. Fiction must begin with the inward life of character, sensibility, psychology, or whatever other words can be used to define it. The second great anti-thesis was the idea that, although the writer should examine among other things the moral nature and the moral behavior of mankind, he ought not to jeopardize his position as a true observer by taking on another role as judge to assign guilt and innocence. As Chekhov said, it was for the artist to pose the great questions, not to decide on them, and the completely satisfying novel is one that sets all the problems correctly. Or, as D. H. Lawrence said, true morality in the novel is a balancing of things in the scales. When a novelist exerts his own ideological prejudice, it is like putting his thumb on the scales to give false weight to one side.

Thus these two related ideas, the first a concept of form and the second a concept of aim, resulted in an entirely new development in fiction. It is impossible to discuss one without the other, and so it will be useful to begin with a general phrase that is descriptive of the modern novel and that distinguishes it from the tightly plotted dramatic novel. That phrase is "organic form."[2] It is to a large ex-

---

[2] This term was employed by Coleridge in his Shakespearean criticism. He made a distinction between the shape or form that is imposed on material (which would include the plot) and organic form. He said that organic form "is innate; it shapes as it develops itself from within, and the fullness of its development is one and the same with the perfection of its outward form." He compares it with

tent an inheritance from the great Russian writers of the nineteenth century, and their preference for a casual kind of freedom in the planning of fiction. The important thing to them was not careful structure, which hindered them, but theme; it was this they were always intent on following. (There were exceptions—Leskov, for instance—and none of them threw plot entirely overboard.) In the short story, we can see the development of theme through Turgenev's *Sportsman's Sketches* to Chekhov's short stories. The thing that one keeps in mind—that is always brought to mind by vivid illustration—is not "what-happens-to-cause-something-else," but thematic ideas. To take a few random examples, there is the theme of betrayal in Turgenev's story, "The Tryst"; or of tyranny in "The Steward"; or of loving identification in Chekhov's "The Darling"; or of ingratitude in his "The Chorus Girl." This kind of story is simple in the sense that it does not have an artful complexity of events. It is the clear windowpane through which we can view the emotional relationships and development of people—and it is in them that the subtle and complex theme lies. The best of Chekhov's stories are extremely fragile to try to handle in criticism. They hang together and make a theme just by a miracle of perfect touches. They cannot be outlined by their events because that reduces them to meaninglessness, nor can the theme ever be as baldly stated as it is above. It is true that "The Chorus Girl" is about ingratitude, but that is only one facet of the theme. It is also about a natural generosity, a kind of hypocrisy, a false pride, an insensitivity to others, shallowness, stupidity—and a simple perplexity about all of these things. Plotted short stories have a necessity of narrowing toward the end so that they can focus on a single meaning (i.e., Aristotle's "single effect"). The Chekhovian story—and this includes those by his successors in the line—is quite open.

n.b.

This can be seen in the frequent (and somewhat overworked) comparison between the stories of Chekhov and those of Guy de

---

a force of nature, which shapes a growing thing, and he thought that it operated in Shakespeare's plays as the conscious artistic skill directing "a power and an implicit wisdom deeper than consciousness."

Maupassant, the most expert of all French short story writers. Maupassant was almost always driving toward a single point and his stories leave the reader with one (grimly ironical in most cases) meaning about life to weigh in his mind. The Chekhovian kind of story keeps making the admission that life is impure; that whatever happens may have something that is ridiculous, something touching, something contemptible, something bizarre about it all at the same time. The plotted short story keeps its mind on its business and exerts its will to keep out the superfluous and to drive ahead. The Chekhovian story ends with the feeling that life is a mixed business that we can't judge simply or absolutely, but that there are certain recurrent themes in it which, when treated by a master writer, can clarify our feelings about the complexity of life without ever making it seem less complicated. About the people in one kind of story we feel: they did certain things that led to a fated end. Of those in the other we can say: some behaved badly and some behaved well in different proportions, but in the end we can recognize that they were human.

The Russian writers (Turgenev particularly) had their impact on the generation of Henry James and Joseph Conrad, but it was not until the second and third decades that their whole style became absorbed by writers in English. Beginning with Katherine Mansfield, who sometimes wrote almost direct imitations of the Russians, it affected decisively the work of any number of other short story writers. In the novel, Tolstoy's and Dostoevsky's influence was more generalized and not so specific as Chekhov's was on the short story in English.

We can begin to understand what is meant by "organic form" in the novel by realizing that it has some affinities to both "plot" and "story." "Real life," to repeat Ivy Compton-Burnett's remark, "has no plots." But it does have recurring patterns and forms. We are born, we mature, we grow old, we die. That is the given form for human life. But, within that big outline, there is a more specific cycle common to most of us. We go to school, we fall in love, we marry, have children, provide for their early lives, part from them as their cycle enters maturity. This is all, of course, "story" within a certain pattern. There is a kind of novel which the Germans call a *Bildungsroman,* which follows the course of a life from early stages to later ones and which depicts the growth of a person. This is coming closer to organic form, but it is still not the same thing.

Here it is worthwhile to pick up, for a moment, a particular example. *War and Peace* (leaving out the historical novel of Napoleon, etc., and the essays on history) is a story of several people going through fifteen years of their lives, from youth to approaching middle age. Their stories, which intersect, veer apart, then come close again, throughout the novel, are governed by two great sequences: the historical events of their time and the sequence of growing up, falling in love, marrying, taking on the roles and responsibilities of their class. The historical sequence goes from peace, through war, and returns to peace again. That has a deep effect on the development of each private life, which, nevertheless, has its own pattern. It passes through the stage of youthful independence, through the turbulence of dealing with emotions and ideas in early manhood or womanhood, then arrives at the peaceful settlements of maturity.

Cause and effect play a part in the construction, and chance does, too, at certain points. There is a sense of direction and a procedure toward destination, as in a plot. Yet, in *War and Peace,* these things have a quite different quality because their purpose is different from that of the same things in the plotted novel. They are not meant to unravel a secret or to combine to make a denouement. They are a part of the common events of life and the cycle of life. This is not to say that Tolstoy had a deeper sense of life than had some of the other great writers who employed a very definite plot, but those writers had to expend certain amounts of their energy and skill in convincing us that their extraordinary version of life does, in the end, have a fidelity to experience.

Plot strategy imposes a form on the writer's material and the purpose of this form is to impose moral decisions about life. Its archetype is a trial in a court of law, with the evidence and the characters of the personae gradually revealed, conflicting testimony given, facts introduced, a certain eloquence of defense and prose- cution, a summing-up, and a verdict in the denouement. The story or novel that moves according to organic form is not cumulative in that way, does not cumulate *morally*. But, then, does it have any moral nature at all?

D. H. Lawrence's two novels, *The Rainbow* and *Women in Love,* are a study of the complexities of love and marriage followed through three generations of the Brangwen family. The theme that is constantly played on in the various man-and-woman relationships of the two novels is that of maintaining individual freedom in con- trast to, or conflict with, the demand to sacrifice individuality for a perfect union. Critics have denied that the second novel is a sequel to the first, and, in a restricted sense, they are probably right, even though both novels deal with the same milieu and the same family. The important point for this discussion, however, is that there is a common theme and that the over-all structure through which Lawrence presents this theme covers both books.

The design of the novels is an interesting example of organic form. There are five major examples of a love relationship, the first three (in *The Rainbow*) being progressively deeper and more com- plex explorations. The first simple statement of the theme is in the account of the marriage between Tom Brangwen and the Polish girl, Lydia Lensky. In this account, Lawrence is content to indicate some of the areas of attraction and tension he intends to develop anew later on and his treatment is conventional and naturalistic. The love between Anna, Lydia's daughter by a former marriage, and Tom Brangwen's nephew, Will, elaborates the theme and, symbolically, deepens it. But this is still preparatory and indicative. The third and final relationship in *The Rainbow* is between Ursula (who is the daughter of Will and Anna) and the young officer, Skrebensky. In this version of the theme, the psychic conflicts that Lawrence has touched on in the earlier stories are dominant, and the affair ends in failure. Lawrence is always suggesting that the potentiality of disaster and the potentiality of completion are inherent in any love relationship, and here it is the dark side of his theme that he stresses.

Yet this threefold plan of *The Rainbow* is not successful because the Ursula-Skrebensky affair, which is intended to be the most searching and profound development of the theme, falls somewhat short. As Graham Hough says, in *The Dark Sun: A Study of D. H. Lawrence,* "The attraction and the failure between Ursula and Skrebensky *ought* to be a mystery, but in fact it becomes a muddle." Lawrence's structural scheme at the end of *The Rainbow* was still incomplete and unsatisfactory because he had not fully worked out for himself all the implications of the "polarity" he sensed in relationships of love.

In *Women in Love,* he divided his theme, therefore, into two different treatments in the concurrent stories of Ursula Brangwen with Rupert Birkin and her sister Gudrun with Gerald Crich. Each side is an exposition—through the usual Lawrentian process of struggle, doubt, passionate affinity, and passionate rejection—of the theme anew and one side of the story ends in catastrophe while the other ends in concord. Or partial concord—there is still another aspect of the theme of love which has been produced throughout the novel and which hangs over the final scene like a question.

It is not in the interests of this chapter to try to give any full or critical account of these novels; the intention is to give some sense of how organic form appears in certain books and how it reveals its meaning. With each progressive movement of the story, Lawrence tried to work out his theme with variations in approach and with increasing intensity. That gives a general shape or structure to the fiction. But, unlike the dramatic novel, its meaning is distributed throughout the whole work and is not reserved for the weight of culmination. Graham Hough has put it very aptly, remarking, "What the novel has to say about ultimate things, about the human condition in general, can only be said through incidents, scenes and character which must all be particular and actual. Lawrence is primarily drawn to this manner of presentation: not man alone with his destiny, but a particular man in a particular situation. . . ." Lawrence insists, through the actions of his characters, on impressing us with moral insights; but he ends *Women in Love* not with a verdict but with a question.

This last is—for the present purpose—the significant thing about Lawrence's work. The particular structure and the method of using the structure are only one means to an end. Other modern novelists have chosen other designs that act within this same general philosophy. Joyce's *Ulysses,* for instance, is a novel of many superimposed designs—the analogical connection with Homer's *Odyssey* being only one of them. *Mrs. Dalloway* is a rather elaborate pattern of crisscrossing time and space in the several consciousnesses of her characters as they move about London in the course of one day. But neither of these, nor any other novel of organic form, is "teleological," that is, directed toward a definite and strictly definable end. All of these novels discuss values, but always as the characters meet them along the way. This (as Lawrence's novels illustrate) gives the author a much greater flexibility in treating these values. Previously, Frank O'Connor was quoted as saying that the novel of plot made characters "show their paces." Questions of equity or morality, too, are limited to the "paces" in order to fit the final purpose.

Edmund Wilson, discussing *Ulysses* in his critical volume, *Axel's Castle,* describes organic form in the novel from a slightly different angle:

It [*Ulysses*] is an organism made up of "events," which may be taken as infinitely inclusive or infinitely small and each of which involves all the others; and each of these events is unique. Such a world cannot be presented in terms of such artificial abstractions as have been conventional in the past: solid institutions, groups, individuals, which play the part of durable entities—or even of solid psychological factors: dualisms of good and evil, mind and matter, flesh and spirit, instinct and reason; clear conflicts between passion and duty, between conscience and interest. Not that these conceptions are left out of Joyce's world: they are all there in the minds of the characters and the realities they represent are there, too. But everything is reduced to terms of events . . . which make up a "continuum," but which may be taken as infinitely small. Joyce has built out of these events a picture, amazingly lifelike and living, of the everyday world we know—and a picture which seems to allow us to see into it, to follow its variations and intricacies, as we have never been able to do before.[3]

SYMBOLISM

A symbol is a meaning-bearing device. Its barest definition is, "something that stands for or represents something else." Along with this goes the idea of a disproportion or disparity between the symbol and the thing symbolized. That is, a concrete thing comes to denote an abstract idea or a cluster of abstract ideas. A small thing represents a much larger thing. A specific action may symbolize a whole complex of human attitudes.

There are several classes of perfectly conventional symbols with fixed and recognized meanings that usually come from a long history. Such things as scales representing justice, gold representing the idea of wealth, laurels for achievement, the color white for purity, or the cross for Christianity are traditional symbols of our society. Folkway symbols are such things as a clover leaf for good luck, red hair for a fiery temper, business as representing efficiency, etc. In literature, the most elaborate and systematic use of symbolism is Dante's *Divine Comedy,* which is based on the established symbols of Christianity—a rather different kind of thing because they are all related in a system of logic.

The symbolist movement of the nineteenth century introduced a radical concept of the symbol as a quite idiosyncratic thing, depending on the sensibility of the individual author rather than on reference to accepted meanings. Certain images were intended to suggest sensations in a highly private and logic-defying way, more often producing a mystery than an accessible statement of any kind.

In fiction, two kinds of things can bear symbolical meanings. One is the object; the other is the event, whether physical or mental. The vital necessity in technique is to make the symbol belong so naturally to the course of the story, to its furnishings or to the be-

[3] New York: Charles Scribner's Sons, 1931; p. 222.

havior of its inhabitants, that it does not announce itself as manufactured, imported, a false way of underlining some meaning.

An example of a small and rather modest use of symbolism appears in one episode of *Le Père Goriot*. Parisian society of fashion
and wealth is one half of the book's milieu. The hero, Eugène de
Rastignac, is trying desperately to make his way into that society,
but he is Balzac's young man from the provinces and he has no
sense of how hollow and cruel it is. Balzac, while viewing it chiefly
through Eugène's dazzled eyes, is always suggesting the reality to
his reader. Beautiful and aristocratic women are in the foreground
of the scene. One of them is the Vicomtesse de Beauséant, a
distant relative of the young man. She introduces him into this
world; he finds her kind and generous, and—when her great love
affair fails—even tragic. "In his eyes, Madame de Beauséant had
the magnificence of one of the goddesses in the *Iliad*."

Just after her disaster is certain, she gives a brilliant ball. She
asks Eugène to recover her letters from her former lover and, when
he returns, there is a brief scene in her room. She announces her
departure to bury herself "in the depths of Normandy." She is overcome by an agony of grief. But she says that she wishes to give
Eugène some final token of her friendship, because he seems to
her so noble and frank "in a world where such qualities are rare."
Then there is a moment of hesitation—it seems that Madame de
Beauséant has not actually thought of these sentiments before this
moment, and so she glances around the room hastily to find something that might be appropriate. " 'Ah, yes,' " her eye falls on her
glove box. It might seem to us rather difficult to make anything
out of that, but the lady has considerable dramatic resources:
" 'Here is the box I used to keep my gloves in. Every time I took
them out, before going to a ball or theatre, I felt I was beautiful,
because I was happy, and I never touched it without leaving some
pleasant thought with it.' " Thus far, the speech is plausible and
even affecting. We are with Eugène. But then in the last sentence,
she reaches the chute—or the one inevitable false note that suddenly reverses the meaning: " 'There's a great deal of me in it, a

whole Madame de Beauséant who no longer exists.' " Of course we remember that the box is quite empty.[4]

This is a minor but expert employment of symbols. The lady wishes to make a symbolical gesture. She lights, by chance, on the glove box and, with her pretty little speech, tries to make it out as a symbol of the happiness she once enjoyed. But Balzac makes the symbol work both ways and become ironical; if Eugène is "good, noble, and frank," it is absurd to give him a symbol of the vain life that has brought her such sadness. Thus, the manufactured symbolism of gesture and object—which, nevertheless, they both seem to take seriously—*does* take on a real and sarcastic kind of symbolism for the reader.

It is a small incident and its importance should not be exaggerated; yet it is so deft because it arises so naturally in the story. Beyond that, it touches the Balzacian theme of the corruption of character in the world of money and fashion.

In *Anna Karenina* Tolstoy uses just such unobtrusive symbolism —but there it is not a matter of separate symbols belonging to isolated incidents but rather a recurrent and thematic kind of symbolism. One of the most interesting examples of this repetitive device is the number of scenes having to do with railway stations and journeys, serving to remind us of the underlying theme in the story of Anna and Vronsky, which is one of travel and escape. It is as if the lovers were always trying to move on in order to avoid the knowledge of their love's terrible insecurity, a suspicion of which comes to them only in repose. They first meet in a railway station in Moscow; they meet again in a station, after the first step in their affair has been taken, on the way back to Petersburg. Anna's suicide takes place in another station and Vronsky is seen for the last time at a railway station as he departs for war.

That is a rather plain and direct kind of symbolism that Tolstoy is content to leave simply there; it reminds us of a theme but bears little weight of meaning beyond that. Mingled with it, however, is another kind of symbolism, another linked series of symbols

---

[4] Trans. Katherine Prescott Wormley (Boston: Little, Brown and Company, 1899), pp. 312–313.

of quite a different order. The station as a symbol belongs to the ordinary rationale or the ordinary psychology of the story; the second series of symbols relates to feelings of guilt and premonitions of death. When Anna first arrives in Moscow and is being greeted on the platform by her brother, an accident occurs. The train has backed up and has crushed one of the guards. In the train, on her way back to Petersburg, Anna has a few moments of delirium and hysteria; when she gets out on a snow-swept platform, "The bent shadow of a man glided by at her feet and she heard sounds of a hammer upon iron." A "peasant with a sack" is also noted in just a glimpse.

Later on, when the affair has been fully established, there is a strange coincidence of dreams. Vronsky dreams that "a little dirty man with a disheveled beard was stooping down doing something, and all of a sudden he began saying some strange words in French." He recalls the dream "with a chill of horror." Just afterward he goes to meet Anna, who tells him that she is certain that she is going to die and that she has been warned so by a dream. This bears an incredible resemblance to Vronsky's in some particulars. Anna has dreamed about going into her bedroom and seeing something standing in the corner—" 'and I saw it was a peasant with a disheveled beard, little, and dreadful-looking. I wanted to run away, but he bent down over a sack, and was fumbling there with his hands. . . .' " As he fumbled, the peasant was saying, " 'Il faut le battre, le fer, le broyer, le pétrir.' " (" 'The iron has to be struck, pounded, kneaded.' ") Immediately someone is telling her that she is to die in childbirth.

During Anna's last railway journey, she looks out of the carriage window and sees "a misshapen-looking peasant covered with dirt, in a cap from which his tangled hair stuck out all round . . . stooping down to the carriage wheels." Anna thinks that there is something familiar about him and then remembers her dream. A few minutes later, she gets out at the next station and commits suicide by throwing herself under the wheels of a train. As she is dying, she imagines that "A peasant muttering something was working at the iron above her."

This recurrent symbol has something of an omen, something superstitious and melodramatic about it in contrast with the simpler one with which it is associated. This image of death—which has a reminder of the mediaeval folk tale about it—reflects the fateful and melodramatic side of the story. Even though it is something of a jar in the midst of a realistic novel, Tolstoy has risked its use in order to suggest the aura of doom that surrounds the romantic figures of Anna and Vronsky.

Both of these instances from Balzac and Tolstoy are examples of a very relevant kind of symbolism. They pertain directly to Eugène or Anna and their force is channeled back into the story. Probably most fictional uses of symbols belong to this order. Mr. Jaggers in *Great Expectations* is always washing his hands—a symbolic cleansing of a guilt-feeling. In Katherine Mansfield's story, "Bliss," Bertha Young identifies a beautiful pear tree as a symbol of her own happy life—and then discovers the notion to be only an anthropomorphic fallacy. And so on. But there is another class of symbols, whose intention is much more ambitious.

These are the symbols that attempt to relate some figuration in the story to a larger, and perhaps very involved, concept that stands outside the story. They infer not so much a local truth (Mr. Jaggers is a man who feels guilt) as a general truth toward which the fiction is reaching. Joseph Conrad's *Heart of Darkness* offers one quite clear and simple example. Marlow is on his way to the Congo when he observes this scene:

"Once, I remember, we came upon a man-of-war anchored off the coast. There wasn't even a shed there and she was shelling the coast. It appears the French had one of their wars going on thereabouts. Her ensign dropped limp like a rag; the muzzles of the long six-inch guns stuck out all over the low hull; the greasy, slimy swell swung her up lazily and let her down, swaying her thin masts. In the empty immensity of earth, sky and water, there she was, incomprehensible, firing into a continent. Pop would go one of the six-inch guns; a small flame would start and vanish, a little white smoke would disappear, a tiny projectile would give a feeble screech—and nothing happened.

Nothing could happen. There was a touch of insanity in the proceeding. . . ."[5]

It is, of course, a symbolic image of futility. Europe, with her puny weapons of technology, is trying to subjugate the immense primeval continent, the "heart of darkness." Although the incident is complete in itself, it does have a relation to Marlow who also is going to attempt, in his own way, to master Africa—and it is an intimation of Kurtz's disaster to come. But its major purpose is to light up for a moment a larger theme which hovers over the whole story.

This kind of outreaching symbolism is seen in a more systematic way in those novels which succeed in being microcosms of a society. Jane Austen is hardly a "symbolic" writer in any strict sense, yet she gives a very strong impression of Mansfield Park as a kind of concentrated symbol of the dominant class in the society of England in her day. In the novel, she puts into action practically all of the moral and material values, the preoccupations with manners, class, money, family, status, etc., that ran so deeply through relationships in the real world. Thomas Mann, in *The Magic Mountain*, consciously symbolized the sick and disordered society of prewar Europe in the small world of a Swiss tuberculosis sanitarium.

This discussion is meant, however, to be no more than an introduction to some of the ways in which symbols can bear an important weight of meaning in the work of fiction. It is far from being any complete or adequate account of a subject that has attracted a great deal of modern critical attention—nor is it necessary to attempt here any analysis of those writers, such as Melville, Kafka, or the later Joyce, whose work is very largely based on some system of symbols. A considerable body of criticism about them is readily available.

The apprentice writer should approach the matter of symbolism with considerable caution. Symbols are not ornaments to be hung on the Christmas tree of the story; they cannot be fabricated in an attempt to give the fiction an air of depth and significance; they are serious and useful only when they are born from the narrative itself.

[5] *The Portable Conrad* (New York: The Viking Press, 1957), p. 506.

The brief scene from Balzac is a good example of how a natural turn in the story can be given a little symbolic stress, and this is probably the kind of effect the young writer should try for in the beginning. It is very likely that most readers would follow that passage without the feeling that they had come face to face with a symbol—most readers are not literary critics. On the other hand, no intelligent reader could scan that scene without getting a deeper sense of Balzac's meaning than the dialogue displays on its surface.

The case of those symbols in *Anna Karenina* is somewhat different. It is apparent that they are extraordinary, even symbolic, details. Tolstoy wanted to cast a shadow of desolation around the figures of Anna and Vronsky. It could be baldly stated: "Anna then began to have a premonition of disaster"; but that would be simply a matter of the author instructing the reader, not convincing him. Thus Tolstoy wanted something of a symbolical kind to delineate this rather delicate and chancy conception. The interesting and important thing about his method is that he worked from the material of Anna's psychology to produce the symbol. She had, during her return trip to Petersburg, glanced at a peasant with a sack and also at a railway worker testing the carriage or engine wheels with his hammer, but she had barely noticed them. They have nevertheless lodged in her unconscious as visual images connected with guilt (she has met Vronsky twice on station platforms) and with death (the worker who was crushed by the train). In this way, all of the elements fuse together in her nightmare. The figure proceeds directly out of the disturbance in Anna's mind—and any psychological symbol that is to be used must have the same sure basis.

THEME AND MEANING

Some important considerations in understanding the ultimate meaning of any piece of fiction are these:

Its general kind or category as a literary form.
Its more specific type or genre.

Its plan or structure as an aim toward meaning.

Its theme or themes as a producer of meaning.

As for the first, René Wellek and Austin Warren (see their *Theory of Literature*) distinguish two kinds: one is "romance," which is any fiction with a predominant strain of the imaginary. It is the heir of the epic, the myth, and the fairy tale. The second is realistic fiction, which sticks close to plausibility and which derives from reportage. (The actual terms used by Wellek and Warren are romances and novels.)

This informs us of a very general intention. The more specific type or genre gives us a little better definition of it. That is, a satire intends to ridicule something, usually with implied comparison to an ideal. The negative mockery is one part of the meaning and the implied ideal is the other. Tragedy, comedy, and tragicomedy all have their traditional types of meaning. Branching out of them are numerous subspecies; such as the novel of manners, the novel of romantic love, the novel of adventure, etc. This classification, of course, is no more than a broad indicator of what final meaning may be, and one should avoid the mistake of certain librarians who have shelved *Crime and Punishment* with the detective novels and *Moby Dick* with the sea tales for boys.

Plan or structure as culminating in certain kinds of meaning have been discussed in the chapter on plot and the section on organic form.

When we arrive at theme or themes as the producer of meaning, we have narrowed down to the thing that makes every piece of good fiction unique. It is true that a theme can, for classroom or other purposes, be rudely summarized in some such statements as "the futility of trying to recover the past," "idealism, even though defeated at the moment, lives on," or "life is absurd and all our actions are pointless." But this is a useful lie, as every intelligent reader knows. He knows perfectly well there are so many nuances and qualifications that would have to be added to prove the statement true or false that it would take, say, 325 pages. Characters would have to be brought in to illustrate certain delicate points, scenes would have to be introduced to give just the precise tone to this or that point about the theme; it ought to be at least as well written as the original novel because style has a good deal to do with the coloration of theme, and . . .

Though the theme diminishes to no more than a lump of logical statement after the process of critical boiling-down, its feeling ought to be clear and coherent enough. Around that essential thing there can be discussion, interpretation, and illuminating insight. Two examples of writers who do this extremely well are Frank O'Connor and V. S. Pritchett, both of whom—significantly—are authors of fiction as well as essayists.

FALLACIES[6]

On the negative side, here are a number of the ordinary fallacies that often enter into the judgment of meaning in fiction:

The didactic fallacy results from evaluating the meaning of any piece of fiction by its moral intentions alone. The sermon preached from an imaginary pulpit may be highly salutary (or, at least, you agree in thinking so) but it may be dull, verbose, and badly expressed. You may condemn it because, though brilliant and well expressed, it does not agree with your moral outlook. Or, you may say that the moral point is subordinated or nonexistent in the fiction, and thus the fiction fails.

The historicist fallacy is that of judging a work by its symptomatic relevance to its times: "An English lady who writes quiet novels about vicarages and country life can't possibly be of importance because she was living in a bustling age when England was fighting great wars, amassing money, and building an empire." Or: "The Lanny Budd novels of Upton Sinclair are major works."

The intentional fallacy is that of estimating a novel or story by what the critic (or reader) has arbitrarily decided to be the *real* intention of the work. Such critics delve into what they take the

---

[6] For a very fine summary of some of the fallacies described here, we are indebted to Allan Rodway's "What the Critics Really Need," which appeared in the Winter 1963 issue of *20th Century*.

author's subconscious to be and brush aside any indications of meaning expressed by the author himself.

The naturalistic fallacy is the judgment of fiction by its fidelity to fact alone. Alteration of fact is significant only when it leads to mistaken general conclusions. Even the realistic novel may have reasons for changing actuality around to fit its purposes.

The formalist fallacy is that of measuring the novel or short story in accordance with what the critic thinks to be the only correct form. Somerset Maugham used to berate Chekhov a great deal because "his stories have no plot."

The fallacy of "good taste" is that of praising or condemning an author solely by the critic's personal notion of what is agreeable or disagreeable. Balzac, Chekhov, Zola, and dozens of other important writers have all been attacked for showing the "sordid," "depressing," or "decadent" side of life. It is a fair subject for comment, but not for arbitrary judgment.

None of these things need bother the writer as he sits down to start his piece of fiction—in fact, they should be banished from the mind as needless handicaps. Too many writers labor under one or another of these superstitions and the results can be crippling to their work. On the other hand, the beginning author, who is in the process of learning his craft by reading the best work of those who have gone before him, should be aware of these various traps of judgment.

HOW TO MAKE YOUR FICTION HAVE AN ULTIMATE MEANING

Now you have arrived at the point where your sketchy map leaves off. Your guides, your equipment-bearers, the other members of the climbing party have all stopped at various shelter points along the way. The peak of the mountain rises up in front of you. You are all alone. The only comfort you have is the recollection that nobody ever reached the highest point unless he went by himself.

EXERCISES AND WRITING SUGGESTIONS

1: CONCEPTION: THE ORIGIN OF A STORY

A. Examine a story such as Henry James's "The Next Time" in the light of what the author has said about its conception. In the case of James, how much remains of his original idea to "Trace the history of a charming little talent . . . that has been exactly the martyr and victim of that ineffectual effort . . . to make, as it were, a sow's ear out of a silk purse"? (See *The Notebooks of Henry James* for his account of the conception.) The idea for "The Next Time" was a result of James's own experience. Why doesn't the autobiographical element intrude in the finished story? List some of the ways in which James leads away from himself and toward his characters—that is, toward an achievement of the imagination.

B. Now look at some of your own completed stories. Has the conception been treated too casually, too much in terms of yourself? What are its further possibilities? (A reading of James's notes for "The Next Time" may suggest to you a fruitful kind of "dialogue" which an author can carry on with himself—making suggestions, raising objections, asking questions, and so on.)

C. Go through your notes for possible stories with these questions in mind.

1. Is this merely a happening in my own life which at the time seemed to me strange or exciting or touching? Can I recover the original emotion? Can I recreate the situation in a way that will

interest any readers the story may find? Or is this idea, seen now in retrospect, really so commonplace or so limited that it will yield nothing to the exercise of the "moral imagination"?

2. Is the idea too "literary"? Did it come more from my reading than from anything I have observed for myself and felt myself deeply engaged with?

3. Is this too baldly an anecdote?—original and amusing, perhaps, but incapable of any kind of significant expansion?

4. Did this idea come from some striking public event—such as the scandal that launched Trollope on the Barchester novels? If so, can I do as Trollope did: launch my story from the headlines without making it simply a rehash, thinly veiled as fiction, of events sufficiently known to everyone? Do I have a particular point to make? Is the point what really commands my imagination, so that the actual events of the case won't hamper my imaginative working with it?

D. Here are five brief story ideas. As an exercise, take each and see what kind of development you can devise for it:

1. They were a devoted couple for years, yet when her mother died and she was free to marry him their relationship came suddenly to an end.

2. When the promotion went through, and he had every reason to expect that there would be another within seven or eight months, he began to drink heavily; then he deserted his wife and children and lived for a time with another woman in a shabby downtown hotel; and now he's left town and as far as his family and ex-employers know is gone for good.

3. They were exceptionally handsome and intelligent children, both of them, yet there was something secret and morose about the boy, something almost frightening.

4. Nobody liked her—and really there were any number of good reasons. Yet when she died suddenly a number of people felt a deep sense, not only of loss, but of guilt.

5. It was a scandal in the parish, of course. And then the papers got hold of it—not the worst part, fortunately. The question now is whether they'll keep on digging—and how much we're all going to be involved before they're done.

2:   BEGINNINGS

Take as an example one of your own short stories with which you are reasonably satisfied and review it in the light of some of the suggestions contained in Chapter Two.

A. Read the ending over very carefully and try to determine exactly what theme or meaning the story has led up to.

B. Is there some suggestion—either direct or oblique—of this theme or meaning in the opening of the story? Do beginning and ending have some harmony, either of idea, mood, observation, or plot? Could that beginning have belonged equally well to another story?

C. If after this examination the opening passages do seem too remote from the main theme of the story, read through the first few pages to try to determine where the story actually does begin.

D. Underline the parts in the beginning that fill in necessary background information (or, that answer *Who? What? When? Where? How?*).

E. Has this information been packed too heavily into the first few paragraphs of the story? Is there any of it that can be cut out? Is there any that can be reserved to be introduced naturally at some later point in the story? Has the reader, in short, been given just enough information to orient him securely without being overloaded with facts?

F. If the beginning outlines a situation in being, have you made the salient points of the circumstance clear enough? If you are dealing with the relationships of two or more characters, have you made a sharp definition of their attitudes toward one another?

G. What elements have you introduced at the beginning of the story that suggest interesting questions to be solved later on? How early do they occur? Are they early enough to attract the reader's attention at the outset? Do these anticipations deal with matters of real importance in the story—or are they simply the tricks of an eye-catching beginning?

H. Write three new beginnings for the story, employing different methods for each (for example, portrayal of a single character; establishment of some situation among characters; description of an action; introduction of a problem faced by one or more characters). If possible, choose a different chronological point for each of the three. Now compare the various beginnings, trying to decide for yourself which one most successfully follows the general guidelines suggested in Chapter Two. If you now have a beginning that is superior to the original one yet not quite consonant with the story that follows, this may be a sign that the story could be recast to better advantage.

I. Examine the beginning chapters of four or five nineteenth-century novels by well-known authors. Note the methods and characteristics of each. Now look at the opening chapters of novels by such contemporary authors as Saul Bellow, Evelyn Waugh, J. D. Salinger, Joseph Heller, Kingsley Amis, William Golding, and William Styron. Observe differences in the introduction of factual material, the use of scenic or character descriptions, the handling of action, or the establishment of situation in these beginnings. With reference to the principles suggested in Chapter Two, decide for yourself which one of these beginnings is most effective, and why.

J. Assuming that you are about to begin a novel, choose what kind of tone and subject you might use for a "low" beginning and what might be appropriate for a "high" beginning. Try your hand at sketching both.

3: STYLE AND SPEECH

A. Take one of your own stories and examine it for these stylistic deficiencies:

1. Is the language repetitious?
2. Are there commonplace words or phrases which no longer have power to evoke character or scene or mood?
3. Are you using two or three words where one, carefully chosen, would make the point more effectively?
4. In general, is the language of the story an example of economy rather than of wordiness?
5. Is the prose easy and idiomatic? For instance, when you read it aloud does it flow smoothly, or are there awkward passages resulting either from poor construction or stilted expressions?

B. As an exercise in making your style flexible enough to deal with a variety of subjects and themes, imagine for yourself several different kinds of situations at their climactic moment, and then try to write a paragraph or two in which your language explores that moment fully. (You might, for instance, describe a widow's feelings as she prepares to spend her first night alone in the house she and her husband have lived in all their married life. Or the moment when a man's infatuation for a foolish woman leads him to make an irrevocable commitment to her. Or the panic of someone new to teaching as he or she faces the very first class. Or a moment of intolerable shame in the life of an admirable person.)

C. Read carefully a few passages from stories or books by writers of serious standing—say, *A Portrait of the Artist as Young Man, Between the Acts,* "Old Mortality," "Spotted Horses," "Big Two-Hearted River," *The Death of the Heart.* Can you identify some of the characteristics of each style?—those things which mark it unmistakably as a passage from (for instance) James Joyce rather than William Faulkner, or from Virginia Woolf rather than Katherine Anne Porter?

D. Analyze the dialogue of several modern writers who are particularly skillful in their use of idiomatic language. (These might include Eudora Welty, Ring Lardner, J. F. Powers, Nelson Algren, Angus Wilson, Mordecai Richler.) How do they make speech a revelation of character as well as an advancement of the narrative?

E. Look at the speech of the characters in one of your own stories.

1. Does all of it deal, as Elizabeth Bowen says, with "something unprecedented"? That is, does every speech add significantly to the reader's knowledge? Or are there places where readers will guess that you're marking time while you try to work your dialogue in the direction you next want to take? If this is the case, can you effect a rapid transition, perhaps by narrative, from the last significant speech to the next one?

2. Do all of your characters tend to sound very much alike—and probably very much as you do? Ask yourself whether the failing is one of carelessness or whether it indicates an imperfect knowledge on your part of the essential qualities of your people.

F. Using one of your own stories, try to make the speech of each character so recognizably his own that you can eliminate almost all attributions like "he said," "she replied," and so on.

4:   CHARACTERIZATION

A. Analyze one of your stories in terms of Henry James's dictum: has the character determined the particular situation in which he finds himself? Does that situation, in turn, throw fresh light on the character? If you can trace no cause-and-effect development, try to discover where the trouble lies. Perhaps you began the story before you had an adequate sense of your character. On the other hand, perhaps you have tried to impose a mechanical plot on a believable and appealing person who is resisting the arbitrary handling that a hard-and-fast plot line requires.

B. Write set-piece characterizations of two or three people in stories you have completed or plan to write. Include everything which it will ever be necessary for the reader to know: appearance, mannerisms, speech, past, location, and so on. Then go through each description and determine how much is of immediate importance to characterization and what can be deferred until later. Rewrite each paragraph in accordance with your decision. Has the character now been brought before the reader with the maximum economy? Does he, nevertheless, emerge as someone both memorable and interesting?—someone the reader will want to follow through the rest of the narrative?

C. Even if you feel generally satisfied with your revisions, look at them again with as much critical detachment as you can achieve. Is every adjective, is every noun, as precise as you can make it? Despite your revisions, have you perpetuated any of the errors pointed out in the commentary on the passage from Disraeli's *Coningsby*? In addition, have you avoided all comparisons so complicated or bizarre that they bring the reader to a halt?

D. Go through one of your stories and label all of the characters either "flat" or "round" according to their function in the narrative. Look closely at your flat characters: are they consistent, or are there places where you have enlarged on their role without adequately preparing the reader for their sudden increase in importance? Have you misjudged their relative effect on the action? (Forster believes that on occasion flat characters may assume a temporary roundness; it is up to the writer to decide when this is the case and when he has simply miscalculated the character's relevance. All writers have anecdotes about minor characters who have suddenly run away with a narrative. These are extreme occasions, of course, but it is often the case that some characters diminish in stature, and others come prominently forward, during the writing of a fiction. This can leave the reader with a sense of serious inconsistencies in characterization, however, unless the writer is at pains to rework his story in terms of its conclusion.)

E. Let us suppose that you are putting in too much description of the physical setting. Let us suppose further that all of it is necessary, but that handled straightforwardly it slows the story down. Can some of the setting be seen through the eyes of one of the characters? that is, can you combine, as Mann did in "Death in Venice," both setting and state of mind? Take a passage of description which seems to lend itself to this treatment and try writing it from the viewpoint of someone who is possessed of a strong emotion which colors everything he or she looks at.

F. Look at the gestures your characters make, the amount of moving around they do. Are they like puppets being jerked meaninglessly? If so, what can be done to give their movements significance? If, conversely, your characters seem lacking in animation, could some revelatory habit or mannerism be brought in which would not only enhance the reader's sense that these are real people but also give some movement to the narrative?

G. Read one of the current French antinovels; for instance, Claude Mauriac's *The Dinner Party*. Then recast one of your briefer stories in the "objective" form. What has been gained? (Probably a sense of intimacy and immediacy.) What has been lost? (Probably a degree of intelligibility.) Do you think it possible to combine some of the techniques of objective fiction with some of the more traditional techniques? How would you set about the job, and what elements of classical characterization do you think would have to be permanently abandoned? Is Henry James's view of characterization still valid?

5: POINT OF VIEW

Following are some exercises intended to help the student toward a better understanding of the problems of point of view in fiction.

A. If time permits probably the best way to get some idea of the limitations and possibilities of various points of view is to write the same story three or four times, employing a different central intelligence each time. It is suggested that you take a very short story of your own and that you retell it as follows:

1. From the point of view of a child who participates in the action.
2. From the point of view of an adult participant whose feelings and prejudices are deeply involved.
3. From the point of view of a narrator-agent who conforms to the definition given in this chapter.
4. From the viewpoint of the omniscient author.

In this exercise the important things to notice are (*a*) how greatly the narration of the story is affected by the technical problems of remaining within a specific point of view; (*b*) how much the style, tone, theme, and even the idea of the story are governed and made individual by the particular viewpoint. You can improve your judgment in this matter by asking of any story—either a published story or one of your own—two questions: Could the story be more varied and interesting if another viewpoint were adopted? How would the adoption of that alternate possibility affect the main theme and the final meaning of the story?

B. Select a first person narrative—either novel, novella, or short story—by some author you respect. Try to define for yourself the reasons for the choice of first rather than third person. Does it seem to you that the "I" narrator is sufficiently personified? Or, on second glance, does he seem to be too indistinct and too obviously a device for the author's autobiographical recollections? In this case, would the story lose a special and personal quality if it were told in the third person? Or would it gain from a somewhat more objective telling?

C. Find, in one of your own stories, a scene that is told from an individual viewpoint, whose meaning relies on the distinctions and value judgments belonging to one person. Now try to rewrite the scene as if you were a playwright (that is, reporting speeches and actions by objective descriptions, though still using the mode of fiction). Try to translate the comment formerly afforded by the personal point of view into a comment that can be deduced from evident attitudes, speech, and action. What is now different about the final effect of the scene? Has it suffered any loss of meaning in the shift from explicit value judgment to implicit? Have you succeeded in making the scene more dramatic?

D. Try to find a novel and a short story that are particularly good examples of the authorial point of view. Notice (*a*) at what points the author borrows an individual consciousness to record certain events of the story and when he has felt the objective or "theatre" method necessary to carry his narrative; (*b*) when the commentary, generalization, or value judgment is introduced and how it is introduced; (*c*) the transitions from one viewpoint to another and from one scene to another; (*d*) the instances of panoramic observation.

6:   BACKGROUND; PLACE; SETTING; MILIEU

A. In your mind, you probably have a complete sense of the physical background or setting of the next story that you plan to write. As a preliminary project, describe that setting completely: its history, geography, topography, architecture, local customs, varieties of trees and shrubs, and so on. After doing this, go back through your material and decide which details are relevant to the particular story you want to tell, and which—no matter how delightful or vivid—must wait until another time. (An incidental benefit may be the discovery that your landscape can provide you with ideas for several other stories.) Ideally, an exercise such as this one should show you exactly the degree of importance that your setting has to the story. If you found, as your description lengthened, that you were getting more and more distant from your central concern, then probably the setting is of minimal importance. If, on the other hand, you found yourself discovering more and more details that were significant because of their effect on life and character, then it would seem that the place where your story happens is going to need very careful attention when you begin your writing.

B. Look at one of your completed stories in the light of what you have just learned. How much of the detail is irrelevant? How much should be expanded? And, most to the point, have you used your setting as effectively as you know how to?

C. Review the comments in this chapter on Sarah Orne Jewett's story, "The Mistress of Sydenham Plantation." Then look at your own stories with this question in mind: did I write any of these only because I wanted to make use of a setting which had particularly appealed to me? Have I succeeded in doing better than Miss Jewett did, or have I perpetrated the same mistakes?

D. Try a few paragraphs as a "poet" on interior decoration. Using, for example, *The Custom of the Country* as a model (see the quotation in this chapter), select the details of a room or a house which, in your opinion, would characterize the occupants in terms which the educated general reader would find revealing; for instance, tasteless but well off; austere, critical of other people's possessions, but not really very discriminating; indifferent to surroundings; extremely aware of every detail of a room's finish, from the polish on the paneling to the carving of the furniture. Obviously, your descriptions (however good in themselves) must not exist for their own sake but must cast a considerable light on whatever group of people you would assemble for a story.

E. As an exercise in developing your powers of observation, the next time you are in an unfamiliar setting—a house, perhaps, or a museum—try to observe as many details as you can. Then, when you are home again, write a paragraph incorporating all that you have seen which seems expressive of the place.

7: NARRATIVE STYLE; TIME AND PACE IN FICTION

These suggested exercises deal with the subject of narrative style and the problems of time and pace in fiction.

A. Take a story you have already written, or have outlined to write, and note where the main scenes, i.e., those that are fully explored and detailed, fall. Indicate with no more than a sentence or two where the narrative bridges would appear. From this kind of scenario you can now get an idea of the pattern—or of the lack of pattern—in your story. Look at it from the viewpoint of balance. Does it, for instance, begin with a long narrative summary followed by three or four scenes bunched closely together at the end? Or does it open with one important scene, continue with extensive narrative summary, and end with another important scene? Is it largely scenic throughout, though going on to end in a substantial passage of narrative? None of these methods is necessarily wrong, and any one can be used if important considerations of plot or theme demand it. But, if there are no such overriding demands, it is best to work out some kind of balanced pattern for the placement of scenes. Can the sequence of the scenes be changed around to better effect?

B. Now examine the parts of the story that have been assigned to narrative summary. Are there any potential scenes that might be rescued from the summary and developed into a part of the dramatic pattern? In other words, have you narrated something that might be more effective and more useful to your scenario pattern if the characters themselves were to act it out?

C. Try rewriting some scenes from your fiction exactly as if they were very brief one-act plays. That is, introduce some sort of opposition or mystery, deepen and develop it, and finally bring it to a climax or revelation. This should not, of course, be the pattern for every fictional scene, but it is a most useful practice because many of your scenes will demand this technique.

D. Look at the narrative parts—the "stage directions," as it were—within any dramatic scene you have written. Are they cumbersome and not very meaningful to the action or idea of the scene? that is, in getting a character out the door, do you note how he takes five steps across the room, puts on his hat, grasps the knob, says good-bye, opens the door, steps through it, and closes it behind him—or the equivalent in any physical action? See how much of this kind of narrative can be omitted or cut very sharply. (Why not say simply "Parker left the room.") Try to relate as much of the incidental action as possible to the meaning of the scene or to a revelation of character.

E. Note whether in the scene under examination you have used one technique as a kind of backbone for that scene; e.g., dialogue; description of physical action or actions; the reflection and commentary of one character on what he sees and hears going on about him. Have you used this technique consistently? Or have you reported some dialogue directly, yet some other equally important dialogue by indirect summary? or, perhaps, reported fully one or two impressions by your point-of-view character, while omitting his observations on some salient matter? Try rearranging the technique of writing the scene so that one method dominates it throughout while the others supplement.

F. Select an example of skillful narrative method from a novel you have been reading. Note how the author has varied the mere summary of events and where he has employed incidents, generalizations of his own; how he has covered considerable stretches of time in a brief report; and—most important—how he has made the narrative build up an approach to a new development of the story through scene.

G. Examine some work by Henry James, Joseph Conrad, Ford

Madox Ford, or Marcel Proust for examples of the time-shift and note how they are used.

H. Take some piece of your own work, either finished or unfinished, and find some places where you might introduce a scene from the past with good effect. First write a simple flashback transition, trying to make it work as smoothly and unobtrusively as possible.

I. Now take the flashback passage and, referring to the last section of Chapter Seven, elaborate it so that it becomes a time-shift. Moving from a particular scene to abstract ideas and then again to a particular scene of the past has been noted as one typical method of shifting time, though it is not the only one. Can you think of some other devices writers have used to make the transition?

8: PLOT AND STORY

Undertake the following exercises as a way of determining for yourself some of the uses of plot in fiction and some of the problems connected with it.

A. Write a one-paragraph summary of a simple story, according to E. M. Forster's definition. Now take exactly the same elements in your summary, shift them around so that they create a plot (still in Forster's terms), and write a second summary paragraph. Finally, write a third paragraph, using any device you can invent to make the plot fit the description, "It is only at the end, when the events have reached culmination, that the pattern is complete."

B. Take two or three published stories you admire and outline them just as the Moravia story in this chapter is outlined. That is, note briefly the establishment, rising action, crisis, recognition, and denouement scenes. If any one of these elements seems to be lacking in a story, try to explain to yourself why it has been omitted. Does the omission strengthen or weaken the story? If the story is told in a way quite different from this "classic" plot development, try to decide the author's reasons for avoiding it. Could the story be recast in the classic mold? Would it then be more effective or less effective?

C. In your reading of fiction, note several examples of events that happen by chance but that seem to you to be natural and believable. How has the author prepared for them so that their plausibility will not come into question? Now find some examples in fiction of coincidences that seem strained or incredible. What is it that makes them so? Note how the plot is weakened by their employment. Try to decide what necessity of plot logic has impelled the author to use them. In each case, pose exactly the same plot problem to yourself. Could the coincidence be dropped without radical alteration in the structure of the story? Or could it be changed and modified into some form that will not arouse the incredulity of the reader?

D. Write a one-paragraph plot outline of a surprise-ending story (either one you have read or one you can invent), in which the mystery depends on *who?*, *what?*, or any other question of fact. Now try to rewrite the summary, removing the surprise ending and the emphasis on a factual answer. Substitute a *how?* or a motivational kind of mystery. Notice which of these emphases gives the greater opportunity for the development of character. Notice which one stimulates the imagination to go beyond the set outlines of the plot.

E. Write out a simple statement of a theme that might be used in a long story, a novella, or a novel. Think of two different opposed or contrasting treatments of the theme that might form a plot and subplot. Try to decide at which points the two could reflect, comment on, or complement each other—either in terms of characters that might be used or in terms of actions that might take place. Select some well-known English or American novel in which two or more plots are employed and analyze it according to how the plots are woven together and how they interact with each other.

F. Read several stories by authors mentioned in this chapter, with the idea of determining how the plot structure does—or does not—lead to a moral conclusion for the story. Does the moral judgment at the end seem to be perfunctory and stereotyped? Or has the plot method led to an interesting and individual moral statement?

9: ORGANIC FORM AND FINAL MEANING

Because it is impossible to suggest any practical written exercises that would give the student a better insight into the subject of organic form and final meaning, the authors here furnish a few questions that may serve as guidelines for self-criticism and a greater awareness of objectives.

A. Try to sum up for yourself the meanings inherent in the conclusions of various pieces of fiction you have written. Do you find that you tended to work toward one single effect in idea? Could these final meanings, as a rule, be expressed concisely in a brief assertion or aphorism? Do your stories seem to narrow down at the end to make a moral or didactic point?

B. On the other hand, do the conclusions of your stories offer difficulties of interpretation to others who have read them? Do other readers often suppose a meaning quite remote from the one you had in mind? In a story which follows the general procedures of organic form no two readers will arrive at precisely identical meanings; nevertheless, do those who have read your stories find meanings that fall within the scope of your own intentions? Do you find that they conceive of the theme in much the same way you have meant it?

C. One useful exercise in reading would be to look at a number of stories or novellas with the idea of trying to define the author's essential theme—then paying close attention to the conclusions and trying to decide for yourself how well the endings succeed in deepening and rounding off the thematic ideas. (It might be well to begin with Chekhov, in such stories as "Ward No. Six," "The Duel," and "The Woman with the Dog."

D. On rereading some of your own stories, do you find that you have consciously attempted to use symbols in certain places? In the light of what has been said in Chapter Nine, do they seem to work naturally and functionally in the stories? Or do they seem to be artificial appendages? Would the stories express their meaning perfectly well without these symbols?

E. If you are interested in the technique of symbolism in your writing, it is suggested that you attempt to work out some careful treatment of a symbolic action or object similar to the technique in the example from Balzac discussed in Chapter Nine. You should be sure, of course, to introduce the symbolism in a place where it can effectively bear some meaning for the story and can contribute to the development of a theme.

F. In your reading, notice some of the varied kinds and uses of symbolism. It might be useful, for your own purposes, to write a brief analysis of the symbols and systems of symbols in stories by such authors as Hawthorne, Kafka, James, Melville, Bernard Malamud, and so on. (This is not suggested as an exercise in literary criticism but as a practical examination of technique.)

A SELECTIVE BIBLIOGRAPHY
OF BOOKS DEALING WITH
TECHNIQUE

Allen, Walter. *The Writer on his Art*. New York: McGraw-Hill Book Company, Inc., 1949.

Allott, Miriam. *Novelists on the Novel*. New York: Columbia University Press, 1959.

Booth, Wayne C. *The Rhetoric of Fiction*. Chicago: Chicago University Press, 1961.

Bowen, Elizabeth. *Collected Impressions*. New York: Alfred A. Knopf, Inc., 1950.

Cather, Willa. *On Writing: Critical Studies on Writing as an Art*. New York: Alfred A. Knopf, Inc., 1949.

Chekhov, Anton. *The Personal Papers of Anton Chekhov*. New York: Lear Publishers, 1948.

Cowley, Malcolm (ed.). *Writers at Work: The Paris Review Interviews*. First and Second Series. New York: The Viking Press, Inc., 1959 and 1963.

Forster, E. M. *Aspects of the Novel*. New York: Harcourt, Brace & World, Inc., 1954.

Glasgow, Ellen. *A Certain Measure*. New York: Harcourt, Brace & World, Inc., 1943.

Humphrey, Robert. *Stream of Consciousness in the Modern Novel*. Berkeley: University of California Press, 1955.

James, Henry. *The Art of Fiction*. New York: Charles Scribner's Sons, 1948.

James, Henry. *The Art of the Novel*. Oxford: Oxford University Press, 1947.

James, Henry. *The Notebooks of Henry James*. Oxford: Oxford University Press, 1947.

Joseph, Sister Miriam. *Shakespeare's Use of the Arts of Language*. New York: Columbia University Press, 1947.

Kronenberger, Louis (ed.). *Novelists on Novelists*. New York: Doubleday & Company, Inc., 1962.

Lubbock, Percy. *The Craft of Fiction*. New York: The Viking Press, Inc., 1957.

Muir, Edwin. *The Structure of the Novel*. London: The Hogarth Press, 1954.

O'Connor, Frank. *The Lonely Voice: A Study of the Short Story*. Cleveland: The World Publishing Company, 1963.

O'Connor, Frank. *Mirror in the Roadway*. New York: Alfred A. Knopf, Inc., 1956.

Pritchett, V. S. *The Living Novel*. New York: Harcourt, Brace & World, Inc., 1947.

INDEX

INDEX

225

Printer and Binder: American Book–Stratford Press

79 12 11